A VISIONARY NATION

A
VISIONARY
NATION

Four Centuries of American Dreams
and What Lies Ahead

ZACHARY KARABELL

Perennial
An Imprint of HarperCollinsPublishers

A hardcover edition of this book was published in 2001 by Harper-Collins Publishers.

HarperCollins books may be purchased for educational, business, or sales promotional use. For information please write: Special Markets Department, HarperCollins Publishers Inc., 10 East 53rd Street, New York, NY 10022.

First Perennial edition published 2002.

Designed by Nancy Singer Olaguera

The Library of Congress has catalogued the hardcover edition as follows:

Karabell, Zachary.
    A visionary nation : four centuries of American dreams and what lies ahead / Zachary Karabell. — 1st ed.
        p.   cm.
    Includes bibliographical references.
    ISBN 0-380-97857-1
    1. United States—Civilization. 2. United States—Social conditions—1980– . 3. National characteristics, American. 4. Technological innovations—Social aspects—United States. 5. Perfectionism (Personality trait)—Social aspects—United States. 6. United States—Civilization—21st century—Forecasting. I. Title.
E169.1 .K318   2001
973—dc21   00-053935

ISBN 0-06-008442-1 (pbk.)

02   03   04   05   06   ❖/RRD   10   9   8   7   6   5   4   3   2   1

CONTENTS

Acknowledgments vii

A Visionary Nation 1

PART ONE   THE PAST 11

One   Religion 13

Two   Individualism 31

Three   Unity 48

Four   Expansion 67

Five   Government 84

PART TWO   THE PRESENT 117

Six   The Market 119

Seven   The Internet 158

PART THREE   THE FUTURE? 191

Eight   Connectedness 193

Notes 217

Index 237

ACKNOWLEDGMENTS

As with any major undertaking, this book could not have made the journey from unfocused ideas to printed, bound pages without the enthusiasm, prodding, and encouragement of a wide array of people.

This book began with a phone call from Hamilton Cain, then at Bard Books, a division of Avon Books, which unbeknownst to either of us would soon be acquired by HarperCollins and the News Corp. Hamilton asked what ideas I had for a book on American history; drinks were had; follow-up conversations followed; and a book was outlined. To Hamilton, my deepest gratitude for picking up the phone and thinking of me. Without him, the rest would not have happened.

Trena Keating at HarperCollins took up stewardship of the book after the merger, and her editing and her passion saw the book to its realization. Her belief in its potential contributed immeasurably. Tim Duggan then shepherded the book to publication with his usual combination of steady calm and enthusiasm. To both of them, and to their assistants, David Semanki, Christine Walsh, and Kristen Schmidt, my thanks also for various and sundry, including their toleration of more than one curious or concerned phone call.

My research assistant, Lauren Winner, found more material more efficiently than I would have thought possible. She also added her own store of knowledge about new trends within American Christianity. She's moved on to her own book, and it will, no doubt, be as impressive as everything else she's done.

Then, a number of people agreed to take me to task for what I had written and offered critiques of earlier drafts. As usual, credit goes to them for any improvements, while I take full responsibility for any remaining problems that resulted from not heeding their advice. Nods, in no particular order, go to Timothy Naftali (for being a devil's advocate), Fareed Zakaria (for general sagacity), Laura Moranchek (for setting me straight about the origins of the Web), Tiffany Devitt (for a view from the Silicon trenches), Fred Logevall (for giving me an academic perspective), Phil Weiss (for telling me to cut and state), Eric Olson (for pushing me to think about how businesspeople think about business), Nicole Alger (for giving me an honest response), David Denby (for good-natured dissent), Bruce Feiler (for illuminating the bookend problem), David Callahan (for his boundless exuberance), and Jonathan Tweedy (for ruminations and Rue B).

With the draft more or less complete, there remained the problem of the title. The impasse was finally broken one night at dinner, when I sat with Nicole Alger, Alex Alger, and Dan Chung and they indulged me with their efforts to find the right title. Also pitching in was our waiter, who had the apt but improbable name of Tennyson Bardwell. To all of them, and Dan in particular for coming up with it, thank you.

As usual, John Hawkins occupies a large space in my heart. Yes, he did the deal, but he also helped me and supported me, and that has been priceless. And to Moses, Holly, and Matt, all of John Hawkins and Associates, my thanks as well.

At HarperCollins, Josh Marwell, Nina Olmstead, and Jeannette Zwart sold the book; Christine Caruso and Diane Burrowes marketed it; and Patti Kelly organized the publicity. Without them, and without the support of Carie Freimuth and Cathy Hemming, this would have remained a manuscript.

And finally, to Nicole, who has enriched my life and who has put the writing of a book into perspective. It is wonderful to be able to express ideas and passions on paper, but without someone to share them with daily, there would be far less joy. For her electrical charge, I thank her.

A VISIONARY NATION

A VISIONARY NATION

The e-mail went out to everyone in the company. "You can change the world!" Robert Wrubel, the vibrant former CEO of Ask Jeeves, often sent out these messages, to buoy morale and get people fired up. It was a clever management technique, but the sentiments were genuine. Wrubel infused the company with a vision: that Ask Jeeves will enable people to be more educated about everything in their lives, to be better connected with other humans, better connected to information, products, and services. Oh yes, he was fond of saying, we are driven by a passion to change the way companies are organized, the way people interact, and most of all, the way the market works. "In almost everything we do, we are fueled by a degree of enlightened utopianism."

Based in an office park in Emeryville, California, just across the bay from San Francisco, Ask Jeeves is a search engine. Ask Jeeves lets users ask questions the way they would ask them in real life and then provides answers. Go onto the web site and ask where you can buy a used Lincoln Continental and Ask Jeeves will tell you where to go. Ask a harder question, and Ask Jeeves often gets stumped. Internet purists have derided the company. Its stock price has declined from its highs, but as of early 2001, the publicly traded Ask Jeeves was still worth several hundred million dollars. It is one of the twenty most popular web sites in the world, and by the standards of Silicon Valley and popular culture, it is a modest success.

"I want to give people Perfect Information," Wrubel said during a 1999 speech to a group of New York editors and webbies. "Perfect

Information is power, and the closer we can get, and the closer each person can come to it, the more each and every person will have the power to shape and determine their own lives." Perfect information—the ability to know precisely what you want to know—sounds like some latter-day equivalent of the Holy Grail. While Ask Jeeves knows that perfect information will always be a dream, the company is energized by the belief that it's possible to come close and that it's possible to connect people with the information that they need when they need it. That may not be perfect in the sense of complete and all-encompassing, but it might be perfect in that it would transform how people interact with one another, with companies, and with the world as a whole in myriad ways.

Perfect information would give individuals the capacity to make informed decisions. That sounds fairly innocuous, but it isn't. Suppose you want to buy that Lincoln Continental; perfect information makes lemons impossible, price gouging obsolete, and marketing ineffective. Want the ideal lover? How about a dossier that provides all the data, except for the actual experience. Have a question that is at once pressing and obscure? Perfect information means that all you need to do is ask. If knowledge is power, then Ask Jeeves aspires to be the ultimate leveler. If controlling access to knowledge has been one means that governments, companies, and individuals have monopolized power, then Ask Jeeves has the potential to be more than a search engine; it just might be a vehicle that will transport us to genuine democracy.

Like all new ventures, Ask Jeeves faces an uncertain future. After a dismal six months during which its stock, like the stock of many Internet companies, lost most of its value, Rob Wrubel resigned as CEO in December 2000. Though revenues continue to grow, so do losses. In the coming year, Ask Jeeves could establish a solid niche and become profitable. It could be acquired. Or it could burn through its remaining cash and go bankrupt. Whatever its fate, however, its rapid growth and its ebullient approach to business are part of the larger phenomenon of the New Economy.

The employees and executives at Ask Jeeves look at the future warily but optimistically. In 1999, the company was the flavor of the month in the business press. In late 2000, it was hard to find anyone touting its prospects. That's the rollercoaster of being a New Economy start-up, and people at Ask Jeeves try not to pay too much attention to the ebbs and flows of how they're being portrayed. They rely instead on the conviction that they're involved in something big. David Birnbaum, a thirty-three-year-old producer, with a shock of wavy hair and perfect teeth, spent eight years working for the U.S. Customs Service before joining the company. "At Customs, everyone was just pushing paper. It was impossible to get anything done effectively. I'm not saying that people in the government weren't capable and earnest, but there was no sense of excitement, even when I was doing things that probably affected as many people's lives as I am now." He shakes his head in bemused amazement: "I thought that the grass would be greener working in this environment, and man, is it ever. In the government, it was just a job, a good job, but a job. But here, there's the potential to shape the big picture."

You could get a similar response from almost anyone who works at Ask Jeeves. As Enrique Salem, senior vice-president for research and development, told me, "We're changing the world and we might also get rich. What could be better? I've been in the high-tech world for twenty years, but when I told people in the mid-1980s that I was working on Windows, they wondered what I was talking about. Now, I tell people I'm doing something on the Web, and everyone's eyes light up." Then he pauses and gives that slight shake of the head, the wake-me-I-must-be-dreaming smile. "People come here because they want to be part of history being written. They want to be a part of culture being made, and of course, there's the financial upside." And there he sat, busy, frazzled, surrounded by activity, changing culture and hoping to get rich.

"All that we're trying to do," Wrubel said a few months before his resignation, "is connect people to what's important to them. That may be another product, but more often than not, what they want isn't another trinket. It's connection, to something they want, yes, but mostly to other people. What they want is community, which includes commerce, but it's bigger than that." And then that infectious grin, which said more than any words could, We are on the cusp of a brave new world, so enjoy the ride.

The Internet is new, but the vision is not. The magical fusion of the Web, the computer, and the stock market is a unique product of our cultural moment; the presence of visionaries who believe that they are fundamentally transforming culture is not. The New Economy is simply the latest of a series of utopian dreams that have defined American society since the time of the Puritans.

The United States is a visionary nation. Americans believe in the promise of a better world. Unlike other societies, the United States has no shared ethnicity, no common religion, no sense of historical heritage. Instead, there is an idea. Running through the currents of our history is a presumption that it is possible to have it all. And not just that a few people can have it all, but that all of us can.

In comparison to other cultures, that's unusual. Human needs and desires exist on a spectrum from the material to the nonmaterial. Most people most of the time, for much of human history, have clung to the hope that they can have enough to live and be content. Americans believe that all needs can be satisfied, that we can have wealth *and* happiness, homes *and* spiritual fulfillment, comfort *and* community, sated appetites *and* satisfied souls. The only thing missing is how. Convinced that abundance is possible, we continually strive for it and are always looking for the means to achieve it.

The truth, of course, is that nothing can give us everything. Even if Robert Wrubel and Ask Jeeves are one hundred percent right, even if the Internet provides every one of us with Perfect Information, and the stock market, in its symbiotic relationship with the Web, revolutionizes the economy and leads to fifty years of economic prosperity the likes of which the planet has never seen, we will still be left with nonmaterial needs that the New Economy can't address. The clichés will out: money can't buy love, happiness and worldly success keep remarkably little company. The New Economy may or may not draw us nearer to God, or help us understand our psyches, and a booming Dow and technological advances may extend life but will not obviate the fear of death. In short, the wonders of the New Economy not withstanding, we have yet to square the circle in such a way that our nonmaterial and material needs are simultaneously provided for in equal measure.

Yet we keep expecting to find the magic formula, and at any given moment in our history, there are visionaries who think they have found it. That makes the culture vibrant, dynamic, and creative. It ensures that society will always be striving for something more, something better. But visionaries are rarely realists, and their reach is greater than their grasp. They promise a better world, but with such high expectations, the vision always falls short of its goals. At their best, visionaries do not acknowledge the possibility of failure, and they charge ahead. At worst, they can be downright totalitarian and refuse to consider alternate perspectives.

That only hastens the end. Unable to see where the vision falls short, visionaries resist criticism, and people do what they always do when their needs aren't met. They become dispirited, and they look elsewhere. The obverse of the utopian impulse is a dread that everything is going terribly wrong. Yearning for the ideal, Americans easily switch from giddy optimism to grim pessimism. Heady images of a perfect future quickly turn to dark pictures of a society going down the drain. People become disillusioned. They reject the vision for not satisfying all of their needs, and then they invent a new vision, a supposedly better one. A new stage forms, and the pattern begins again.

The same cycle continues today. Over the course of nearly four hundred years, visions have come and gone, each seemingly dominant in its day and in its place. What remains constant is the conviction that utopia is possible.[1] What changes is the prism, the language, and the method. The belief remains, but the paradigms shift—and we tend not to be aware of those shifts when they are happening. Given how consumed we become with the utopia du jour, we usually lose sight of what has happened before and fail to notice the changes that may be occurring even now.

What this means is that sooner or later, whether or not the stock market rises to astronomical heights or crashes to earth, whether or not the Internet empowers every single person beyond our wildest reckonings, the era of the New Economy is finite. In fact, it will certainly be eclipsed within our lifetimes, and given how rapidly things change in today's world, it may be in the process of being eclipsed even as you read this.

This cycle of vision followed by vision has been going on for centuries. In the pages that follow, you will read about seven stages of American culture. Five of these are historical, one describes the present, and the last one, the seventh, lies in the future. These stages are loose formulations. They are not objective markers; they are not rigorous categories, and they are not meant to be. Some of them are apples, while others are oranges. Someone else writing a similar book might have cut the historical pie in a different way.

The stages are ways of describing utopian visions that have been prominent during different eras.[2] Our world today is formed by the cycle of stage giving way to stage. Shakespeare said that what is past is prologue, and it's a vital prologue. At heart, however, this is a book not about our past, but about who we are now, how we came to be that way, and what that means for our future.

The first stage, the Puritan vision for a City on a Hill, was prominent in New England in the seventeenth century. The second stage, the eighteenth-century amalgam of individualism, freedom, and liberty, seized the imagination of Americans during the American Revolution. The third stage, the drive to create a national union, which began with the Constitution and lasted through the Civil War, was of concern primarily to a small group of political leaders and of little interest to most Americans until the 1850s. The fourth stage, the late nineteenth-century period of territorial and economic expansion, affected all Americans, but only a few thought of it as a vision for a better world.

The fifth stage revolved around government. The New Deal in the 1930s and the Great Society in the 1960s framed every major social question in reference to what went on in Washington. Whether you were conservative or liberal, Republican, Democrat, or apolitical, the federal government was the leitmotif of American culture. During this period, government was the predominant vision, the axis around which the culture revolved, in much the same way that the New Economy is now.

The second half of the book plunges into our present. The failed promise of the Great Society, the rise of Ronald Reagan, the odd peregrinations of the Clinton administration, and the innovations of Silicon Valley brought the fifth stage—the government stage—to an end and led to the triumph of the sixth stage, the New Economy. As with each prior stage, the sixth stage is defined by visionaries. The champions of the New Economy occupy the same cultural space that the Founding Fathers did during the Revolution. Though most people do not fully share the idealism of Silicon Valley or the great expectations of venture capitalists who have funded start-up companies, the culture bears their stamp. Though most people listening to Rob Wrubel hold up their hands to say, "Now wait a minute," it is men and women like him who create the cultural framework that we all experience, even if we disagree with the vision, even if we see its limitations. We live in a world of the market and the Net, whether we want to or not.

But that will not last. As people notice what the Net and the market do not provide, murmurs will grow that the current stage isn't all that it is cracked up to be. In fact, this is already in evidence. It may be that doubts and questions will coexist with the current paradigm for years before a new stage emerges. The critique of government developed in the 1960s, but it was nearly three decades before government actually faded as a cultural stage. The same may be true with the market and the Net.

Eventually, however, the New Economy is doomed, either because it will fail spectacularly with a market meltdown and economic depression or because it will reach the limits of possible success. Either way, a seventh stage will follow. My suggestions about what the future will hold are based, as are all such predictions, on what the present paradigm leaves out. The New Economy is at its most tenuous in the way that it addresses the yearnings of the spirit, the desire for community, and the intractable challenges of family, love, aging, and death. But reasonably or not, people expect those needs to be satisfied, and they will become disillusioned as it becomes clear that the New Economy doesn't effectively fulfill those needs. In time, that disillusionment will lead to the seventh stage, and the mores of connectedness and community will supplant those of the New Economy.

Even then, however, the cycle that this book describes is likely to continue. The seventh stage might replace economic goals with communitarian ones, and it might embrace the language of the New Age rather than the patois of *The Wall Street Journal*. But the seventh stage will be no more balanced than any of the other previous stages. Its visionaries will be just as convinced that they are right, and they will be just as sure that their formula for utopia will succeed. And so like past visionaries they will overreach and make grandiose claims, and they will raise the bar of high expectations and sow the seeds of deep disillusionment. In short, driven by the same visionary extremism, the seventh stage will in time be followed by an eighth, and the eighth by a ninth, and so on, in an endless cycle.

But the very act of identifying a pattern can change it. Twentieth-century physicists grappled with the problem of how the observer shapes what is observed. Similarly, tracing cultural patterns can potentially alter them, or at least alter our relationship to them. As we become more aware of the impulses that characterize American society, we might be able to change its trajectory.

We have, over the course of our history, thrown out an awful lot of acquired wisdom in the process of replacing it with the next new thing. The early visions all spoke to something central in American culture, and each responded to needs and desires that have never disappeared. Religion may no longer define the ideal world as it did for the Puritans, but the United States is still a deeply religious society. Our language, our institutions, and our government reflect that heritage. Government may not be the linchpin it was during the Great Society, but government continues to be a force in the economy and in daily life, even if it no longer commands passion and even if it no longer defines the zeitgeist. American society is a layer cake of previous stages.

Yet we tend to forget the wisdom of the past and instead attempt to reinvent the wheel. Over the course of four hundred years, Americans have come up with numerous visions, and then have forgotten the answers suggested by previous generations. That historical myopia has some benefits. It allows the culture to shift, cyclically and regularly, without any deep awareness of those cycles. Furthermore, a utopian impulse can be aided by historical ignorance. If you pay too much attention to how familiar the patterns are, you might throw up your hands and conclude that there's no reason to hope for radical change. Visionaries are often able to do what they do because they dream of new worlds and dismiss the answers of the past as inadequate.

But it might be time to grow up a bit and integrate the past into our visions. We do have a history, and we do have a long legacy of trying out different frameworks and being disappointed. In a Peter Pan quest for the ideal world, we never quite notice that we've done this before and it hasn't worked. But what if we identified the cycle? What if we saw it for what it is: an unrequited quest that remains unrequited partly because it is unrealistic and partly because we expend too much energy discarding previous visions rather than incorporating them? Does it need to be *either* individualism *or* unity, *either* government *or* the New Economy, *either* material abundance *or* spiritual abundance?

The past may be set, but the future is not. The transition from the sixth stage to the seventh might be as jarring and extreme as the previous transitions. But we could also change the story. We could recognize that we are stuck in a cycle that has brought us frustratingly close to our dreams while keeping us agonizingly far. The cycle, dynamic though it is, could be altered and improved. We could progress more holistically, blending several visions rather than clinging to one. And if we make that adjustment, instead of a future of endless, unrealized utopias, we might actually create the society we have dreamed of.

But let's begin at the beginning. The quest for perfection has been a hallmark of American culture since a group of settlers embarked from the old world to create a City on a Hill. They didn't succeed, but they made a compelling start.

PART ONE

THE PAST

ONE

RELIGION

In the spring of 1583, the half brother of Sir Walter Raleigh set off from Plymouth, England, intending to settle the east coast of Maine, near the inlet of the Penobscot River. Sir Humphrey Gilbert hoped to tap the rich fishing waters that lay between Newfoundland and the northern peninsula of North America, and on the voyage across the Atlantic, he often sat in his cabin with a book, reading to pass the time. According to most accounts, the book he was reading just before he died in a blustery September storm in 1584 was *Utopia*, by Sir Thomas More.[1]

More depicted an ideal society, an island which he called "utopia," a Greek neologism meaning "not a real place." More's utopia quickly became synonymous in Western Europe for a world only dreamt of, a society that forever lay on the distant horizons of human potential. Though More depicted his utopia as a land of religious tolerance and democratic equality, he ran afoul of England's Henry VIII and was executed for high treason in 1535 and later canonized by the Catholic church.

Most of the men and women who fled England for the shores of the New World had little time for religious tolerance or for democracy, but like More, they envisioned a utopia. They had to. Every aspect of moving to the New World was fraught with danger. If you wanted to undertake the journey, you had to board a tiny, rickety ship that might or might not get across the ocean. The journey took long weeks, and when you arrived, you arrived nowhere. The New World may not have been total wilderness, but the presence of Native American tribes was a mixed blessing. They might help you find food or they might kill you. True, in the early seventeenth century, life was nowhere easy, and the prospect of a new beginning was worth the very real possibility of premature death. The Spanish and Portuguese had settled in South America with a far less coherent vision than those who created the colonies of New England, and the choices in early modern Europe were never without risk. Still, emigration posed a formidable challenge and for that reason, those who made the journey tended to be those who saw in the New World the possibility of an ideal world.

Not everyone who emigrated shared that hope, and along with the Puritans, the Pilgrims, and the Quakers came thousands of hangers-on, fortune seekers, military men, and servants. Whether or not they, too, were propelled to construct a society unlike any other we will never know. Their voices are silent, though judging from the writings and sermons that the leaders of the various settlements left, these fortune seekers and military men were likely to pass their time getting drunk in a tavern, speaking lewdly, scheming for ways to accrue wealth, and laughing at the sanctimony of the clergy. But the culture wasn't determined by the opportunists or the servants, especially not in New England, where the Puritans controlled not only the pulpit but the law. The culture was a Puritan culture, and the energy and vision of these early Puritans is woven in the heart of American society.

The settlers emerged from an England that was in a slow burn caused by a combustible tension between Anglicans and Puritans that would soon erupt into civil war. In truth, the first English settlers weren't Puritan at all, nor did they arrive in New England. The men who founded Jamestown in Virginia in 1607 were Anglican, and they were looking for precious metals. Within a few years, they realized that no gold or silver was to be had in the swamps of Virginia, and they slowly turned their attention to a lucrative new crop called tobacco. But though they had commerce uppermost in their minds, an English life in these years was a life suffused with God and faith. Even Captain John Smith, the mercenary, hard-bitten hero of the colony's early years, attributed the survival of Jamestown not to the efforts of men but to the will of God. Explaining how rescue ships from England arrived just in time to save the colony, during the "starving times" of the winter of 1609–1610, Smith wrote that "the God that heard Jonah crying in the belly of hell, he pitied the distress of his servants. . . . This was not Ariadne's thread, but the direct line of God's providence." Virginia may have been a chartered company created to bring profit to its shareholders, but its settlers nonetheless viewed reality through the prism of seventeenth-century Anglicanism.[2]

Smith himself was a rugged soldier who was very much out for financial reward, as were most of those who gravitated to Jamestown. But the era was suffused with religious mores, and even the most venal inhabitants of the colony would have agreed that their fate was in God's hands and that they could and should thank God for their success. And if the colony thrived and made them and the shareholders wealthy, that would be a sign that they had pleased God. Still, Jamestown did not attract religious firebrands, nor was the settlement a welcome place for Anglican separatists. The religious utopians gravitated to the north.

The first wave to embark for New England was an innocuous group of separatists who set sail from Leyden in the Netherlands, where they had fled from England in 1608. Believing that they would face increasing persecution at the hands of the Anglican clerical authorities who answered to James I, these separatists wanted only to find a place where they could celebrate God and work toward their own salvation in peace. But while Leyden was hospitable, the group feared that their children would be absorbed into Dutch society and lose their sense of identity and mission. So the Leyden separatists set forth once again, across the sea to the new colonies. Intending to migrate to Virginia, they found funding from English investors and secured a patent from the English crown that would allow them to live in the new world "unmolested." But their ship, which set sail in 1620 with barely one hundred passengers (of whom less than half were from the Leyden separatist community), drifted off course and landed at the end of a peninsula hundreds of miles to the north of their intended destination, at the site of modern-day Provincetown.

Suffering from malnutrition and scurvy, the passengers aboard *The Mayflower* didn't have the strength to reembark for Virginia. And so the separatists signed a covenant that bound them together to obey whatever laws they might jointly pass. They disembarked and, in the words of the future governor, William Bradford, "fell on their knees and blessed the God of Heaven who had brought them over the vast and furious ocean and delivered them from all the perils and mysteries thereof." They soon moved up the coast to Plymouth and built some ramshackle houses. Had they known that within six months half of them would be dead from exposure and starvation, they may have been less thankful, but the Plymouth colony persisted, infused with Pilgrim piety, for seventy more years. Its chronicler, Governor Bradford, described a community that never ceased to struggle for financial security and that narrowly avoided being absorbed into the more powerful Puritan colony of Massachusetts Bay. Yet, in spite of, or perhaps because of, these challenges, the Pilgrims never ceased to believe that all that mattered was the doing of God's will, and they felt certain that they were setting a noble example. "As one small candle may light a thousand," Bradford wrote, "so the light kindled here hath shone to many, yea in some sorte to our whole nation."[3]

THE PURITAN VISION

Where the Pilgrims were quiet in their devotion and content to withdraw from the Anglican church, the Puritans, who fled by the thousands to the areas around Boston after 1630, were more ambitious and more contentious. They wanted to transform the English church, and if that meant retreating to the New World until such time as Charles I had died, and with him his archbishop William Laud, then that is what they would do. The men who led the venture that created the Massachusetts Bay colony were well connected, Cambridge-educated Puritans who were coming under increasing pressure from Laud and the Anglican establishment. Among them was the forty-one-year-old John Winthrop, who owned a small manor in Suffolk and had recently lost his government commission. With their connections and their positions in society, the founders of Massachusetts Bay were able to arrange for multiple ships and gather more than a thousand settlers, who streamed into New England beginning in 1630.

Winthrop soon emerged as one of the guiding lights of the colony. Strong-willed and stern, Winthrop epitomized the Puritan spirit. Portraits depict him as an angular man, with a long, drawn face, sharp eyes, and pursed lips. Some have said that he was by nature kind, but that is not the impression he has left to history. Instead, he appears as an autocratic leader, who served as either governor or deputy governor for the next twenty years. Intent on building a stable settlement, he steered a firm course and tried to keep dissent to a minimum. Like many Protestant reformers, Winthrop believed that God had but one will, and that right and wrong were unambiguous categories. Men are fallible, but God is not. Men require laws and rules to force them to walk the path of righteousness; left to their own devices, people will quickly succumb to temptation, to sin, and to the devil. They might succumb no matter what, but at the least those entrusted with governance could endeavor to keep vice and sin in check.

That was Winthrop's mandate. Recognizing that people are weak and easily tempted, he was determined to construct a community that worked as one unit toward salvation. Like all the leaders of the settlement, and like Protestant reformers from Calvin onward, Winthrop believed that only God could save souls, and that salvation was a mystery bestowed by His grace. That led to a conundrum that bedeviled the Puritans: if only God could determine salvation, how would people know who was saved and who was not? Most Puritans thought that a saved person would behave in ways that an unsaved person would not. Though salvation was a mystery, the Puritans thought that people displaying the traits of a saved person, consistently over time, were probably among the saved. While hypocrisy was an ever present danger, the Puritans came to the conclusion that unsaved people could only exhibit righteous behavior for so long before they did something sinful which made their true state clear to everyone.

Upright behavior, or what the Puritans called sanctity, could be tested and observed; it could also be policed. And men such as Winthrop saw it as their task to make sure that people acted in a sanctified manner. But no matter how obsessed the Puritans were with behavior, behaving well was not in and of itself a guarantee of salvation. You could pass numerous laws governing behavior, from how much someone could drink to what they were allowed to wear. You could demand strict accountability for actions that today we would consider to be private. You could outlaw cursing and dancing, and you could preach loudly against cardplaying, as the Puritans of Massachusetts Bay did, but no matter how strict the authorities were, in the end, it was all in God's hands. You could know a saved person by his good works, but good works could not save you.[4]

Behind these rules, behind the obsession with probity and morality, was a clear vision. Heading toward New England on the *Arbella*, John Winthrop and his cohorts felt that they were on an errand. They wanted nothing less than to construct a Godly paradise. "For we must Consider that we shall be as a City upon a Hill, the eyes of all people are upon us," Winthrop wrote.[5] Centuries before, the great theologian Saint Augustine of Hippo wrote his monumental *City of God*, which gave expression to the never-ending Christian desire to re-create Eden. Winthrop and the New England Puritans may have been stern, uncompromising men and women, familiar to us as black-clad figures, never smiling, speaking portentously as in Arthur Miller's *The Crucible*. The portraits of Winthrop and others of his day only reinforce those impressions, as do the countless sermons by seventeenth-century ministers railing against the inherent sinfulness of men. But beneath that harshness bubbled the waters of utopia.

Assuming that his writings genuinely reflected his spirit, then in the depths of his soul, Winthrop was convinced that Massachusetts Bay was a noble experiment, a rare moment in human history when people earnestly banded together to live as pure a life as they could. The fact that the new colony was suddenly swamped with settlers after 1630 only confirmed that view. As Archbishop Laud tightened the pressure on the Puritans, they departed England in droves, thousands upon thousands streaming onto ships and across the sea, where the unsentimental, severe Winthrop welcomed them.

In 1638, at the height of what became known as the Great Migration, when, during the summer months, twenty ships arrived carrying more than three thousand passengers, Thomas Tillam wrote a poem to capture his feelings. "Hayle holy-land," he said, "wherin our holy lord hath planted his most true and holy word. . . . methinks I heare the Lambe of God thus speake. Come my deare little flocke, who for my sake have lefte your Country, dearest friends, and goods, and hazarded your lives o'er the rageing floods, possess this Country." Yet, Tillam warns, "beware of Sathan's wylye baites. He lurkes amongst yow, Cunningly hee waits." As long as every man and woman fought against Satan and stayed true to the path of Christ, then their lives would be for the greater glory of God, and He would reward them.

The idea was simple: if the Puritans worked on their own purification and sanctification, then God would grant them peace, security, and material bounty. The ideal was a seamless link between this world and the next, between the seen and the unseen, the flesh and the spirit. Everything flowed from God's grace. The purer the spirit and the more dedicated the community, the more worldly success there would be. The link between the spirit and the flesh was explicit, and for the Puritans, logical. While the point of this life was to prepare for the next, material prosperity was seen as God's gift in return for fulfilling the covenant with Him. Surrender to God, renounce pride, and own up to your sins, declare that God's wisdom was infinite, and you would be admitted to the ranks of the elect, declared a "saint," and be guaranteed a prosperous life, in all ways. Provided they kept their covenant with God, then He, "with his Wonder-working Providence" would shower the Puritans with his abundance. As Winthrop observed, "The end is to improve our lives to do more service to the Lord, the comfort and increase of the body of Christ . . . that ourselves and posterity may be the better preserved from the Common corruptions of this evil world, to serve our Lord and work out our Salvation. . . . We are entered into Covenant with him for this work. . . . Now if the Lord shall please hear us, and bring us in peace to the place we desire, then hath he ratified this Covenant."[6]

The Great Migration of English Puritans, which brought more than 20,000 people across the ocean, transformed New England from a modest outpost into a complex and thriving society. Most of these settlers shared the vision of a City on a Hill. But they hardly agreed on the best way to create it. No matter how autocratic Winthrop or the other leaders were, their theology ensured that there would be constant debate over what was permissible and what was not. Only God could save, and only God knew the truth. Most Puritans agreed that the community could monitor behavior and that each congregation could assess the sanctity of its members, but their disputes were intense and constant. Just as Protestant sects today in the United States debate vehemently and are constantly fragmenting, the early

Puritans squabbled, and the contests were often bitter. Some people simply refused to abide by the authority of the first wave of the Puritan migration, and new settlements were created. Like branches from a tree, the Puritans radiated out from the Boston area, down the coast, up the coast, inland into the Connecticut Valley, and toward Narragansett Bay and what would become Rhode Island.

QUESTIONS, DISAPPOINTMENTS, AND ALTERNATIVES

Almost from the moment it coalesced, the Puritan movement began to dissipate, not from an absence of fervor or a failure of vision, but rather as a natural outgrowth of the belief system. Like other Protestants of the sixteenth and seventeenth centuries, the Puritans based their theology on the assumption that each person confronts God alone. No relationship was more personal and more central than an individual's relationship with God. Believing that God attends to the salvation of each living soul, the Puritans celebrated individualism. This wasn't an individualism in the contemporary sense. People weren't free to behave however they wanted to, and the Puritans legislated public morality to a degree that even the most conservative among us today would find repugnant. Instead, people were free to be saved or to sin; they were free to be a member of the church and free to be damned. In the meantime, the civil authorities would do their best to foster a climate of sanctity, but at the end of the day and the end of the line, each person would stand, alone, in front of God and be judged.

This vision undermined both civil and religious authority. If individuals were ultimately responsible for their salvation—and salvation mattered more than anything else—that made it hard to force people to accept the authority of men. The English Puritans in 1640 revolted against King Charles I, and ultimately executed him, and though the Puritans could be authoritarian, their religious beliefs led to the questioning of all human laws and all human rules. In New England, though Winthrop and the leaders of Massachusetts Bay tried to enforce rules of conduct, people dissented and struck out on their own, and slowly the prism of faith began to shatter.

In addition, the inhabitants of New England were not the only ones who had a utopian vision undergirded by religion. Other settlements in the New World were motivated by religious ideals. In Maryland, the proprietor, Cecilius Calvert, who succeeded his father as Lord Baltimore and was himself a practicing Catholic, carved out a sphere where English Catholics could worship without reprisal. In 1649, partly to placate the government of Oliver Cromwell in England, Maryland passed the first religious tolerance act in the colonies. Several decades later, William Penn managed to secure a patent from Charles II, making him the proprietor of a vast tract of land that would later become Pennsylvania. Unlike most proprietors, Penn himself moved to the New World and helped create Philadelphia, which in his vision would be a haven for the inner light and truly a city of brotherly love, as it meant in ancient Greek. Penn was a devout Quaker, a radical pacifist sect of Protestants who believed that faith and salvation were a private matter between God and each individual. According to the Quakers, no mediation was possible or necessary. No priests, no council of elders, no congregation of saints could do anything but hinder the free working of God's grace. Furthermore, no one could interpret the scripture for anyone else. Penn, an ardent Quaker, was also an ambitious proprietor, and by the end of the seventeenth century, Philadelphia was a thriving multiethnic city.

Like the Pilgrims and the Puritans, the Catholics of Maryland and the Quakers of Pennsylvania were motivated by a religious vision of a new world. Penn was driven to make his vision real, and almost single-handedly, he established a colony that would exert a strong influence on the course of subsequent American history. The Quakers have been called radical "antinomians" because they rejected the notion of churchly authority, but the Quakers of Pennsylvania were not embattled. With Penn at the helm, they were the dominant sect. That wasn't the case in Massachusetts, where the antinomians fought what amounted to pitched theological battles with the Puritan establishment. And as a result of these battles, long before Pennsylvania was founded, the Puritan utopian vision began a slow transformation into something else. As would happen repeatedly in American society, the prevailing paradigm was challenged. People began to question its validity and its efficacy. They began to doubt; they became disillusioned, and then, slowly, a new stage emerged.

The impulse to create godly communities has never disappeared.

Long after the first stage ended, groups of Americans withdrew from the larger society motivated by a religious desire to construct a City on a Hill. Believing that the larger society was unredeemable, these groups moved to rural areas where they could live by their own rules and raise their children uncontaminated by the outside world. Some of these groups are familiar because they have survived to this day. Others lasted for a time and then faded. In the late eighteenth century, a group calling itself the Millennial Church of Believers formed settlements in New Lebanon, New York, and in Ohio and Kentucky. Commonly known as the Shakers, these groups eschewed the outside world, practiced celibacy, and waited quietly for the Second Coming of Christ. They continued to attract adherents until the early twentieth century. Another group, the Amish, were German settlers who believed that society was corrupt and that technology was a primary cause. In an effort to construct a community devoted to God's grace, they shunned contact with outsiders, and they continue to live apart to this day, in Ohio, Pennsylvania, and parts of the Midwest, having made compromises along the way but never abandoning their vision.

Animated by the same impulses that led to the establishment of Massachusetts Bay, Plymouth, and Pennsylvania, similar groups today form and dissipate all around us. Some of them quietly remove themselves, home-school their children, and try to wall off their lives from the impurities that surround them. They want no publicity, only to be left alone. But their utopianism is often colored by extreme intolerance for those who don't share their vision. The unwillingness to brook dissent and the willingness to damn any who disagree with the vision are the dark sides of the utopian impulse. The Puritans are no exception. In mid-seventeenth-century Massachusetts, when the prevailing paradigm was questioned, the response was swift and harsh.

The first major challenge to the Puritan orthodoxy came from the dual figures of Roger Williams and Anne Hutchinson. Others had questioned the leadership of Winthrop, some quietly, some not so, but nothing compared to the divisions caused by the Antinomians. Roger Williams arrived in Massachusetts in 1631, and, like Winthrop and many of the early Puritan notables, he was an ordained minister and had been educated at Cambridge. But unlike many of the other settlers, Williams was a separatist. Like the Pilgrims at Plymouth, he believed that the Church of England was unrepentantly corrupt and unredeemable. For several years, he preached at various churches in Massachusetts, particularly in the thriving town of Salem, and from the pulpit he denounced the hypocrisy of Puritans who still clung to the hope that they could reform the Anglican church. And he assailed the whole notion of a Bible commonwealth, claiming that there was no scriptural justification for the kind of government headed by Winthrop.

Williams was the first genuine American Baptist, and as such, he challenged the notion of the covenant. It was up to every individual to cement his or her relationship with God, and God was not bound by any prior commitment. People, said Williams, stand as individuals before God, not as members of a covenanted group. Not surprisingly, Williams triggered a reaction. Though he could be outgoing and had a reputation as a charming, engaging man, his theology undermined the foundation upon which Massachusetts Bay rested. The ministers in Salem and Boston acted quickly and banished him. Though they meant to send him back to England, he was warned by a not entirely unsympathetic Winthrop and was able to flee south to Narragansett Bay, where he founded the town of Providence. Before his banishment, Williams wrestled with the question of how any of us can know whether anyone else is saved, and for a time, he concluded that the only people he could be sure of were himself and his wife. Oddly enough, once he was free of Massachusetts, he became less exclusive. As John Winthrop wryly observed, in Rhode Island, Williams "having, a little before, refused communion with all, save his own wife, now would pray with all comers."

Over the next fifty years, Williams built a colony composed of assorted outcasts—Quakers, mavericks, and Indians. The Massachusetts minister John Cotton believed that for Williams, banishment was "not counted so much a confinement as an enlargement." Williams, the founder of Providence, devoted his considerable energy to converting the local tribes. He learned several Indian dialects and was treated with great respect by the Native Americans. Rhode Island became a haven for religious tolerance. Once he accepted the impossibility of knowing who was elect, Williams embraced any who seemed to be striving to be saved. His colony was a place of little hierarchy, and there was no clerical establishment that resembled the

Puritan churches of Connecticut and Massachusetts. In Rhode Island, each person confronted God on his or her own, and the church did not presume to meddle.[7]

The moment he disputed the idea of a covenant, Williams began to undermine the Puritan vision. After he rejected the Bible Commonwealth, he opened the door to personal liberty. Williams may have been a man of his times, a man who shared more with John Calvin than with Thomas Jefferson, but in challenging the role of the church, any church, any congregation, he opened up a new vista. Puritans such as Winthrop wanted to build a City on a Hill that would be composed only of the saved and governed by the elect. Their vision held that each congregation would determine the sanctity of its members. But Williams pictured a different type of world, one in which individuals united by their striving would live together in harmony. Their commonality was not the status of their souls; it was their commitment to live a pure life and draw ever nearer to the Lord. Rhode Island would be a place where individuals gathered freely and voluntarily, united by a common cause.

Williams was the first glimmer of the second stage of American culture. Soon after he was banished from Massachusetts Bay, another controversy erupted, this time over the theology of Anne Hutchinson. Like Williams, Hutchinson challenged the reigning orthodoxy, and like him, she provoked a reaction. Maybe because she was a woman, maybe because her manner was uncompromising, she was brought to trial for her views, and though she lost her contest with the authorities, her legacy had a lasting influence. We know comparatively little about Hutchinson; she left no writings, and most of the descriptions of her come either from her enemies or from her great-great-grandson Thomas Hutchinson, who was lieutenant-governor of Massachusetts on the eve of the Revolution. She had been a follower of the minister John Cotton in Lincolnshire, England, and when he was banished to America by Archbishop Laud, she, her husband, and her many children followed. Soon, she began to disagree with Cotton over the fundamental principle of church membership. Like Williams, she doubted that any group of fallible people could possibly discern God's grace, and she vehemently argued that no amount of good works could ever prove that someone was saved.

Winthrop may have grudgingly respected Williams, but he

thought that Hutchinson was a witch inspired by the devil who would tear the colony apart unless she was stopped. The mid-1630s were a period of acute spiritual questioning in the colony, and Hutchinson at first had the support of influential ministers such as Cotton, simply because of her passionate enthusiasm. But when she preached a theology that invalidated the authority of those ministers, they turned on her. In the fall of 1637 she was "examined" by the General Court of Boston. After several days of testimony, she was excommunicated for heresy and banished. She left for the friendlier land of Rhode Island, but soon departed for the wilds of eastern New York, where she was killed by Indians in 1643.

"Here is a great stir about graces," she is reported to have said, "and looking to hearts, but give me Christ, I seek not for graces, but for Christ, I seek not for promises, but for Christ, I seek not for sanctification but for Christ, tell me not of meditation and duties but tell me of Christ." Hutchinson distrusted anyone who made a show of striving for grace. Church membership in Massachusetts Bay depended on a public statement of faith, but Hutchinson dismissed the idea that anyone could demonstrate salvation. In fact, she said, the very act of demonstrating was a sure sign of the lack of grace. In short, if you felt that you had to show that you were saved, you weren't, and any congregation that demanded a demonstration was corrupt.

According to the records of the trial assembled by Thomas Hutchinson a hundred years later, Governor Winthrop began the examination by charging her with spreading ideas that "troubled the peace of the commonwealth and the churches here." He added that she led meetings and conducted other activities that were "not fitting for her sex." And then he continued with a litany of accusations, including the violation of the fifth commandment and dishonoring the fathers of the commonwealth. Most grave of all, he accused her of invalidating the covenant of works, a charge she was unquestionably guilty of. The question, then, was whether the covenant of works itself was valid. Whatever her skill as a preacher or a debater, she wasn't going to win that argument in the general court. The leaders of the colony believed in a covenant of works. They had to, because that was the basis of their vision and the foundation of their authority. Without it, no minister and no congregation could claim that it had the right to govern or to determine who would be admitted to church membership.

These debates may seem arcane but they went to the core of what Puritan society wished to be. Would it be a world ruled by an oligarchy of the elect, who would determine the rules for the rest? Or would it be an egalitarian community, where the only thing known was the unknowable authority of God?

Hours and hours passed, as various ministers probed Mrs. Hutchinson on her theology. She spoke about the soul as pure light and about the nature of the Resurrection, while Winthrop, Cotton, and others took exception with her stance on good works. But the climax of the trial occurred when she was asked how she had come to her teachings. "I bless the Lord, and he hath let me see which was the clear ministry and which the wrong . . . He hath let me to distinguish between the voice of my beloved and the voice of Moses, the voice of John the Baptist and the voice of antichrist, for all those voices are spoke of in scripture. Now if you do condemn me for speaking what in my conscience I know to be the truth I must commit myself unto the Lord."

She was then asked how it was she knew that it was God's spirit that inspired her. "How did Abraham know that it was God that bid him offer his son, being a breach of the sixth commandment?"

"By an immediate voice," the deputy governor replied.

"So to me by an immediate revelation," she answered.

One can imagine the gasps and the dismay that filled the room when she said this.

"How!" The deputy governor exclaimed. "An immediate revelation."

"By the voice of his own spirit to my soul," she repeated. And with that, her fate in the colony was sealed.[8]

In declaring that God had spoken to her, Anne Hutchinson raised the specter of chaos. For if ultimate authority was the voice of God heard by each of us alone, then who could test that? Who could challenge that authority? What could prevent anyone and everyone from standing up and announcing that God had spoken to them and told them that they were free to act however they pleased? By elevating her own experience of revelation above all else, Hutchinson allowed for the possibility of a community of self-guided individuals.

Over the next centuries, American faith would evolve along precisely these lines. For many Americans, religion is an intensely private experience that consists of personal and immediate experience of God. But for the Puritans, that was a dicey proposition. They didn't trust what would happen if personal revelation was permitted, and they banished Hutchinson in an attempt to keep that particular lid on that particular kettle.

But her influence and the principles of Antinomianism were infectious, and slowly, New England began to change. The vision of a Bible commonwealth started to hold less appeal, particularly to the second generation of settlers and to the children of the first wave. After the initial decades of hope and euphoria, reality was sobering, and for many, disillusioning. As more settlers arrived and New England diversified, society began to look not like the dreamed-of City on a Hill, but like any other human society, with all its wonders and weaknesses. The Puritans had managed to carve a settlement out of a wilderness, and they had successfully fended off hostile Native American tribes. But when they looked around in the latter half of the seventeenth century, ministers saw a familiar landscape of human failings. They lamented the public vice, the drunkenness, and the general moral turpitude that was increasingly prevalent. The rules governing church membership were relaxed, and from the pulpits, the clergy despaired that the vision of a utopia would remain just that. In jeremiad after jeremiad, they fulminated against the fading enthusiasm.

New England remained an intensely religious place nonetheless, and though the initial vision was diluted in the second half of the seventeenth century, no new template took its place. If the sermons are any reflection, the citizens still, throughout the seventeenth century and into the eighteenth, conceived of themselves as belonging to a society dedicated to Winthrop's vision, and Rhode Island remained a haven for religious striving.

But then something happened. Around 1740, New England was seized with a religious fervor that resembled the passion of the founding years. Known as the Great Awakening, this period seemed to presage a reinvigorated Puritan ideal, a second wave of religious utopianism. But instead, it marked the beginning of a new cultural moment, the passing of one cultural paradigm and the birth of an another.

Jonathan Edwards was an unlikely instigator of a religious revival. A serious, scholarly minister who had trained at Yale and was the grandson of the great divine, Solomon Stoddard, Edwards was devoted to his Northampton, Massachusetts, congregation, and devoted as well to unraveling the mysteries of faith. He wrote copiously; his sermons were sober, and his essays were dense and meticulously argued. But at their core was a message similar to what Williams and Hutchinson had preached, and similar as well to the essence of the Quakers. He preached that God had it in His power to save or to damn, and that the best we can hope for is to throw ourselves on the mercy of the Lord. Otherwise, we will be damned.

Side by side with his grim fatalism, Edwards held out the promise of spiritual rebirth. He believed in the possibility of a lightning conversion. Suddenly, the sinner has a direct experience of God and it is as if a veil were lifted. He called this a "new birth" and he taught that no one was exempt. Worldly status made no difference; education or manners made no difference. Everyone was equal in the eyes of God.

Edwards understood that his teachings might be unsettling, and that they might lead to excesses of zeal and occasional disruptions of orderly society. "Many that are zealous for this glorious work of God," he wrote, "are heartily sick of the great noise there is in the country, about imprudence and disorders." But, he reminded people, better those excesses than what normally passed for "regular" behavior. Regular behavior just meant that people were "asleep, or cold, or dead in religion" rather than "alive and engaged in the things of God."[9] Edwards was a deeply rational thinker, but his preaching stressed the preeminent importance of God's grace. In short, according to Edwards, you can't reason your way to God.

Edwards might not have become so influential if it hadn't been for the preaching of George Whitefield and Gilbert Tennant. Whitefield, born in Gloucester, England, where he honed his theology, ventured to the colonies in 1738 to spread his gospel. He had a musical voice and a spry gait that allowed him to dance across the stage and mesmerize a crowd. Gilbert Tennant of Philadelphia lacked Whitefield's learning and grace, but his coarseness added to his popular appeal. Audiences could identify with him. After 1740, these two stoked the Awakening, and they established the model for fire-and-brimstone sermons. Thundering against sin, warning of eternal damnation, Whitefield roused his audiences to a frenzy and demanded that they let Jesus Christ into their hearts. Listening to one of Whitefield's jeremiads, Edwards himself wept uncontrollably. Revivalist meetings today have become such a part of the American landscape that it's hard to fathom how much the Great Awakening shook American society. Even more, it shook the established clerical order of New England, and later, of the Southern colonies. Some of the meetings broke up into anarchic dancing, shrieking, book burning, wailing, speaking in tongues, and assorted convulsions.[10]

The teachings of Edwards cemented the legacy of the Antinomians, and threatened to make churches and ministers irrelevant to individual salvation. The old congregationalists of New England resisted the new teachings, and even Edwards was cast out of his church. But the change was irreversible. The reformists set up their own institutions and their own congregations, including the College of New Jersey (founded in 1746 and later renamed Princeton), Dartmouth (founded by evangelical minister Eleazar Wheelock), as well as Brown and Rutgers. These new colleges were designed to be homes to the new theology, and places where ministers who would spread the new word could be trained.

The Great Awakening both reinvigorated the religious vision of the first Puritans and transformed it. It was a period of creative destruction. What emerged would have surprised, and to some degree dismayed, the leading lights of the Awakening. Having dealt a lethal blow to the traditional religious establishment, the "New Lights" inadvertently weakened the hold of faith and religion. Whereas the cultural template of seventeenth-century New England had been primarily religious and the vision primarily that of a City on a Hill, after the Great Awakening, it shifted toward the individual, toward the freedoms of man in a civil society, and the possibilities of what free men could do. Out of this ferment, the second stage arose.

The first stage meant a society organized around God and God's will. It meant liberty circumscribed. "It is a liberty," said John Winthrop, "to do that only which is good, just and honest." Liberty to do good was not the same as liberty to do what you wanted.[11] The first stage was created by religious utopians who believed that individual freedoms existed only within the context of God's law and God's grace. Though the Puritan mainstream stressed the existence of a covenant that bound men and God, its theology opened the door to personal revelation, and try though they might, the leaders of Massachusetts Bay and Connecticut could never shut it. The leaders of Pennsylvania didn't even try. With the Great Awakening, the Antinomians ruled the day, and the religious establishment lost its hold on the culture.

The first stage, however, never disappeared, it just seemed to, as the cultural life of the colonies came to be dominated by those who agitated against the rule of George III and the English Parliament. The colonies, and later, the United States remained a deeply religious society, even though religion occupied a less dominant role. In the middle of the eighteenth century, there was a decisive shift away from the ministers and toward the squires, away from the Puritans of New England and toward the gentry of the mid-Atlantic states—who were never as enamored with the religious ideal as their northern neighbors. Boston remained a vital center of colonial society, and an important leader in the revolution, but the relative influence of New England declined. From Virginia came new champions of the rights of man and the freedom of the individual. They envisioned a different type of City on a Hill, a commonwealth of law, not of God.

The first stage began with a flurry of activity in New England. The vision moved tens of thousands of people to emigrate to a dangerous, unstable new world where the chances of early death were high. But like all subsequent visions, its ultimate goals proved elusive, and people became skeptical and dissatisfied. The process of shifting from the Puritan vision to the next was slow, confused, and messy, but eventually, its place was taken by another vision, one that would help create the United States.

TWO

INDIVIDUALISM

Every year, thousands of schoolchildren read *Johnny Tremain*. Written by Esther Forbes in 1944, the book tells the story of a young silversmith on the eve of the Revolution, who loses his hand in an accident but is still able to witness the great events of those years. The story drips with every image every American has of the Revolution: the Boston Tea Party, the battles of Lexington and Concord, Paul Revere's ride, the winter at Valley Forge, the signing of the Declaration of Independence. It depicts a tumultuous time, when two million colonists rose up and stood against king and Parliament in defense of their rights and their liberties. It also evokes American individualism. By telling the story of great events through the eyes of one boy, Forbes made the Revolution a personal story of a young man coming of age and recognizing his heritage.

Individualism, freedom, liberty, rights: today we use these terms loosely, and they seem to be slightly different facets of the same idea. Americans have come to think of themselves as a people defined by the rights of the individual and by personal freedoms, as established in the Declaration of Independence and the Bill of Rights. American identity emerged from the ferment of the latter half of the eighteenth century, but it did not emerge fully formed. At the time, freedom and liberty were contested ideas and debated heatedly. American colonists argued among themselves and with the English over rights. And as for the term "individualism," it was never used.

But this period was the crucible of American individualism. Though the actual word wouldn't come into vogue until the French introduced it in the nineteenth century, the attributes of American individualism were visible everywhere on the eve of the Revolution.[1] The Great Awakening roughly pushed the church aside, and that left the individual to stand alone in front of God's judgment. The Puritans had already eroded the traditional hierarchies of Europe, and the Great Awakening went even farther. But other obstacles remained—the king, represented in the colonies by royal governors, and Parliament. With the Seven Years War and its aftermath, these were challenged as well.

THE REVOLUTIONARY VISION EVOLVES

Unlike the vision of the early Puritans, the second stage was less coherent. It developed in fits and starts. The people who united to challenge the Stamp Act of 1765 did not have a clear sense of the world they were trying to create, and the world that the Boston radicals or the Virginia gentry envisioned in 1770 was still a fuzzy version of the world they decided to fight for in 1774 and 1775. They were often reactive, and they disagreed about what they were demanding from the British. But in the end, their disparate ambitions, motivations, and ideologies wove together, and the result was a revolutionary war for freedom, liberty, and the rights of the individual.

The Stamp Act was a tax on paper passed by Parliament to defray the costs of the Seven Years War. From the perspective of the British prime minister, the act was both justifiable and innocuous. The war had removed the threat of the French in North America, and it had been expensive. A tax to recoup costs made sense, and Parliament was the supreme legislative body for the British empire. But colonial leaders didn't see it that way. Rarely had Parliament attempted to intervene in the domestic affairs of the colonies, and the few previous attempts, such as the ill-fated attempt to create a "Dominion of New England" in the late seventeenth century, had been abandoned in the face of colonial resistance. The colonists saw the Stamp Act as an illegitimate infringement of their rights as British citizens, and they reacted angrily.

Throughout New York and New England, opposition groups calling themselves "sons of liberty" discussed ways to resist the act and force its repeal. In Virginia, the charismatic twenty-nine-year-old Patrick Henry compared the English king to Julius Caesar and Charles I, and he hoped that some American would assume the role of Brutus or Oliver Cromwell and stand up to tyranny. Under the leadership of James Otis of Massachusetts, nine colonies sent delegates to a "Stamp Act Congress" in June of 1765, which then dispatched a petition to King George III. The Congress resolved "that His Majestie's liege subjects in these colonies, are entitled to all the inherent right and liberties of his natural born subjects within the kingdom of Great Britain. That it is inseparably essential to the freedom of a people, and the undoubted right of Englishmen, that no taxes be imposed on them, but with their own consent, given personally, or by their representatives. That the people of these colonies are not . . . represented in the House of Commons in Great Britain." Few Americans not in high school or college history classes remember the Stamp Act, but it is from this resolution that we get the familiar phrase: "No taxation without representation."[2]

This phrase was widely contested in England. In the words of Soame Jenkyns, who was a member of Parliament for forty years, "No Englishman . . . can be taxed but by his own consent as an individual: that is so far from being true that it is the very reverse of truth." No one, continued Jenkyns, is ever willingly taxed, and left to individual consent, no taxes would ever be collected. The fact that he felt the need to refute this contention, however, reflects the degree to which the American colonists were making it.[3]

Faced with riots and varying degrees of active and passive resistance, Parliament rescinded the Stamp Act. The English government remained determined to shift the financial burden of governing the colonies to the colonists themselves, and that meant taxes and a heavier administrative hand. Over the next decade, as the number of new taxes mounted, colonial resentment grew and deepened. Different leaders began to think more rigorously about the place of the colonies in the empire, and about the rights of the Americans. As each side became more bitter and positions hardened, the colonists started to think of what their world would be if the English crown were no longer hovering over it.

These colonists were a disparate, thriving hodgepodge of two and a half million people. Stretched from Maine to Georgia, from the Atlantic to the Appalachians, most of them had seen immense changes in their lifetimes, as the menace of the French rose, as the fires of the Great Awakening spread, and as the economy thrived and society became more complex. The Puritan seafarers of Boston, the Dutch landlords of the Hudson, the merchants of Philadelphia, the tobacco gentry of Virginia, and the rugged farmers of the North Carolina back country shared little except a common legacy of English law and religion. That was enough to instill a vague common bond, but until the outbreak of hostilities with the British, the differences were at least as apparent as the similarities. The needs and interests of a Virginia grandee such as Thomas Jefferson bore scant resemblance to the interests and desires of a Bostonian such as John Adams. Yet, floating through the cultural ether were currents of individual enterprise, traditions of local autonomy, and an unshakable conviction that Americans bowed to no one in their potential.

The archetype for the colonial American was Benjamin Franklin, the self-made maverick whose career spanned most of the eighteenth century. He was at one time an apprentice, a printer, a publisher, an aphorist, an inventor, a diplomat, a financier, an investor, an organizer, a politician, and finally, a statesman. Born in Boston in 1706, he moved to Philadelphia as a young man and became a life-long resident, except for extended stays in France and England representing first the colonies and after the Revolution, the new Confederation. Like many leading colonials, Franklin was a late convert to the idea of independence. Until 1774, he believed in the British Empire and believed that the American colonies were best served by being a part of it. He was an advocate for greater unity and organization amongst the colonies because he thought that the more cohesive the colonies were, the more effectively they would be able to have their voices heard at the royal court in London. Franklin was also a rabid speculator, investing in numerous schemes to purchase and settle the vast lands to the west of the colonial settlements. And in his eclectic musings, many of them published during his lifetime, he emerged as the composite American, replete with all the attendant contradictions: lusty, frugal, ambitious, curious, crude, devious, farsighted, astute, and above all, without a sense of limits.[4]

In his autobiographical writings, Franklin comes across as a man who rarely doubted that he was the agent of his own destiny. That sense of individual self-determination has become a central aspect of American culture, but in the context of the mid-eighteenth century, it stood in stark contrast with the Puritan ideal. Franklin was hardly alone in his worldview, but he was a remarkably pure icon of the American individual. Even when he discussed religion, he talked not of the awesome power of God but of the importance of a measured faith and a dutiful acknowledgment of the Lord. The virtues he preached, such as "early to bed and early to rise makes a man healthy, wealthy, and wise" and the injunction that a person "keep his nose to the grindstone" are secular versions of the sermons preached from the Congregational pulpits of New England and taught informally by the Quakers of Philadelphia. The Puritan emphasis on work and rectitude as reflections of grace were transformed by eighteenth-century Americans such as Franklin into recipes for economic and political success. As Franklin flew a kite to test the powers of lightning, so, too, would the colonists test the power of the British imperium.

The tension between London and the colonies mounted in the decade after the Stamp Act, and the colonists were constantly reframing their own past as they searched for rationales to challenge the rule of king and Parliament. In Boston, the stern radical Samuel Adams and his young cousin, John Adams, constructed an intellectual framework to resist the efforts of Parliament to extract more revenue from the colonists. The senior Adams—classically educated and fond of citing the example of the early Romans as exemplars that the colonists should emulate—used the Sons of Liberty as a protorevolutionary organization much as the Bolsheviks would use "cells" to organize underneath the radar of the Russian police in the years before 1917. But Samuel Adams also acknowledged his Puritan heritage, and honored it. In short, he saw the emergent United States as a "Christian Sparta," a country inhabited by people who were at once united, willing to fight, blunt, and deeply imbued with faith in themselves and in God's power.[5]

John Adams, one of the most important of the Founding Fathers, was an irascible, ill-tempered, self-deprecating political genius. In his portraits, he looks perpetually dyspeptic, as if suffering from emotional indigestion. That may be because he was never at ease with himself or with the world around him, and from that inner tumult he questioned and probed, and from that questioning, he arrived at answers about independence and governance that helped create a new nation. In his first published essay, which he wrote when he was thirty years old in 1765, he analyzed the antecedents of American republicanism. Of course, in 1765, America was not yet a republic, so it couldn't very well have antecedents, but Adams was a visionary who saw that one day it probably would. In his view, the Puritans hadn't just been pursuing a religious polity. "It was not religion alone, as is commonly supposed," he wrote, "but it was love of universal liberty . . . that projected, conducted, and accomplished the settlement of America."[6]

Adams constructed an American past that explained the lust for liberty. His reading of that past, however, was more myth than fact. It is difficult to find any Puritan speaking about liberty or love of liberty in the way that Adams claimed. As we've seen, the Puritan framework wasn't liberty but God, grace, and the covenant. A hundred years later, however, the Puritan ideal had lost its hold, and the colonists were actively engaged in formulating a new set of ideals. Adams was one of those who articulated the new vision. Nascent in 1765 and more fully developed decades later, America's second stage imagined a society oriented around the principle of liberty, and the principle that each citizen had rights, which no human authority could legitimately deny.

The chorus of voices supporting this idea grew progressively louder. From Georgia to Massachusetts, disparate people arrived at a similar vision of the American colonies as a land dedicated to freedom and liberty, in opposition to an English crown that supposedly sought to oppress them. The language of liberty and rights was English, and it drew directly or indirectly from sources such as the Magna Carta, the writings of John Locke, and the heritage of the seventeenth-century English civil wars between Puritans and Royalists. But the colonists didn't just build on an English legacy. They were innovators. In the years after the Stamp Act crisis, Americans argued that the colonies were a land of freedom and unparalleled opportunities. They asserted that the only thing keeping Americans from realizing their dreams of a society more affluent, more stable, and more energetic than any the world had yet seen was the tyranny of Parliament and the tyranny of the king.

Of course, many of the people who developed the paradigm of

the United States as a land devoted to freedom and liberty owned slaves. That paradox has haunted the United States. The Virginians who were most adamant in their defense of American liberties denied them to black slaves who worked their land. That hypocrisy was possible only because their conception of liberty and rights and individuals was wrapped up in mores and experiences we find alien today.

For many Americans in these years, freedom was constrained. Individuals had rights and freedom, but that didn't mean that they were free to do as they pleased. Even that icon of American initiative, the singular Paul Revere, one of the Sons of Liberty, silversmith, and freedom rider, understood liberty in a different way than we do now. He saw freedom as inherently limited and he harkened back to a New England tradition that people were free to do right, not free to do what they wanted. In the eyes of the Puritans, people had the freedom to walk in the path of God, but no individual had the right to pursue lust and vice. Genuine liberty was the right to live a moral life.[7]

That was one view. Others saw freedom as absolute for those who had it and nonexistent for those who didn't, namely slaves. The tobacco states such as Virginia and the Carolinas, where slaves made up a considerable portion of the population, were home to some of the most avid defenders of freedom and liberty. Thomas Jefferson owned slaves, as did George Washington and James Madison. Jefferson conceived of himself as an inheritor of the tradition of the English gentry and of the independent yeoman farmer who was free because he owned land. For Jefferson, being a landowner who wasn't forced to work for a living was the foundation of independence, and he believed that it would be the foundation of colonial independence as well. Commenting on the irony that fervent defense of freedom often went hand in hand with chattel slavery in the South, one English observer of the American scene wrote that the Virginians "can profess an unbounded love of liberty and of democracy in consequence of the mass of the people, who in other countries might become mobs, being there nearly altogether composed of their own Negro slaves."[8] In eighteenth-century Europe, class warfare always verged on violence, and advocating equality was a far more complicated social and political issue than in America. Jefferson and other Virginians were able to speak of liberty without worrying that the have-nots would rise to demand their fair share.

Still others, such as Patrick Henry and Thomas Paine, saw liberty and freedom in expansive, absolute terms, similar to how Americans in the twentieth century talked about freedom. Clearly, there was no one definition of freedom and liberty, but the eighteenth-century colonists who defined the Revolutionary era shared the suspicion that liberty was not adequately protected by English common law, by courts, or by written constitutions. Because liberty rested at best on tentative institutional foundations, the revolutionaries believed that it had to be fought for and defended against those who would try to take it away or deny it. And though some Americans thought of liberty in communal terms, while others thought of liberty as highly personal, by the time of the Declaration of Independence, individual liberty became the rallying cry for all.

Until the passage of the Coercive Acts in 1774, which were a set of draconian laws intended by Parliament to force the colonists to cease resisting English authority, America was relatively calm. So calm, in fact, that Sam Adams confessed that he "feared that the people will be so accustomed to bondage as to forget they were ever free."[9] In response to the Coercive Acts, there was a wave of activity that made the protests against the Stamp Act look tepid in comparison. A Continental Congress was convened. Its petition to George III was rejected, and after the king declared the colonies in a state of rebellion, a second Congress met in the fall of 1775. By that point, a nascent revolutionary army had formed, and colonial troops fought against British redcoats at Bunker Hill in Boston. Even then, however, the prevailing sentiment was not in favor of independence. Instead, the leaders of revolt sought some middle ground that would restore the old equilibrium and preserve colonial liberty within the British empire.

By 1776, however, independence began to seem viable and inevitable. Each move by the British was interpreted as an example of tyranny, and as a step down the road to further American bondage. The revolutionary leaders claimed that they were the victims of a royal conspiracy to deprive them of their rights, rights that they had enjoyed until then because they were English citizens. But as the crown seemed to be depriving them of those rights, the colonists formulated an alternate basis for them, one that didn't depend on English citizenship.[10] In this new conception, liberty was something that was God-given to all people, and if that was the case, then no king could take it away.

Where John Adams traced the roots of liberty to the Puritans, Thomas Jefferson and many of the Virginia gentry had little time for religion. In drafting the statute that established religious freedom in independent Virginia, Jefferson wrote that "our civil rights have no dependence on our religious opinions." Instead, Jefferson believed that the colonists, as free inhabitants of the British empire, possessed the right of departing from England to the New World, and so they also possessed the right of departing from the empire and creating a new republic. Like his mentor Patrick Henry, Jefferson envisioned a society composed of and governed by free men. The alternative was slavery, and that was unacceptable. Henry, ever the dramatic orator, and always on the lookout for a rhetorical moment, gave the revolution one of its pithiest and more enduring aphorisms. Falling to his knees in the Virginia House of Burgesses in 1775, he cried out that life was not worth living if it were to be lived in chains. "Give me liberty!" he said, his voice descending to a low rumble, "Or give me death!" That was not quite enough for him, however, and he added a final flourish, imploring his colleagues to bury him where he knelt.[11]

Slowly, a new paradigm was being constructed, one that revolved around the words liberty, freedom, republic, independence, rights, and equality. All that remained was to make the vision a reality by separating from Great Britain. But that required an additional step. It wasn't enough to talk about rights as Englishmen, or rights as a free people, or liberties that stemmed from the Puritan heritage. In order to rouse the mass of people to action, and in order to make the cause of revolution more than simply an elite dispute between wealthy merchants and landowners on the one hand and Royal authorities on the other, a bridge had to be constructed between high principle and every individual American.

That was what Thomas Paine accomplished. He was an improbable visionary. An Englishman with no formal education and no consistent career, the thirty-seven-year-old Paine arrived in the colonies in late 1774 and settled in Philadelphia. Later portraits show him with a twinkle in his eye, a shock of hair, prominent nose, and an air of aggressive confidence. The radical Paine had no love for the English crown, and at an opportune time, after George III had declared the colonists to be in a state of rebellion, he dashed off a pamphlet called *Common Sense* that sold more than 100,000 copies within a few weeks of its publication in January 1776.

Paine took no prisoners. He lambasted the tyranny of the king, and he unequivocally endorsed independence. Unlike many colonists, he had no sentimental attachment to that amorphous thing known as the English Constitution. Unwritten and vague, the so-called Constitution was a catchall for traditional English liberties and for the balance of power between king and Parliament. Paine dismissed the idea of English liberty, and asserted that Americans could never be genuinely free within the English system because there was no genuine freedom in England. Much as the preachers of the Great Awakening roused people to emotional frenzy while the old establishment looked on in shock, Paine eschewed the carefully argued, dutiful petitions that had characterized colonial writings on the crisis. Instead, he went for raw passion, anger, and outrage. Intending to provoke his readers to action, he wrote in common language and careless prose. This offended men such as John Adams, who thought that politics should be a nobler endeavor, but educated men such as Adams were not Paine's intended audience.

Paine directed his polemic to the ordinary men and women of the colonies, to the farmers and small merchants and shopkeepers, to the coachmen and innkeepers and apprentices and servants, to the Scotch immigrants who were acutely sensitive to the perceived depredations of the English crown, and to those who arrived in the colonies on a hope and a promise. As described by the late-eighteenth-century French writer Hector St. John de Crevecoeur, the average American was an immigrant or child of immigrants. On arriving in the colonies, the new American heard the land speak to him: "Welcome to my shore, distressed European; bless the hour in which thou didst see my verdant fields, my fair navigable rivers, and my green mountains! If thou wilt work, I have bread for thee; if thou wilt be honest, sober, and industrious, I have greater rewards to confer on thee—ease and independence. . . . I shall endow thee besides with immunities of a freeman." The language is romantic, but so was the vision.[12]

In *Common Sense*, Paine deconstructed the idea that freedom could coexist with monarchy. Calling George III "the Royal Brute of

Great Britain," he refuted the English conception of liberties and rights maintained within the framework of the crown. In fact, he continued, the colonies were the product of people fleeing the tyranny of England. "This new world hath been the asylum for the persecuted lovers of civil and religious liberty. . . . Hither have they fled, not from the tender embraces of mother, but from the cruelty of the monster; and it is so far true of England, that the same tyranny which drove the first emigrants from home, pursues their descendants still." If the Americans continued to put their faith in the crown, if they looked to England to safeguard their liberties, warned Paine, they would lose what little liberty they had. Instead, they should separate, and form their own constitution which depended not on the king, but on law. "In America, THE LAW IS KING. For as in absolute governments, the king is law, so in free countries the law ought to be king, and there ought to be no other."[13]

The concept that law is the guarantor of freedom and liberty was revolutionary. Instead of a country ruled by a king, Paine described a country ruled by law, under which every citizen was equal. With *Common Sense*, the various threads of colonial political imagining came together. The colonists would form a new nation, governed by law, dedicated to freedom and liberty, and established on a foundation of the rights of individuals.

THE TRIUMPH OF THE REVOLUTIONARY VISION

From Paine it was a short step to the Declaration of Independence. Though some leaders were still cautious, and though some continued to hope for compromise in the form of autonomy or confederation with England, slowly, the options dwindled. The Second Continental Congress went about the task of setting up a nascent state, with an army and various administrative branches, while the thirteen colonies, which were now governed by newly convened legislatures and "committees of correspondence," established state constitutions and debated tactics. Even in late spring, there was no consensus on independence, even though Paine had shifted public sentiment in that direction. The Congress didn't have a mandate for independence; that would have to come from the individual colonies. Many of the delegates were disturbed that independence seemed to be coming even though no decision had been made to declare it. That was how matters stood when Thomas Jefferson was appointed to draft a declaration.

The vision for a new society based on law and the rights of man had come into focus. All that remained was to lock it in place and have it acclaimed by popular will. What had begun as a set of ideas, loose and ill formed, had coalesced into a framework for a society unlike any other. That doesn't mean that the picture was so clear at the time, nor that there was consensus on anything more than high principle. On that count, there was a wide degree of agreement amongst the leaders of the revolt and among people in general. It's impossible to know how many of the two and a half million colonists endorsed the general outlines of this new ideology, or how many were loyalists to their core. But it's fair to say that a substantial majority were in favor of moving toward independence, and for that reason, the provincial legislatures instructed their delegates to the Congress in Philadelphia to announce it to the world.

In later years, Americans came to view the Declaration of Independence as a love song to equality, liberty, and the rights of the individual. Those elements were certainly present in the draft penned by Jefferson and in the final document edited and approved by the Continental Congress. "We hold these truths to be self-evident, that all men are created equal, that they are endowed by their Creator with certain unalienable Rights, that among these are Life, Liberty, and the pursuit of Happiness." These words became enshrined in popular consciousness by subsequent generations. But for the Founding Fathers, Jefferson included, the declaration was meant to be a brief sketch of the reasons for severing the bonds with the crown.[14] Most of the text is an eloquent laundry list of grievances, not an articulation of a new creed. However, it was the section on rights that endured and became central to our founding myths.

Within fifty years of its signing on July 4, 1776, the Declaration was popularly understood as the ultimate triumph of a vision. It was celebrated as the foundation of a society based on the ideal that individual human beings have rights that no other human and no government can legitimately deny. Placing the individual's rights at the center of society required a new conception of social and political organization. The United States only became real because of that promise and that hope.

That doesn't mean that the leaders of the Revolution were united. They differed widely over what institutions would replace the crown. Some wanted thirteen independent states, others called for a republic, and a few suggested a federation of autonomous states. There was an anarchic quality to the Revolution. People agreed about what they were fighting against, but rarely about what they were fighting for. Of course, with British armies attacking from the Carolinas to Canada, there was not much room for calm deliberation about the future. Survival was the first priority. The colonies were united only insofar as they shared the basic ideology of rights and the desire to be rid of the crown (though even here, many Tory Royalists resisted the revolution). Some have described the Revolution as a civil war as much as anything else, and the internal divisions were acute.[15]

Having transformed a vision into a nascent reality, the new entity that would become the United States was buffeted by war, internal disputes, and intractable questions about what to do with independence. Following the Declaration, state conventions wrote constitutions. Variations notwithstanding, the states were all conceived as republics, that is, as societies governed by the authority of their citizens, who would deliberate and make laws to serve the public good and preserve liberty. The state constitutions were then ratified by popular vote. The men who drafted them looked to the model of ancient Athenian democracy for inspiration, and they placed a premium on virtue. They believed that only a virtuous citizenry would act unselfishly, and only virtuous citizens would be able to understand the need to balance individual, local, and national interests.

In addition, the Continental Congress drew up the Articles of Confederation, which spelled out how the states would relate to one another and what the responsibilities of the central government were. The states agreed that the Congress needed to have the power to raise an army in order to coordinate strategy against the British, and the authority to negotiate with foreign powers. But the Articles did not give the Congress the right to raise taxes. Disputes over taxation had instigated the revolt, and the states zealously guarded the principle of taxation with representation. Given that the Congress represented the states only indirectly, through delegates appointed not by popular will but by state legislatures, it was not granted the authority to tax. That was to be its most crushing liability.

For the next seven years, America's war with Britain was the pre-eminent concern, but after the settlement in 1783, the new country was racked by economic crises and an inability to act in a unified manner. The debts incurred by the Continental Congress during the war were crushing, and there was no easy way for the Congress to meet its financial obligations. Meanwhile, the states were going their separate ways. Without a common enemy, it wasn't clear what the common bonds were. If all they shared was a belief in liberty and rights, that was not sufficient to form a union. In fact, those beliefs mitigated against unity. Classical notions of republicanism held that only small groups could be effectively democratic. Relative to that standard, the states were already unwieldy, especially behemoths like New York, Pennsylvania, and Virginia. While the states recognized the necessity of some coordination, they balked at ceding control to a central government, particularly one with the power to tax, to print money, or to raise an army.

The 1780s were a period when state governments exercised their hard-won freedoms and reveled in the absence of a more powerful government telling them what to do. In one sense, it was an intensely democratic period. More people had the right to vote and to have a voice in public affairs, and political participation was extraordinarily high. The states issued their own currency, debated the nature of society, and passed laws touching on most aspects of life. The arguments in the various legislatures were involved and heated. Never before had so many had so much to say and so much right to say it, and never before had there been such focus on setting up governments dedicated to preserving freedom.

At the same time, these years saw what many people termed the "excesses of democracy." The newly empowered state legislatures passed so many laws that it was hard to keep track of them, and the thirteen states were so focused on flexing their autonomy that they worked at cross-purposes. Not only was the economy in chaos because of the debts and damages of the war, but the credit system was in shambles. International credit was tight because of the constant defaults on debts, and the animosity between the states prevented any effective joint action on repayment. Legislatures printed paper money with abandon and then passed stringent laws to collect debts. The states also competed with one another for primacy in settling the frontier to the West. And American shipping was constantly preyed upon by the British navy, while the Continental Congress watched helplessly and depended on the voluntary efforts of the states to provide men, ships, and money.

Individuals throughout the new United States celebrated their freedoms and were highly reluctant to submit to any authority, even if it was in their best interests. Republicanism was the order of the day, but it was often interpreted in a manner that recalled the Antinomians. Many people assumed the right to determine what was right, to assess whether or not a particular course of action was consonant with the principles of individual liberty. The old hierarchies were no longer respected, and the traditional deference of the lower classes, be it to wealthy merchants in New England or landed gentry in Virginia, disappeared. The Revolution wasn't just against the English crown; it changed the social order of the former colonies.[16]

DISILLUSIONMENT

As problems mounted, many people concluded that democracy had run amok. Throughout the colonies, men such as John Adams, James Madison, Gouverneur Morris of Pennsylvania, John Jay of New York, and William Paterson of New Jersey worried that the United States was descending into chaos. Looking at how democracy was working, they concluded that strong states and a loose federation were not a viable combination. As George Washington wrote to John Jay, "Our affairs are drawing rapidly to a crisis." Convinced that a stronger union was needed, these men became known as the Federalists, and they took a dim view of the American political scene. They looked around and found little virtue. Instead, they saw a surfeit of selfishness. They feared that economic collapse would leave the United States vulnerable to attack and maybe even to reabsorption by the British. At best, they saw a sprawling continent of disunited states that were undermining their collective future.

The Federalists began to talk and to ponder, and they concluded that the Articles of Confederation needed to be discarded and another system created. But they couldn't announce that directly. Too many people in too many states distrusted their motives, and staunch republicans such as Patrick Henry warned that the revolution could

be turned back by reactionary aristocrats who supported the Federalists. When the delegates assembled in Philadelphia to amend the Articles in 1787, they did so under the pretense that they were simply
recommending revisions. They had no mandate and no authority to
establish a new constitutional system, but that is what they proceeded
to do.[17]

Many of the state governments looked on warily, believing that
there was a hidden plot. When proposals to amend the Articles were
first introduced, delegates from Massachusetts sounded the alarm:
"Plans have been artfully laid, and vigorously pursued, which . . .
would inevitably have changed our republican governments into
baleful aristocracies." If the Federalists had their way, claimed the
Massachusetts delegates, Congress would acquire vast powers that
would reduce the states to a vassalage not unlike what had previously
existed between the colonies and the English government. Distrust of
the motives of the framers of the Constitution was present at the
start, and in later years, some historians would interpret the Constitutional Convention as a second revolution that saw the triumph of
conservative elites over popular democracy. That is unfair. The
motives of the framers of the Constitution may have been complex,
but these delegates believed in a unified nation, governed by a strong
central government that was more powerful than the individual state
governments. Their vision was a reaction against the individualism of
the Revolution, but it was no less pure.

As the fifty-five delegates gathered in Philadelphia, one of the
fears of George Washington came to pass. Asserting their own autonomy, a group of farmers in western Massachusetts took up arms
against their state. The farmers who followed Daniel Shays in 1787
were not preaching democracy; they were taking desperate action
against taxes they could not pay and against the harsh measures that
the state was taking to collect them. The only way to prevent the local
courts from foreclosing the farmers' property was to prevent the
court from convening, and the only way to do that was to seize the
courthouse. In order to seize the courthouse, the farmers needed
weapons, so they raided an armory in Springfield. Shays had served
Massachusetts during the revolution, and he had settled in Pelham.
Though his ragtag group succeeded in taking some weapons, they
were disorganized and soon routed by the militia. However, for more

than a month, it looked as though Shays's movement might ignite a wider rebellion. "My name is Shays," began a ballad written soon after, "in former days/In Pelham I did dwell, Sir./But now I'm forced to leave the place/Because I did rebel, Sir./Within the State I lived of late/By Satan's foul invention,/In Pluto's cause against the laws/I raised an insurrection."

Though Massachusetts appealed to the Congress for help in suppressing the revolt, there was little that Congress could do. That alarmed the Federalists. Shays's Rebellion was interpreted as an omen of what could happen to the United States unless a new constitution was written. Thomas Jefferson, hearing about the episode in Paris, where he was representing the Congress, dismissed the rebellion as benign. "A little rebellion now and then is a good thing; the tree of liberty must be refreshed from time to time with the blood of patriots and tyrants." Notwithstanding Jefferson's rhapsody, Shays was just a poor, desperate farmer who barely escaped with his life to Vermont, hardly the patriot described by Jefferson.[18]

Shays's Rebellion signaled that there was precious little loyalty to government, any government. No one fought for the United States. No one rallied to defend Massachusetts, and Massachusetts was at best lukewarm about amending the Articles to prevent a repeat of Shays's movement. The Revolution had succeeded in carving a new world based on a set of principles, but those principles weren't sufficient. The world was new, but old problems remained and new ones beset the United States. A doctrine of republicanism was fine and well, but what about trade and economics? What of currency speculation and banks? What of the new lands to the West and transportation? The Revolution had been silent on such matters, and the Articles gave Congress little authority to address the issues. The vision that sustained the Revolution wasn't enough to forge a union.

By the late 1780s, republican individualism had lost much of its shine, even in the eyes of men such as George Washington who had been among its most avid defenders. The second stage of American culture saw the blossoming of America, the land of the free. The next stage would create a United States.

THREE

UNITY

The celebration of liberty and individual rights had fueled a revolution, but it had not established a perfect society. Removing the English crown had led to its own set of problems. Looking back centuries later, the 1780s may not seem like a period of "excessive" democracy. In fact, it's possible to see the period just after the Revolution as a rare moment of republicanism in practice. But that was not how many members of American society felt at the time. They did not see the glories of individualism and liberty but the perils of anarchy. Anxious about such dangers, they reacted, and they conceived of an alternate paradigm.

The framers of the constitution tended to be well-to-do. They owned land, or were wealthy merchants. They had led the Revolution and fought against the British, but most of them were not identified with the masses. For that reason, their motives have often been criticized by later generations as reactionary and conservative. The framers were certainly conservative, in that they were uncomfortable with the social extremes that accompanied the Revolution. But they weren't reactionary. They simply had a different vision.

A Vision for a New Nation

The new vision was for a "union." At various times in the past, Americans had spoken of unity and union. Even Thomas Paine, the icon of the revolutionary paradigm, understood the virtues of union. "It is not in numbers," he wrote, "but in unity that our greatest strength lies."[1] But the defenders of the culture of the 1780s saw those who called for union as aristocrats who wished to put democracy in an early grave. To a degree, the opponents of the Constitution, the Anti-Federalists, were correct. Some of the Federalists, represented most notably by Alexander Hamilton, did have antipathy for popular democracy and preferred a government by the elite. Even more, men like Hamilton were so alarmed by the problems of the 1780s that they denigrated democracy and individualism. As the new vision took shape, the old one fell into disrepute.

Given his origins, Hamilton was a surprising defender of privilege. He was a bastard child born on Nevis in the West Indies (today's Caribbean) who was orphaned as a boy and made his way to New York as a teenager. He was a charismatic speaker and a gifted writer, and he took the opportunity of the Revolution to make a name for himself as an aide on Washington's staff. By the late 1780s, Hamilton had become an ardent Anglophile who exerted his formidable energies and utilized the contacts he had built up during the war to push for a constitutional convention. Though he was not an active participant during the meetings in Philadelphia in the middle months of 1787, he was instrumental in getting the new constitution ratified.[2]

The convention that drafted the constitution grappled with countless issues, from the basic structure of the government to the larger philosophical questions of slavery and sovereignty. Would large states have more say than small? Would slave states count slaves as part of their population? Would the federal government have the right to raise an army? What powers would the president have? How would dangerous factionalism be avoided? What would be the division of power between the states and the federal government? All of these questions were debated as the document was drafted. Then the draft was debated state by state and put to a ratification vote that narrowly passed in key states such as New York and Massachusetts.

In the end, the Constitution was established as a compact between the people of the United States rather than between the states. That made all the difference. Rather than a union of states, which was what the Articles of Confederation had been, the Constitution was a union of free people. Of course, not everyone involved in framing and ratifying the Constitution saw it that way. Many of the

Southerners, including such leading Virginians as Jefferson, believed that states' rights preceded the Constitution and that whatever the powers of the federal government, the states retained a large measure of autonomy and authority. The Constitution itself was not internally consistent. It began, "We the people of the United States, in order to form a more perfect Union, establish justice, insure domestic tranquility, provide for the common defense, promote the general welfare, and secure the blessings of liberty to ourselves and our posterity, do ordain and establish this Constitution for the United States of America." This seems to be a clear statement that the union is composed of individuals. But then, to satisfy those who were uncomfortable with that principle, the tenth amendment was added, which said that "The powers not delegated to the United States by the Constitution, nor prohibited by it to the States, are reserved to the States respectively, or to the people." The ambiguity of the Constitution was an accurate reflection of divided opinions at the time. Even though the Constitution was eventually ratified, those divisions remained, and the question of whether the United States was a union of people or of states became the central fissure for the next seventy-five years.[3]

The debates over ratifications were acrimonious. The Anti-Federalists accused the Federalists of tyranny, and the Federalists warned that if the Constitution was not adopted, there would be anarchy. George Mason of Virginia, a leading Anti-Federalist, declared that the Constitution created "one consolidated government" with the power of direct taxation, and that state governments would be overwhelmed and destroyed. "It is ascertained by history," he said, "that there never was a government over a very extensive country without destroying liberty." Following Mason, Patrick Henry granted that while the document had "beautiful features," they appeared to him as "horrible." In time, he warned, the president would become king, the senate would be a tool for minority control, and liberty would expire.[4]

The Federalists had to convince the public that the Constitution would be a stronger guarantor of liberties than the alternatives. George Washington put the matter plainly. The only way to decide on ratification was to answer the question, "Is it best for the states to unite, or not to unite?" Believing that it was best, three men penned a series of "letters" published in newspapers in key states. Written by Hamilton, James Madison, and John Jay, the Federalist letters boldly made the case for ratification. The intent, according to Hamilton in Federalist letter No. 1, was to prove "the utility of the Union to your political prosperity—The insufficiency of the present Confederation to preserve that Union." Madison, the Virginia planter who earned the sobriquet "Father of the Constitution," argued in Federalist No. 10 that the great dangers of republican democracy were "faction" and the tyranny of the majority. Factions, Madison contended, acted in their own interest and hijacked the common good.

In arguing against factions, Madison described the Constitution and the resulting Union as the pathway to a better world. He claimed that with its checks and balances, the Constitution would create a federal government that was above faction and above the selfish interests of individual states. And with factions in check, human pettiness and provincialism would be contained, people would be secure, the common good would be served, and the interests of the minority would be protected.[5]

With the Constitution, the Federalists supplanted one utopian vision with another. Some of them were aware of just how utopian the endeavor was. "This is a new event in the history of mankind," said Governor Samuel Huntington to the Connecticut ratifying convention. "Heretofore, most governments have been formed by tyrants and imposed on mankind by force. Never before did a people, in time of peace and tranquility, meet together by their representatives and, with calm deliberation, frame for themselves a system of government."[6] The arguments for ratification eventually carried the day, though not without some tense moments in late 1787 and early 1788. The Constitution was adopted by the states, and a new government assembled in Philadelphia in 1789.

The vision that a national union would preserve liberty and generate prosperity was no less idealistic than the belief, in the late 1770s and 1780s, that the virtue of individual citizens would lead to a smoothly ordered society. The Federalists had created a national government out of the conviction that a strong union was imperative. Having won that battle, they found themselves embroiled in others.

They had created a federal government stronger than any one individual state government. They had endowed it with responsibilities and a structure. But there was as yet no national identity, and no consensus about what the United States was. Was it a nation of slavery or of freedom? Was it a society of democracy or aristocracy? Was it agrarian or mercantile? Did it look toward Europe or the Western frontier? To England or France? And how would the federal government actually govern? These were the questions that arose in the coming decades, and to an extent, they all revolved around the larger puzzle of who would define the United States and what its definition would be.

In essence, the vision of the third stage was constantly challenged until the Civil War. Many Americans felt that the Union should go no further than the rudimentary framework established in 1789; others believed that the ideological limits of the Union were reached during the Jacksonian era. With each challenge, the defenders of the third stage were forced to come up with new twists. Each contest led to a more sophisticated articulation of the vision.

It's important to keep in mind that these were debates largely between elites. The questions were argued in Congress, raised in cases before the Supreme Court, and addressed by the president. But the federal government was a small arena in the late eighteenth century, and it remained small in the first decades of the nineteenth century after the capital moved to a fetid marsh off the Potomac named in honor of George Washington. Institutionally, the federal government was tiny, with several hundred people actively employed. There is no comparison, in size or scope, between the federal government of the nineteenth century and the federal government of the twentieth.

That meant, for instance, that farmers in Kentucky had little say, and perhaps even less interest, in the minutiae of elitist politics in Washington. The debates over the nature of the union were not of deep interest to the frontiersmen who settled the Mississippi region or to the mill workers of New England. Nonetheless, the battles between Federalists and Republicans, between the Jacksonian Democrats and the Whigs, and between North and South, were essential to the formation of a national American identity. The men who participated in the federal government, or contributed to the debates surrounding it, shaped the vision of the third stage. In multiple ways, this vision filtered through society, and in time, influenced the self-conception of all Americans.

The Debates

The first fault line was between Federalists and Republicans. Though these were not parties in the modern sense, they were factions in the Madisonian sense. The Federalists gathered around Hamilton, Jay, Adams, and the new president, George Washington. The Republicans looked to Madison and Jefferson. The two camps fought over several key issues—a proposed treaty with England being the most contentious—but the larger division was philosophical. The Federalists, the faction of choice for the grandees of New England and the mid-Atlantic states, envisioned a hierarchical nation that would be governed by an elite with the consent and the occasional vote of the people, that focused on trade and "manufactures," and that looked toward Europe and Great Britain. By contrast, the Republicans saw the United States as a country of landed yeomen—small, independent farmers who were the bulwark of liberty. Jefferson had in his mind's eye a classical ideal of an egalitarian republic, with few divisions between classes, little emphasis on commerce or industrialization, and expansion into the great hinterland that lay to the west of the Appalachians.

Leaving office, with people bitterly divided, Washington made a plea. Though he thought of himself as a man above faction, Washington was part of the problem. By 1797, he was closely identified with Hamilton and the Federalists, and Hamilton actually wrote significant portions of Washington's farewell address. Seeing the need to close the fissures, Washington tried to encourage Americans to identify themselves with the national government. Though the farewell address is remembered for its isolationist policy of nonentanglement with foreign powers, Washington also spoke about union. "While, then, every part of our country thus feels an immediate and particular interest in union," he began, "all parts combined cannot fail to find in the united mass of means and efforts greater strength, greater resource, proportionably greater security from external danger. . . . To the efficacy and permanency of your union a government for the whole is indispensable." He called on all Americans to adhere to the national government and to the idea of unity.[7]

After an unhappy and divisive presidency under Adams, Thomas Jefferson won the election of 1800. He called the victory a "revolution" that would return the United States to the republican principles that characterized the Revolutionary era. Having become even more passionate that the Union was a limited compact between states, Jefferson now found himself in the awkward position of being at the head of a powerful federal government. Jefferson looms large in the American national consciousness. He was a vastly curious and creative man, whose interests ranged from architecture to politics, from farming to philosophy. He was also inconsistent. He could vociferously defend the rights of the individual while simultaneously rationalizing slavery. He could be a champion of states' rights while being a heavy-handed chief executive of the federal government. Jefferson's gyrations were not necessarily more extreme than those of others in his day, but they have marked us.

Preaching the virtues of union at his inauguration, Jefferson extended a hand to his adversaries. To the surprise of the Federalists, he stated that "We are all Republicans, we are all Federalists. If there be any among us who would wish to dissolve this Union or to change its republican form, let them stand undisturbed as monuments of the safety with which error of opinion may be tolerated where reason is left free to combat it. . . . I believe this . . . the strongest Government on earth. . . . Let us then, with courage and confidence pursue our own Federal and Republican principle, our attachment to union and representative government."

But he was clearly uncomfortable in his new role, and he shunned the trappings of power and prestige that the Federalists had acquired. His White House, in the swamps of Washington, was an unpretentious place, and Jefferson made sure it stayed that way. He had few servants, he lived simply, and he spent two terms futilely trying to maintain the United States as an agrarian land of liberty.

By the time he left office, the United States had more than doubled in size, and its character was more Hamiltonian than ever, even though Hamilton himself died after a duel of honor with the traitorous onetime vice-president, Aaron Burr. As one historian of the period observed, "Americans still maintain a pharisaical reverence for Thomas Jefferson, but they have in reality little use for what he said and believed. . . . What they really admire is what Alexander Hamilton stood for." That is overstating the case, but Jefferson believed in a republic of farmers, not a nation of industrialists. He was suspicious of Europe, and while he waged an aggressive foreign policy to keep

European markets open to American goods, he saw the old world as a threat, and preferred the vast North American hinterland. So he obtained the Louisiana Purchase from France, hoping that the new land would ensure the Republican character of the country, hoping that it would be "an empire of liberty."[8]

Jefferson shared with the Federalists a utopian vision of a republic. But his imagined republic had a different character from theirs. Though the Federalists were in retreat, they weren't dead yet, and they fought. They saw Jefferson's policies toward Great Britain and France, then embroiled in the Napoleonic Wars, as inimical to trade, and they distrusted the motives behind the Louisiana Purchase. They thought that Jefferson wanted to weaken American commerce and industry, and they may have been right to suspect him. The irony was that in declaring an embargo against the French and the British during the Napoleonic Wars, Jefferson inadvertently spurred the growth of American industry. Unable to import many of the products that they had come to depend on, Americans after 1807 began to make those products themselves. The embargo and its aftermath were a time of economic recession, but the country emerged from Jefferson's presidency more geared toward commerce and industry than ever before.

The final clash between Federalists and Republicans erupted during the War of 1812. The Republican James Madison had succeeded Jefferson, and he led the country into a war against Great Britain. Relations had been deteriorating for some time, and settlers in the territories of the West were eager to end the British dominion over Canada. The so-called War Hawks, a class of young, aggressive representatives in Congress who came from new states such as Ohio, Tennessee, and Kentucky, wanted to prove once and for all that the United States was a nation—strong, independent, and not to be taken lightly by the imperious British. The resulting war, supported and declared by the Republicans, alarmed the Federalists of New England. They feared that their control of the country was slipping away. First, the party of Jefferson had eclipsed them, and now Jefferson's children in the West were determining the future. In an act of desperation, a group of Federalists met in Hartford in 1814.

The Hartford Convention angrily denounced the war and recommended constitutional amendments that would curb the power of the Southern states and prevent the admission of new states without a two-thirds majority of Congress. The Union was being defined without them, and the Federalists made a last effort to halt the progression of power away from New England and away from their vision. But the war ended with Andrew Jackson's victory at New Orleans, and the Hartford Convention was utterly discredited. With it, the Federalists all but ceased to exist as a cohesive movement.[9]

The struggle between the Federalists and the Republicans had added flesh to the skeletal idea of union. After 1815, the United States was a country defined by a synthesis of the two perspectives. The nation was unequivocally commercial, and the economic policies of the government derived directly from Hamilton. But the values were Republican and democratic. Even so, there still was no consensus on the role of the federal government in fostering the Union. Some believed that the government should actively work to strengthen the bonds holding the nation together. Others, who were wary of a federal government that was powerful enough to hold the nation together, wanted a limited role for Washington, and they preferred the problems of a weak government to the dangers of a strong one.

During these decades, aspects of the earlier stages continued to exert a pull. The strains of both religion and individualism coursed through popular culture, particularly in the territories to the west, and particularly in the form of another religious revival, known as the Second Great Awakening. Beginning at Cane Ridge, Tennessee, in 1801, tens of thousands of people gathered for vast open-air revival meetings where they listened in rapt frenzy to sermons of hellfire and damnation. The Second Great Awakening gave rise to American denominationalism, and Baptist and Methodist churches proliferated throughout the West, preaching a message of individual salvation. The frontier settlements were full of men and women who drank profusely, lived profanely, and then repented, people who seethed with ambition to make something of themselves and whose religion was intensely personal, totally voluntary, and frequently dramatic. People floated from sect to sect, just as they fluidly migrated to new lands and changed political philosophies. Though this epoch revolved around the question of unity and nationalism, faith and individual freedom were embedded in the culture.

The War of 1812 produced a new generation of leaders, including Henry Clay of Kentucky and Andrew Jackson of Tennessee. Clay's political career would span nearly four decades, and in time, he earned the sobriquet "The Great Compromiser." Time and again, he exerted his charisma, charm, and stirring oratory to defend the Union. And more than once, he convinced his less visionary comrades to make concessions in the interests of preserving unity. Like Jefferson, Madison, and countless others, he owned slaves, and, like them, he detested slavery even though he was complicit. A tall, rangy man, he could command the stage, and he may be the most important American never to be president. That distinction might also be shared by two others who alternately battled with him and worked with him in these decades: Daniel Webster of Massachusetts and John C. Calhoun of South Carolina. Together, these three formed what has been called "The Great Triumvirate," after the Roman triumvirates that ruled during the waning days of the Roman republic before it became an empire. Webster was a powerful orator who argued before the Supreme Court, was frequently drunk, always in debt, and often angry, and he schemed and fought for his own fame and for the Union. Calhoun was a scowling tight-lipped Southerner with hawk eyes who defended slavery and states' rights with every ounce of his considerable intellect, while only grudgingly acknowledging the limited virtues of Union. Clay was a passionate frontier compromiser. The Great Triumvirate put their stamp on the political culture to a degree that is unimaginable today.[10]

And then there was Jackson, "Old Hickory," victor at the Battle of New Orleans. A bundle of contradictions, Jackson was a fiery man, who fought multiple duels to defend his honor against slights, real or imagined, and waged violent campaigns against Native American tribes in Florida. He was a lawyer and a land speculator, loyal to the Union and deeply suspicious of it, and, ultimately, a defender of the common man. Jackson became a master of political patronage and a hero of popular democracy. During his presidency from 1829 to 1837, the country shifted politically and demographically. Along with the division between North and South, the Jacksonian era was marked by tension between East and West, with Jackson firmly in the latter camp. Again, it was a matter of who would decide the nature of the nation. The East stood for established privilege and centralized banking; the West for rugged individualism and "wild cat" banks that issued paper currency worth little more than the paper itself. When Jackson vetoed the bill renewing the Bank of the United States in 1832, he condemned the patrons of privilege in the East in language that was a harbinger for the populism of later decades.

Like the president himself, Jacksonian America was contradictory. Individuals were fully capable of holding incompatible beliefs. Southern Jacksonians could be both ardent defenders of egalitarianism one day and ardent defenders of slavery the next. Many of Jackson's supporters, especially the "Albany Regency" in upstate New York, were powerful landlords who had controlled large estates for generations and who thought nothing of telling their tenants how to vote. And Jackson's rhetoric aggravated class struggle. Unpropertied workers agitated for more rights and more power, and the propertied classes squirmed, even though they controlled a substantial proportion of the country's wealth.

In every arena, on every major question, there was strife, as more and more people championed their definition of the nation and clamored for the power and position to transform those visions into reality. Henry Clay imagined a union held together by bonds both material and spiritual, and he wanted to create an "American system" that would use federal funds and federal initiatives to build canals and roads that would connect the disparate regions of the country. Clay believed that those physical links would not only facilitate trade and help farmers sell their products to wider markets; they would also make the Union stronger. But his plan was attacked as another special interest, and it was defeated by Jackson on the grounds that it was an unacceptable use of federal power. Others focused on unity in other realms. In popular culture, Noah Webster tried to standardize American English, believing that a "national Language [was] a band of national union." The Supreme Court, under the stewardship of Chief Justice John Marshall, advanced the notion that the court was the protector of the nation, and, in case after case, he established the Supreme Court as the arbiter of the Union.[11]

But perhaps the most portentous struggle, and the one whose outcome was most uncertain, was between the states and the national government. One perspective was that the Union was the creation of the states. The other was that the Union originated with the people.

One saw the Union as dissolvable; the other held that the Union was inviolable. The divide grew ever larger, and the reason was slavery. The debate over states' rights had a bona fide philosophical component that talked of rights, freedoms, and liberties. In the eighteenth-century context, fear of a strong central government was more than justified. But as the debate evolved in nineteenth-century America, the issue of slavery versus freedom became paramount. The contest split the country geographically between North and South, economically between agrarian and commercial, and ideologically between states' rights and the Union.

Jackson stared down a major crisis in 1832–1833. Led by Calhoun, South Carolina declared that it would not comply with federal taxes. Believing that the tariffs were an unjust imposition, Calhoun argued that a state had the right under the Constitution to opt out of any law that it did not agree with. Jackson, whose animosity toward Calhoun was personal as well as political, reacted sternly. He declared that if South Carolina persisted, it would be committing treason. "The Constitution of the United States," he said, "forms a government, not a league; and whether it be formed by compact between the States or in any other manner, its character is the same. It is a Government in which all the people are represented, which operates directly on the people individually, not upon the States; they retained all the power they did not grant. But each State, having expressly parted with so many powers as to constitute, jointly with the other States, a single nation, can not . . . possess any right to secede . . . because such secession does not break a league, but destroys the unity of a nation." Jackson granted that in extreme cases of tyranny, secession as a revolutionary act might be justified, but he unequivocally rejected the idea that it was a right. He called on all Americans to rally against what Calhoun and South Carolina were advocating. Only then would "the sacred Union be preserved."[12]

The people of South Carolina didn't embrace Jackson's appeal, but they did back down when he threatened to use the navy and the army to force it to. Calhoun was not ready for civil war, and for the next twenty years, the issues raised by the Nullification Crisis were studiously avoided. They came up again and again, but they were not addressed directly until the 1850s. Slavery was kept out of any debates in Congress by an informal but effective "gag rule," and the question of states' rights was channeled into Western expansion, Manifest Destiny, and war with Mexico.

During these years, Clay continued to advocate for union, while the contest between North and South, slavery and freedom, was waged by proxy in the territories of Texas, Kansas, and Nebraska. By acquiring new land and new states, the South hoped to create an empire of slavery that would be able to hold its own against the pressure of the North. Slavery connoted an entire way of life, from economics to values, and only by expanding did the South believe that the system could be sustained and the nation defined by Southerners. By the 1840s, people talked of the Union as divided between "two great sections," and major issues were argued in terms of the effects on those sections. The annexation of Texas in the 1840s was debated in terms of whether that would strengthen or weaken the Union. The same was true for the Mexican-American War between 1848 and 1850, the admission of California to statehood in 1850, and then the political crises of the 1850s that focused on Kansas, Nebraska, and the emergence of a new Republican Party.

THE CIVIL WAR AND THE TRIUMPH OF UNION

In the decade before the Civil War, the precarious status quo of the Union collapsed. The old parties, which had never been particularly cohesive, frayed and crumbled. The Whigs shredded into sectional pieces, and the Democrats were wheezing badly. Coalitions such as the Liberty Party and the Know-Nothing Party flourished briefly, and then fell apart when they tried to obtain a national footing. The South saw the situation in stark terms; Southerners doubted that the North cared deeply about slavery. Instead, they saw Northern animosity to the extension of slavery into Kansas, Nebraska, and the West as a naked power play.

On the other side, the motives of those opposed to slavery weren't necessarily pure. Some of the staunchest defenders of "Free Soil" were virulently racist. They didn't care about the plight of the slaves; they just didn't want the economic competition that slavery represented. Radical abolitionists such as William Lloyd Garrison condemned the hypocrisy of the North, claiming that defense of economic interests was a violation of the dearest principles of the Declaration of Independence. Garrison's critique of the limpness of many Northerners on the question of slavery echoed the critiques of Southerners who saw the Northern attack on slavery as a convenient smoke screen for more mercantile motives.

Slavery was at the core of the ideological struggle of the 1850s. In order to craft the Compromise of 1850, which admitted California as a free state and created a stringent Fugitive Slave Law as the trade-off, the Great Triumvirate made one last encore. Calhoun, so sick that his speeches were read for him, bitterly denounced the North for its depredations. Aging and ill, Clay roused himself to resolve the impasse, aided by the younger Democratic leader from Illinois, Stephen Douglas, and Webster made one of his greatest senatorial speeches. Declaring that compromise on principles was better than dissolution of the Union, Webster enjoined his listeners that "instead of dwelling in these caverns of darkness, instead of groping with those ideas so full of all that is horrid and horrible, let us come into the light of day; let us enjoy the fresh air of liberty and union." The senate agreed to a compromise, and the Union was preserved.[13]

But for too many, the cost was unacceptable. For years, the tensions had been shunted into various safety valves. The parties themselves had kept the lid on sectional strife by providing a political outlet for social and ideological conflicts. The parties were national, and each contained a Northern and Southern wing. They mimicked the divisions in the country as a whole, and political elites could fight within the parties over the issues that fragmented the nation. After the Compromise of 1850, however, the party system disintegrated.

In the North and the West, the vacuum was filled by a new Republican Party that lacked even the pretense of being a national party. The Republicans were explicitly against slavery, and they rejected the philosophy that the states preceded the Union. Granted, the Republicans were divided over what to do about slavery, and outright abolitionists were a small minority. Most Republicans wanted to prevent slavery from expanding any further, and they hoped that by ghettoizing the slave states, the institution would soon whither and die. The rapid rise and popularity of the Republican party set off alarms throughout the South, and with each Republican advance, Southern paranoia increased.[14]

After 1856, when the Republicans made a strong showing in the presidential election that resulted in a victory for the inept Democratic moderate James Buchanan, the northern Democratic Party fragmented. Significant numbers of former Democrats bolted for the Republicans. The people who joined the Republican party concluded that further compromise on slavery would do more damage to the union than standing for liberty and freedom. Moderate and radical Republicans shared a hatred of slavery and a determination that it would no longer define the Union. The contradiction between the principles of the Declaration of Independence, which held that all men are created equal, and the reality of chattel slavery was intolerable to most Republicans, and for that reason, the Republicans were intolerable to most Southerners.

People in every region lost faith that the party system could hold the country together. Clay and Webster died soon after the Compromise of 1850, and they were replaced by men such as "The Little Giant" Stephen Douglas of Illinois, and the shrewd, ambitious William Seward of New York. Seward found slavery distasteful, but he also rejected the narrow racist nativism of many Northerners. In these years, antislavery sometimes went hand in hand with anti-immigration and anti-Catholicism, and Seward denounced such hateful nativism. This cost him support, but he was one of the most powerful forces in the Republican Party. Douglas, a Democrat, made a fortune assisting the first railroad barons, built a formidable political apparatus for himself in Illinois, and planned to become president. He faced a stiff senatorial campaign in 1858 because of an obscure Republican challenger. Douglas won the election, but it was the loser who emerged enhanced.

Abraham Lincoln is such a commanding figure in American history that it's easy to forget that his political career was astonishingly brief. Though he served a term in Congress in the 1840s, he was little known in the United States until his debates with Douglas in 1858. For the next seven years, until his assassination in 1865, Lincoln was the pivotal determinant of American identity. Seven years. That was all. Yet the country underwent a second revolution during that period, and the struggles that marked this stage were finally settled.

Lincoln, born in a Kentucky cabin, was a gangly frontiersman, a self-taught lawyer, a onetime militiaman, an Illinois congressman, awkward and odd looking, deeply emotional and occasionally depressive, a soulful stalk of a man who always doubted the realism of idealism. A brilliant orator, Lincoln was also unorthodox. Unlike Daniel Webster or other famous rhetoricians of the era, Lincoln eschewed long, complicated speeches replete with flowery phrases and intricate narrative arcs. If he had been a composer, he wouldn't have been Chopin. He was a minimalist. Every word packed a punch. His ideas were pared down, his prose sparse. He believed in saying what he needed to and saying it unvarnished.

He was sickened by slavery and distressed to be a citizen of country founded on a commitment to inalienable equality yet constructed to accommodate the most inegalitarian arrangement imaginable. By the 1850s, Lincoln understood that any alteration in the impasse would come at a price, perhaps at a great price. He recognized that forcing the issue of slavery might drive the South to extreme acts, but he didn't think that it would be possible to preserve the status quo. Even if the North allowed for the extension of slavery into the southern tier of the Western territories, he felt that the issue would have to be decided one way or the other. For him, only one option was morally tenable.[15]

In one of his most quoted remarks, made during a speech accepting the Republican nomination for the Illinois senate race in 1858, he stated his beliefs. "A house divided against itself cannot stand. I believe this government cannot endure half slave and half free. I do not expect the Union to be dissolved. I do not expect the House to fall. But I do expect it will cease to be divided. It will become all one thing, or all the other. . . . Whether this shall be an entire slave nation is the issue before us." For Lincoln, there was no such thing as a nation partly free. For Lincoln, slavery was an antidemocratic contaminant which made a mockery of liberty and distorted the institutions of government. In his debates with Douglas, Lincoln stressed this point, while Douglas argued that slavery ought to be left to the discretion of states and to the settlers who formed new states. Douglas, like his mentor Clay, opted for compromise over principle. But as was true during the Puritan epoch and the Revolutionary era, those driven by a vision of a better world defined the culture. Pragmatists were pushed aside.

Lincoln fought for an ideal Union that would be free. He was confronted by Southerners whose Union was based on slavery. Different values, different economies, and different nations flowed from those different visions, and the result was a Civil War to settle the issue. Had Lincoln lived fifty years earlier, the choices would have been different. In an earlier phase, defining the Union involved different questions. But after the triumph of the Hamiltonian economic vision, after the flowering of Jeffersonian values, after the Jacksonian victory for a society governed by a strong national government, slavery remained unresolved, and Lincoln was an ideologue. As he said in the last of the debates with Douglas, slavery represented "the eternal struggle between . . . right and wrong. . . . They are the two principles that have stood face to face from the beginning of time and will ever continue to struggle. The one is the common rights of humanity, and the other is the divine right of kings."

In short, Lincoln is a pure example of the visionary in action. He conceived of a society that manifestly did not exist, and he devoted all of his energies to make it real. That came at a huge cost. Lincoln ran for president as the Republican nominee in 1860, fully aware of the potential consequences of his election. He was not a passive instrument of the party. He was not "selected." He was, as many have noted, a man of burning ambition, and he willed himself to become president. Confronted with warnings that a Republican victory might mean the end of the Union, Lincoln pressed on. Not everyone took the rumblings seriously, and it was hard for anyone to imagine the storm that was coming. In the election of 1860, several new parties tried to prevent a Republican victory, including the Constitutional Union party. But the Republicans, though they won only states in the North and captured barely 40 percent of the popular vote, gained a majority in the electoral college.

The reaction was swift, as the Southern states had warned. Throughout the south, emergency sessions were convened to deliberate secession and the dissolution of the Union. South Carolina acted first, in December, followed quickly by the rest of the deep South and Texas. A Confederate government was created in Montgomery, headed by Jefferson Davis, and the seceded states announced that the experiment that began in 1789 was at an end. Lincoln and the Republicans disagreed.

Lincoln was only one man, a powerful and influential man to be sure, but he was also the reflection of a much larger body of people.

The same was true for all of the political leaders of the 1850s and 1860s. In fundamental ways, the politics of this era permeated the culture. Slavery was not an elite debate. The settlement of the territories was not just a political sore point. And the nature of the Union was not discussed only by businessmen and politicians. These issues were heated at every level of society, and while the "great men" of the period left an indelible stamp, they could not have had the influence they did were it not for the fact that they represented fissures that would have been clear to a farmer in Illinois, a slave owner in Alabama, and a tavern keeper in Massachusetts.

Lincoln's vision may have been noble, but the result was carnage. Unyielding, he somberly informed the secessionists that their actions were unacceptable and would be met by force, if necessary. "I hold that in contemplation of universal law and of the Constitution the union of these states is perpetual," he announced during his inaugural address. He hoped that there would not be bloodshed, but he also recognized that "there are persons in one section or another who seek to destroy the Union at all events and are glad of any pretext to do it." However, the matter as he saw it was simple. "One section of our country believes slavery is right and ought to be extended, while the other believes it is wrong and ought not be extended. That is the only substantial dispute." He then ended with a fatalistic plea. "In your hands, my dissatisfied fellow-countrymen, and not in mine, is the momentous issue of civil war. . . . The mystic chords of memory, stretching from every battlefield and patriot grave to every living heart and hearthstone all over this broad land, will yet swell the chorus of the Union, when again touched, as surely they will be, by the better angels of our nature."[16]

Those better angels fled the scene. After a standoff, the war began at Fort Sumter in South Carolina on April 12, 1861. Several more states, including the pivotal Virginia, joined the Confederacy. Lincoln called up a million volunteers, and soon both the North and South were mobilized. Men were drafted and forced to fight. Modern guns, antiquated military tactics, and primitive health care produced one of the nastiest wars of the century. More Americans died in the Civil War than in all of America's wars in the twentieth century combined.

It would take four years and nearly one million lives, including that of Lincoln himself, shot in the back of the head by John Wilkes

Booth while watching a play at Ford's Theater less than a week after General Robert E. Lee surrendered at a courthouse in Appomattox, Virginia in April 1865. Though neither Lincoln nor most Republicans entered the war committed to freeing the slaves—they wanted only to freeze the spread of slavery so that in time it would wither— by 1863, the logic of their ideology compelled them in that direction. The war ended with a Northern victory that was as bloody and divisive as it was inevitable. With millions more men behind the Union's cause and an industrial might that the South could not match, only great luck or immense Northern incompetence could have saved the Confederacy. Until 1863, it looked as though the South might accomplish the impossible. But it was not to be.

The nation that was created by the Civil War was a Union, strong and absolute. Never again would the proponents of states' rights mount such a lethal challenge to the primacy of the national government. The Union that emerged from the war was a land of basic freedoms and liberty, in fact and not just in vision.

That didn't make life any easier, and that didn't mean that injustice was vanquished. Far from it. Each vision has its winners and its losers, and in this period, the South lost. Whether or not the mass of people in the North were better off as a result of the war was also questionable. In myriad ways, the United States was still a land of inequality, and it would remain so. In the coming decades, the inequities would grow larger as society became richer. But for better or worse, a Union now existed, and it was created by people who envisioned it before it existed and who dedicated their lives to making it real.

FOUR

EXPANSION

It was, by all accounts, hot, dusty, and desolate. The achievement was remarkable, but the setting was bleak and inauspicious. The Great Salt Lake shimmered in the distance, and the mountains rose to forbidding heights on the horizon. The tracks had been laid, and the two engines approached their meeting. One set of tracks came from the west, from the honky-tonk California town of Sacramento, over the Sierra Nevada mountains, through the pass where Donner and his party had starved and died before the railroads arrived, across the territory of Nevada and toward the Mormon settlements of Utah. The other set came from the East, starting at Council Bluffs, Missouri, and heading over Evans Pass in the Rocky Mountains of Wyoming, tracing a route through lands inhabited by millions of buffalo and thousands of wary, watchful, and understandably suspicious Native American warriors.

The meeting of the tracks at Promontory Point, Utah, on May 10, 1869, was widely reported. News stories went out over the telegraph wires and made headlines on both coasts. The ceremony, presided over by a preacher who thanked God for making the vast continent whole, echoed the recently ended Civil War. The great conflict between the states had transformed the nation into one union, at the cost of lives and blood. The joining of the Union Pacific and the Central Pacific rail lines in 1869 cemented that nation with bonds of iron. A Golden Spike, which may or may not have been made of gold, was ceremoniously driven into the ground by an assembly of notables

that included railroad baron and California governor Leland Stanford. The meeting at Promontory Point meant that the transcontinental United States was now linked forever and no longer sundered
by high mountains and the wasteland of the desert.

Stanford epitomized the Western settler turned industrialist.
After a childhood and early career in upstate New York and Albany,
Stanford did what many others had done and would do: he went
West as a young man to seek his fortune. He began by selling shovels
and other supplies to the men seeking gold in the Sacramento basin
after 1849, and he progressed from there. His railroad ventures are
largely forgotten, but he is remembered for the philanthropic gift that
established the university south of San Francisco that bears his
name.[1]

THE UNION VISION FADES AND A NEW ONE ARISES

The tortuous struggles that marked the third stage of America did
not completely disappear in April 1865. The next decade saw intense
and acrimonious debates over Reconstruction, and even when the
South was fully readmitted to the Union, intractable problems persisted. But the existential question about unity and union no longer
divided the body politic.

The Union vision was partly a victim of its own success, and
partly a victim of the same tendency to become disenchanted that
spelled the end of the previous stages. The promise of the Union
never quite materialized. The Civil War was a victory, but it did not
make the visionary rhetoric of Lincoln any closer to reality. The
nation was made whole, but people were not thereby happier and
more at ease. Slavery was abolished, but that didn't mean that freedom reigned. The goals of the abolitionists and of the Republican
Party, the dream of Jefferson for an "empire of liberty" stretching into
the west, all of those had been achieved, yet the United States continued to be a land of churning, unfulfilled passions.

The era of Reconstruction that followed Lincoln's assassination
was corrupt and often petty. The South watched as Northern profi-
teers, derisively labeled "carpetbaggers," took advantage of the victory. The triumphant Republican party descended into bitter
factional battles between "moderates" and "radicals," and President

Andrew Johnson narrowly avoided impeachment when the senate came up one vote short.[2] After Johnson, the administration of the once revered general, Ulysses S. Grant, degenerated into a series of financial scandals as his advisers parlayed their influence into profit, and the efforts of the Radical Republicans to make the former slaves equal citizens foundered on the shoals of racism. Expecting a better world of national unity, universal liberties, and prosperity, Americans found their country beset by a new set of struggles, rent by factious new leaders, and suffering from new liabilities.

The old vision began to fade. Instead of heated debates between political elites about the balance between the states and the federal government, America focused on frontiers, both real and metaphorical. The contours of the Union were set. Now, a new set of American visionaries went to work transforming it.

The fourth stage of our culture represents a vision of expansion. Like previous stages, it was a vision for a better world. In the eyes of the visionaries of the fourth stage, the United States would only achieve its utopian potential if it expanded economically and geographically. The second half of the nineteenth century was a chaotic era, bustling, violent, and fractious. Because of this tumult and noise, the fourth stage was less apparent during its time than the previous stages, or the subsequent ones. The inhabitants of Massachusetts Bay in 1650 thought and spoke in terms of religious imagery and the City on a Hill (the first stage); the revolutionaries of the 1770s developed a language of liberty and individual freedom that would have been debated and discussed by a wide swath of men and women, from the Carolinas to Boston, from apprentices and servants to merchants and landed gentry (the second stage); and the nature of the Union would have been on the lips of political elites in 1800 and then on the minds of most Americans in the 1850s (the third stage). But expansion per se was rarely an explicit part of the national dialogue, not in the 1860s, when the idea was "Manifest Destiny," and not in the 1890s, when the watchword was "imperialism." Economic expansion, while it was the preoccupation of millions, was described in terms of particular industries such as steel, oil, and the railroads. The specifics were much more noticeable in these years than any overarching theme.

But while the vision of expansion would not necessarily have resonated with most Americans, the reality of expansion would have.

The economy grew rapidly. The population exploded. The lands of
the West were settled. And the intellectual life of the country evolved.
No matter where one looked, the United States was expanding, and
people scurried to make sense of it all. They rarely succeeded. So
rapid was the pace of change that the moment anyone tried to nail
down a definition or a solution, the situation had already shifted. The
United States in these years was its own moving target, and by the
time someone became aware of a new development, it was almost
certainly too late to do anything about it. The populist farm movements of this period fought in the vanguard, trying to prevent
changes in the national economy that were far too strong for them to
resist. The dystopian warnings of a grim urban future were sounded
after metropolises like New York and Chicago had already grown
labyrinthine. Expansion was a reality people could not always name,
but it permeated society nonetheless.

The culture of these years was fissiparous. The men who led the
industrial growth existed in a universe distinct from the rough-
and-tumble worlds of New York's tenements or the one-road towns
of the mythological West. The politicians of Washington, frequently
wealthy men themselves, so much so that the Senate in the 1880s
was dubbed "the millionaire's club," had little cultural connection
to the eastern European immigrants who flooded Ellis Island in the
1890s. But in spite of these divisions, Americans shared a lust for
more.

More land, more wealth, more power. It was as though the Civil
War had seen a dam break, and the waters rushed forth. In the 1840s
and 1850s, there had been talk of expansion into Texas, Mexico, and
the Caribbean. The editor John O'Sullivan wrote that those who
opposed the U.S. annexation of Texas were "limiting our greatness
and checking the fulfillment of our manifest destiny to overspread
the continent allotted by Providence for the free development of our
yearly multiplying millions."[3] But while settlers rushed to California,
and the United States acquired Texas and invaded Mexico during the
war in 1848 and 1849, slavery prevented further expansion in these
years. The South hoped that expansion would increase the sphere for
slavery, and the North was determined to prevent that. The result was
a stalemate and acrimonious strife in the territories just west of the
Mississippi.

But with the abolition of slavery, territorial expansion became a cultural idée fixe. The West was a land of possibility, aptly summed up by editor-turned-politician Horace Greeley's injunction, "Go West, young man." However, there was one obstacle: the Native American tribes. By the mid-1880s, after numerous skirmishes, several pitched battles, and relentless pressure by the U.S. Army on the outnumbered Apache, Lakota, Navajo, Nez Percé, and others, the Native Americans of the West had either been contained, removed, or exterminated. The saga of the Indian Wars is an uncomfortable one, for the Native Americans and for the U.S. Army. Often, the army fought against ill-equipped warriors, and by the last years, against old men, women, and children, some of whom were slaughtered so that the United States could sow fear into the tribes that remained and cow them into surrender.[4]

To facilitate the colonization of the West, the federal government encouraged the growth of a railroad network. In one of the earliest examples of government regulations spurring economic growth, the Lincoln administration passed a law in 1862 that granted land to the railroad magnates of the Union Pacific and Central Pacific railroads. These grants became de rigueur for the railways. A fifth of the land in Montana alone was given to the railroads, and an eighth of the territory in California. This amounted to tens of millions of acres. In the process of laying nearly 200,000 miles of track (more than in all of Europe and Russia combined), the railroad companies sold and distributed the land to homesteaders, many of them immigrants recently arrived in the harbors of Boston and New York. The railroads not only spanned the continent; they were the engine for the settlement of the vast region between the Sierra Nevada and the Great Plains.

In the years after 1870, Americans settled more land than had been settled in the previous 250 years combined. What drew these settlers was economic opportunity. The rail links needed to be built, and though Chinese labor was widely used to lay the tracks, thousands of non-Chinese were employed as well. Towns sprang up to support the workers, and in states such as Ohio and Pennsylvania, steel mills were built to produce the rails. The West itself offered agricultural land, but even more, it offered mineral riches. Mining in Colorado, Montana, Idaho, and the Black Hills of South Dakota drew prospectors. In Nevada of the 1870s, the famous Comstock Lode produced hundreds of millions of dollars of silver and gold, while in the area around Deadwood, South Dakota, recently cleared of the antagonistic Lakota led by Sitting Bull and Crazy Horse, miners created a lawless town of easy money and fast guns—one of the closest approximations to the Wild, Wild West of subsequent myth.

In the Plains, from Oklahoma north to the Canadian border, the extermination of the buffalo that accompanied the defeat of the Native Americans cleared the area for farming and for cattle. Millions of acres came under cultivation and millions more were blocked off for cattle ranching, assisted by the recent invention of barbed wire. By the mid-1880s, nearly 5 million cattle roamed the so-called High Plains, from Central Texas through eastern Colorado and parts of Wyoming and Nebraska. The cattle runs not only enriched ranchers in Texas and neighboring states, but the growing demand for beef led to the boom of the great midwestern city of the era, Chicago, with its stockyards and slaughterhouses and railroad terminals.

Throughout the world, the combined effects of improved hygiene and better access to food led to demographic growth in the second half of the nineteenth century. The population of the United States mushroomed. At the end of the Civil War, it stood at 35 million. Twelve years later, when Reconstruction ended, there were more than 46 million Americans. By 1890, there were more than 60 million; a decade later, 70 million. And on the eve of World War I, in 1914, nearly 100 million. Unlike elsewhere in the world, however, the demographic expansion of the United States received a substantial boost from immigration. From the end of the Civil War until 1890, most of the 10 million immigrants who arrived in America were from Western Europe (primarily England, Ireland, Scotland, and Germany). After 1890, however, that changed. In the two subsequent decades, 15 million immigrants arrived, this time from Eastern Europe, Italy, and Russia. Many of them were Jewish; others were Eastern Orthodox or Catholic. All of them represented a new cultural force.[5]

These additional millions fanned out across the country, but they also gravitated toward the older, established cities of the Northeast. Urban growth in these years was extraordinary, and by 1900, 40 percent of the population lived in cities, compared to just 25 percent during the Civil War. By the end of the nineteenth century, the

United States had fifty cities with a population of more than 100,000; six with a population of more than half a million. And New York City, Chicago, and Philadelphia passed the 1 million mark.[6] Three-quarters of the population of the larger cities were foreign-born. The culture of the new metropolises was widely discussed, often in negative terms. Writers and intellectuals looked with dismay at the crowded, filthy tenements of lower New York, and the teeming neighborhoods of the Chicago wards. The United States, grounded in a Jeffersonian vision of small landowners, had never been a urban nation, and as it became one, as the cities blossomed, the adjustment was neither easy nor smooth.

No matter where one turned, there was economic expansion. Every sector thrived. Even the South, which lagged behind the North, built steel mills in towns like Birmingham, Alabama, and lumber mills which utilized the local woodlands. In the central states, such as Ohio, Pennsylvania, and Michigan, factories proliferated, especially steel mills and oil refineries. Leading the way were individuals who became infamous as the "robber barons" of the "Gilded Age." Immensely powerful, uninhibited by government regulations, and driven, these captains of industry were more influential than any president or national politician between the Civil War and the ascension of Teddy Roosevelt in 1901.

The Visionaries of the Fourth Stage

As a young man, the icy, tight-lipped, stingy John D. Rockefeller undercut and harassed competitors in the nascent oil industry. Owning wells in central Pennsylvania and Ohio, he consolidated production, extraction, refining, and distribution. Though he became more so in later years, he was always a humorless man. An ardent Baptist as devoted to his church as he was to his company, he both cornered the oil market and swept up after services on Sunday morning. He lived a private life of great rectitude, and neither drank nor smoked nor swore nor philandered. Commentators at the time, and biographers since, noted the contradictions. A man who abhorred swearing had little compunction about spying on competitors. A man who preached the ethics of Christ extorted and bribed his way to success. Rockefeller was also an innovator, for good or for ill. His Standard Oil

Company was one of the first to perfect "vertical integration" (production, distribution, and sales). The company carved out a monopoly that would only continue to grow when oil was discovered in Texas and Oklahoma, and when Standard Oil gained foreign concessions in remote areas of Central Asia. Vilified and feared, Rockefeller created a dynasty whose influence a hundred years later is still immense. His fortune endowed the University of Chicago and dozens of other major institutions of culture, and Standard Oil, though it was broken up by the federal government in 1911, still dominates the American oil industry in the form of Exxon (Standard Oil of New Jersey), Mobil (Standard Oil of New York), and Chevron (Standard Oil of California).[7]

Oil was not the only booming industry. Steel production rocketed dramatically, going from less than 3 million tons in 1880 to more than 30 million tons by World War I. The transformation of the steel industry was led by a transplanted Scot, Andrew Carnegie. Arriving in the United States in 1848, Carnegie was determined to do something he knew he could never do in Scotland: get rich. After landing a job with the fledgling telegraph company, Western Union, in Pittsburgh, he became the assistant to the head of the Pennsylvania Railroad. From that position, he came to appreciate the importance of steel to the expansion of the railroads and, by extension, of the United States. Carnegie capitalized on a new process for refining steel developed in the 1850s by the English inventor Sir Henry Bessemer, and in the 1870s, he built a steel empire with plants in western Pennsylvania, including the immense Homestead works. Carnegie's steel was used not only for railroad tracks, but for the Brooklyn Bridge and for the new "skyscrapers" that dotted lower Manhattan, Chicago, Pittsburgh, and other American cities in the 1890s, as the dual inventions of electricity and the elevator made it possible to get people several hundred feet above the ground without the burden of walking up flights of stairs.

A small, compact man, Carnegie had a twinkle in his eye, and his face was framed by a neatly trimmed white beard. One of the most successful industrialists of an industrial age, he was thoughtful and reflective, and he put his thoughts to paper. In an influential essay titled "Wealth," published in 1889, Carnegie philosophized about the Gilded Age. Though he was not seen as ruthless, he was certainly partners with some ruthless men, especially Henry Clay Frick, who used Pinkerton detectives and state troops to suppress a strike at Homestead in 1892.

Carnegie lived during a time when the gap between rich and poor was opening to a chasm (a gap that would narrow in subsequent years before expanding again in the 1980s and 1990s). The richest one percent of Americans controlled more money than the poorest fifty percent. This led to a democratic outcry against the robber barons, whose attitudes and antics were chronicled by skeptical writers such as Mark Twain (who wrote *The Gilded Age* in 1873), editors such as E. L. Godkin of *The Nation*, and critics like Henry Demarest Lloyd, William Dean Howells, and Edward Bellamy. "The association of poverty with progress is the great enigma of our times," wrote Henry George in 1879. He continued, "the contrast between the House of Have and the House of Want" meant that progress was more of an illusion than a reality. "Liberty produces wealth and wealth destroys liberty," lamented Lloyd in 1894. Economic expansion promised utopia, but these writers looked around and found evidence to the contrary.[8]

Carnegie defended the agglomeration of capital by the few. Like many of his day, he adopted Darwinian theories of evolution and applied "a survival of the fittest" interpretation to business. The economy grew, unequally but spectacularly, because a select few were uniquely skilled and able to defeat their competitors. The result was dislocation and suffering, but also the onward march of civilization. "The contrast between the palace of the millionaire and the cottage of the laborer with us today," he wrote "measures the change which has come to civilization. This change, however, is not to be deplored, but welcomed as highly beneficial. It is well, nay, essential, for the progress of the race." He then blasted nostalgia for the past. "The good old times were not good old times." He acknowledged that change came at a price, but he claimed that the advantages more than outweighed the costs. He concluded with a vision of the future: "There remains, then, only one mode of using great fortunes; in this we have the true antidote for the temporary unequal distribution of wealth, the reconciliation of rich and poor—a reign of harmony—another ideal, differing from the communist in requiring only the further evolution of existing conditions, not the total overthrow of our civilization. . . . Under its sway, we shall have an ideal state, in which the surplus wealth of the few will become in the best sense the property of the many, because administered for the common good." With this essay, Carnegie became the lead preacher for what he and others called the "Gospel of Wealth."[9]

There was another element to the incredible economic expansion: finance. The towering individual was J. P. Morgan. To the manor born, James Pierpont went into his father's banking business and excelled. After 1880, the House of Morgan was involved in most of the major industries, from steel to railroads to electrification. Morgan, a large man made larger by a healthy appetite that extended beyond food to mistresses, yachts, and art, had an unfortunate degenerative condition of his nose, which turned it bulbous and red and made a tempting target for the caricaturists of the day. To critics, Morgan represented the worst of the age—the gluttony, the privilege, the disdain for democracy, and the secretiveness of the cabals that pulled the levers. He was a proponent of a novel institution known as the "Trust," which allowed for consolidated stockholder control of entire industries. In 1901, Morgan, along with his partner Charles Schwab, assembled the financing to buy Andrew Carnegie's steel empire for half a billion dollars. He then formed U.S. Steel, a trust that controlled more than 60 percent of the country's steel production and absorbed two-hundred other companies.

Morgan took the business of business seriously. He was an acolyte of the Gospel of Wealth, and he believed that the Trust was a stable, honorable arrangement in an otherwise chaotic, dishonest period. In the absence of government regulation, Morgan took it upon himself to make sure that the economy did not collapse, as it threatened to do in the various panics that occurred cyclically. He agreed that it was the rich who had made the country rich, and that it was the Captains of Industry who were remaking the continent and transforming the United States into a great nation.[10]

None of these industrialists and financiers were oblivious to the dislocations that the economic expansion caused. Nor were they unaware that the rewards were distributed inequitably. There were too many negative voices in the press, too many strikes, and too much unrest; it was impossible to deny that Gilded Age capitalism was often harsh. Riots in Chicago in Haymarket Square in 1886, strikes at the

Homestead works in Pennsylvania and at the Coeur d'Alene mines in Idaho in 1892, strikes by the Pullman workers that led to the intervention of federal troops in 1894—these were only the more famous of the labor disturbances. Several miles south of Carnegie's and Frick's mansions, and less than a mile from Morgan's home, New York City had one of the highest population densities in the world, with hundreds of thousands of ill-fed immigrants living in miserable conditions. The economic expansion of the South, more modest but still significant, did not touch the sharecroppers, both black and white, who eked out a subsistence living. And the inflationary tendencies of the economy made life even more precarious for farmers, who formed political movements such as the Grange, the Greenback Party, and the Populist Party to try to give their grievances a voice. Their greatest hope, William Jennings Bryan, who decried the suffering of the many, lost successive presidential elections in 1896 and 1900.

None of this churning undercut the vision of the Gilded Age. For much of the twentieth century, Morgan, Carnegie, Rockefeller, Frick, and the rest of the "robber barons" were reviled as the worst of capitalism. Certainly, they saw the economic expansion through rose-tinted lenses. Nonetheless, they had a vision for the United States, and they were relentless in its pursuit. They imagined a time when the wealth that was being created under their watch would lift up even the poorest unlettered immigrant, when the slums would be cleared, and factories would be places of community and comradery rather than anonymous pits that consumed men and materials without compunction. Certainly, they could be charged with hypocrisy, as they became richer while watching others become poorer. But they, like most people, wanted to believe that their actions were more than selfish. Carnegie spoke for the era when he projected a future that would see wealth evenly distributed. It was not that he and his peers saw their present differently from dystopians, such as Henry George; it was that they saw, or at least wanted to see, the present difficulties as a prelude to future Shangri-las.[11]

For decades after the Civil War, the federal government was quiet, and the White House was occupied by presidents who were thought of, even at the time, as second-rate leaders. The government did not determine events; the industrialists did. But beginning in the 1890s, the state began to play a more active role, both in regulating the messy, disorganized economy, and in pursuing territorial expansion beyond the frontier of the continental United States. The expansion to the west was all but completed by the 1890s, and the closing of the frontier was announced (somewhat prematurely) by the census department in 1890. Addressing the American Historical Association in Chicago in 1893, the great, though misguided, American historian Frederick Jackson Turner declared that the closing of the frontier would have dire consequences. Until its closing, the frontier had served as a safety valve for tension in the East. If people felt stymied or believed that they had been unfairly shut out of the benefits of the economy, they could pack up and head west to a new life. Now that the frontier was no more, Turner warned, the problems of the industrial age could well explode, and the violence of Homestead and Coeur d'Alene would be increasingly frequent.

Turner exaggerated how easy it was for people to uproot themselves from lives in the East. It was no simple task to pack up and head west, and many people were in debt and couldn't afford to move. Settlers were usually young, or were recent immigrants, or people who already lived to the west of the Mississippi. However, Turner was unquestionably right about the influence of the frontier on American culture, and he did identify a consequential shift. However, just as one arena for expansion shrank, a new one opened up.

Beginning in the 1890s, as the frontier closed, America acquired colonies. Though the U.S. government had purchased Alaska from Russia in 1867, subsequent overseas expansion faltered until the 1890s. Then, with the West delineated, if not fully settled, Americans began to flex their economic muscle abroad in the form of men, ships, guns, and war.

In certain respects, American imperialism was a continuation of the Manifest Destiny of the 1840s as well as a return to the brief flurry of imperialism after the acquisition of Alaska in the late 1860s. In other respects, it was an outgrowth of economic expansion. Cuba in the 1890s was mired in an ugly struggle with Spain for independence, and groups in the United States pressured the administration of the Republican president William McKinley to intervene. The reasons ranged from the plea that the United States had a responsibility to fight for liberty wherever it was jeopardized to the assertion that in order to be a great nation, the U.S. had to acquire colonies. Some even believed that America was destined to expand whether or not the United States government willed it. Said one congressional representative, "I think the influence of our institutions is not to be limited simply to the territory that now belongs to us, but that in the process of time, if our Government remains stable and perpetuated, it is to extend to other lands, and I have no doubt but that influence will, by its own momentum, peaceably and consistently with all our engagements with other nations, bring these as well as the territory adjoining us within the embrace of our institutions."[12]

One of the more fulsome exponents of American expansion in these years was Senator Albert Beveridge of Indiana. Beveridge believed that God had marked Americans as a chosen people who had a duty to spread their unique brand of civilization. His vision was an amalgam of the paradigms of the previous stages. His ideology of expansion explicitly invoked God, a City on a Hill, the greatness of the American individual, the spread of liberty and freedom, and the glories of the Gilded Age economy. "There are so many real things to be done," he announced when running for the senate in 1898, "canals to be dug, railways to be laid, forests to be felled, cities to be builded, fields to be tilled, markets to be won, ships to be launched, peoples to be saved, civilization to be proclaimed, and the flag of liberty flung to the eager air of every sea. . . . It is a moment to realize the opportunities fate has opened to us. And so it is an hour for us to stand by the Government."[13]

Economic expansion had benefitted from government aid in the form of land and propitious monetary policy. But territorial expansion, first in the West in the 1870s and then abroad in the 1890s, required federal action because this expansion required armed forces. The growth of imperialism spurred a growth in federal power, and soon, government came to dominate American culture to an unprecedented degree. A pivotal figure in this evolution was a man who was later known to walk softly and carry a big stick, Theodore Roosevelt.

An affluent graduate of Harvard college, Roosevelt worshiped at the shrine of manly virtues. He gloried in white civilization, and in order to prove to himself that his slight physical stature didn't reflect on his true nature, he went west to become a rancher in the Dakotas in the 1880s. Returning east, he went into government in the 1890s. He also wrote a sweeping epic history, *The Winning of the West*, in which he celebrated the conquest of the Native Americans and the spread of American civilization to the backward, barren lands. Only in his thirties, he became police commissioner of New York City, and aggressively worked to reform and organize what had been a ramshackle organization. A rising star in the Republican party, he was an eclectic mix of reformer and racist, imperialist and Progressive, expansionist and conservationist. He was a bundle of energy, cursed with a high-pitched, squeaky voice and bad eyes, and blessed with immense curiosity and lust for life.

As assistant secretary of the navy in the McKinley administration, TR was a strong advocate of intervention in Cuba against Spain. He believed the United States had a responsibility to protect the supposedly benighted Cubans and liberate them from Spanish tyranny, and he yearned for the glory of war. Public opinion, stoked by the warmongering journalism of William Randolph Hearst and Joseph Pulitzer, swayed McKinley, who was also being pressured by an inner circle of advisers.

The war of 1898 sent American troops to Cuba and the American fleet to the Spanish colony of the Philippines. TR resigned his office and helped form a contingent known as the "Rough Riders," who saw action at San Juan Hill in Cuba. After Cuba had been occupied at the cost of thousands of American troops succumbing to malaria, Admiral George Dewey destroyed the Spanish fleet in Manila Bay. Though the American army was disorganized and even inept, Roosevelt himself had a splendid time and rhapsodized about his experience. He had proven himself "a man who does not preach what I fear to practice, and who will carry out himself what he advocates others carrying out." Buoyed by his popularity, TR was elected governor of New York in 1899 and was then selected as McKinley's running mate in 1900. When McKinley was assassinated by the anarchist Leon Czolgosz in 1901, TR, at the young age of forty-three, became president. Mark Hanna, who had done more than anyone to make McKinley's career, stared out the window of the funeral train and bitterly regretted the tragic turn of events. "Now look," he told his companions, "that damned cowboy is President of the United States."[14]

In the White House, TR put on a show, and he knew it. He blustered against foreign adversaries, countenanced the acquisition of the Philippines; bullied his way into European politics as a negotiator between the increasingly antagonistic European nations; brokered a peace agreement in Portsmouth, New Hampshire, between Japan and Russia; sent the U.S. fleet across the Pacific to let the Chinese, Japanese, and the English know that United States had aspirations as a world power; underwrote the Panamanian rebellion against Colombia in order to facilitate the building of the Panama Canal; and intervened in the Dominican Republic while claiming that in the Western Hemisphere the United States had the right to prevent "brutal wrongdoing, or an impotence which results in a general loosening of the ties of civilized society."

During these years, anti-imperialist sentiment also ran high. Many elites in the Northeast vehemently opposed what was going on, and they saw imperial expansion as a violation of essential American principles. "We hold that the policy known as imperialism is hostile to liberty and tends toward militarism," stated the Anti-Imperialist League in 1899, "an evil from which it has been our glory to be free."[15] Some critics lambasted economic expansion, others condemned territorial expansion. And the critics were often right, in that they pointed to real dangers, real problems, and real challenges. There were people starving in tenements; there were children being worked at a young age; and the American occupation of the Philippines was brutal.

But the critics in these years did not determine the trajectory of expansion. They reacted. They did not propel culture; they tried to channel it in different directions. They didn't build the railroads. The robber barons did. They didn't conquer the West. Carnegie, Teddy Roosevelt, Morgan, Rockefeller, the generals and lieutenants who waged the Indian Wars, they and others like them determined the contours of this vision. Whether or not we think that what they did was good or moral, whether or not we accept the Gospel of Wealth, the people who imagined a powerful nation sitting astride the continent and then the world transformed the United States. They also believed that they were transforming the world, bringing God and liberty to a planet where neither was much in evidence. To a point, they did exactly what they intended. The country expanded, the economy exploded, the railroads were built, the industrial power of the United States surpassed that of every other country in the world, and the armed forces exerted their will abroad.

That is not the end of the story, however. The critics had a different vision, a different lens, and the problems that they identified were too acute to ignore. In time, left unchecked, Carnegie and his cohorts may have enriched everyone, but most people were not willing to wait for that far-off day when wealth would spread itself. The danger of civil strife was too great to let the invisible hand do its work. And most people living in the 1890s can be forgiven for not seeing evidence that a new day of peace and affluence lay just around the proverbial corner. The explanations proffered by the robber barons seemed to many to be self-serving rationales for stealing from the poor. To make matters worse, disillusionment with expansion, which reached a peak when the atrocities committed by American troops in the Philippines were publicized, was widespread.

All of these currents—and the shift from one paradigm to another, from the rhetoric of expansion that characterized the fourth stage to the vision of government that formed the fifth—swirled around Teddy Roosevelt. Domestically, Roosevelt presided over a dramatic growth of the federal government. The evolution of the United States as an imperial nation went hand in hand with the rise of the national government as a regulatory state. Already in the 1890s, faced with the economic panic of 1893 and the increase of labor violence, people began to look to Washington to play a more active role. The passage of the Sherman Antitrust Act in 1890 was a first step, but equally significant changes were occurring at the grass roots level.

In cities throughout the country, reformers looked to improve working and living conditions. The abuses of the period were legion, ranging from price-fixing, to exploitative use of child labor, to unsanitary and unhealthy tenements, rampant political corruption, and companies cutting dangerous corners and selling defective products and tainted food. The reformers, working independently but for similar goals, became known as the "Progressives," an umbrella term that included people as disparate as Jane Addams of Chicago's Hull House, the charismatic Wisconsin senator Robert La Follette, and Teddy Roosevelt himself.[16]

The Progressive movement led to the passage of numerous regulatory laws and Supreme Court cases that tested the constitutional validity of federal action in hitherto private realms. TR earned a reputation as a blustery imperialist who also crushed the monopolistic power of the trusts. He tried to conserve the raw West of the imagination, and under his watch, millions of acres of national parks and wilderness areas were declared off-limits to miners, loggers, and ranchers. Slowly, the ethos of expansion receded, and a new era of government developed.

That shift was not apparent at the time. The first decade of the new century seemed as messy and chaotic as the 1890s, and reformers were more aware of the severity of the problems than of government as a solution. Though Upton Sinclair penned his exposé of the Chicago slaughterhouses in *The Jungle*, though Ida Tarbell peeled away the veils of corporate secrecy and presented an unflattering portrait of John D. Rockefeller to the country, and though the Anti-Imperialist League decried what the U.S. Army was doing in the Philippines, few thought that more government was the answer. Reformers were more focused on the perils of expansion than on alternatives to it. But the disillusionment of the Progressives signaled a shift, away from expansion and toward government.

FIVE

GOVERNMENT

Long before the Progressives, while the United States was still locked in the struggle over unity, President Martin Van Buren addressed Congress in the midst of one of the worst economic recessions in American history. The Panic of 1837 hit the country hard, as hundreds of banks went bankrupt and the savings of thousands evaporated in a storm of inflated, worthless currency. Desperate, people looked to the government in Washington for relief. But Van Buren would have none of it.

"Those who look to the action of this Government for specific aid to the citizen to relieve embarrassments arising from losses by revulsions in commerce and credit," he said sternly, "lose sight of the ends for which it was created and the powers with which it is clothed. It was established to give security to us all in our lawful pursuits under the lasting safeguard of republican institutions. It was not intended to confer special favors on individuals or any classes of them. . . . All communities are apt to look to government for too much . . . especially at periods of sudden distress." Van Buren, the scrappy New Yorker who helped establish the modern political party, warned that if the government took any action, it would do irreparable harm to the Constitution, to American liberties, and to the economy, which was best left alone.[1]

A century later, Van Buren's words would have sounded reactionary. In the midst of the Great Depression of the 1930s, Americans turned to government for assistance in ways that Americans of previous generations could hardly have imagined. By the middle of the twentieth century, government became entwined in American consciousness as fully as religion had been in seventeenth-century Massachusetts. Reaching an apex with the Great Society of the 1960s, the government paradigm promised Americans relief from poverty, protection from dangers both domestic and foreign, and held out the hope that all dreams of the good life could become real.

The rise of government, however, took decades. The imbalances of the Gilded Age led many to question Van Buren's assumptions, but only after years of cacophonous debate was a path to government regulation cleared. Andrew Carnegie tried to spread a Gospel of Wealth, but most of his contemporaries seem to have paid more attention to their own enrichment than to that of society. At least that was the prevailing image of the robber barons. Free competition, said Henry Demarest Lloyd in the 1880s, was all well and good, but only "in a community where everyone had learned to say and act 'I am the state.' " Writing two decades later, however, a Harvard history professor observed that by the turn of the century, the old doctrine of laissez-faire was being supplanted by a new ethos of government control. The belief in individual liberty remained as strong as ever, and the effervescent enthusiasm for economic growth still bubbled over. But at the same time, "the average American" came to believe some "government control" over those disparate forces was imperative, "not to hedge in the individual to restrain his powers, but to clear the field of special advantages. The American theory of business and of government control," the professor concluded, "is summed up in the single phrase, 'a square deal.' "[2]

At some point after the turn of the century, the pendulum swung, and enough people in enough places believed that if the country's culture and economy were left in the hands of the wealthy few, the society as a whole would suffer. The rise of government was supported by millions of ordinary citizens who believed that their interests would be served by government action. But it was also supported by a number of prominent individuals, many of them presidents, who actively increased the scope of government. The age of government, not surprisingly, was also the age of the presidency.

TR, WILSON, AND THE RISE OF GOVERNMENT

As Theodore Roosevelt sadly assumed the presidency after the assassination of McKinley in late 1901, he was determined to expand the
powers of the national government. He didn't believe in government
per se; rather, he wanted to craft a balance between the needs of business and the needs of the larger society. He wanted to curb the
excesses of the former and allow for the greatest good to the greatest
number. That entailed a de facto enlargement of the sphere of government, but it did not yet mean a coherent vision for an activist government. TR himself didn't fully embrace an expansive domestic role
for the federal government until he ran for president in 1912, as a
third-party insurgent. But the glimmerings of a new vision appeared
even in his first message to Congress in 1901.

To assure leading Americans that he remained an avid champion
of the Gilded Age, Roosevelt declared that "the captains of industry
who have driven the railway systems across this country, who have
built up our commerce, who have developed our manufactures, have
on the whole done great good to our people." Much of the criticism
of them, he felt, was attributable to envy. However, that did not mean
that everything was fine. He explained that though government regulation of business required an extremely delicate hand, corporations
derived their rights from law, and hence from government. Therefore, he argued, corporations could and should be held accountable
for their actions by the government. If they acted in such a way as to
cause "injury" to the public, then they should be regulated, punished,
and prevented from continuing to do the public harm.

Roosevelt thought that the Constitution provided only minimal
guidance. "When the Constitution was adopted," he said, "no human
wisdom could foretell the sweeping changes alike in industrial and
political conditions, which were to take place by the beginning of the
twentieth century." He called on Congress to pass laws that would
enable the "National Government to exercise control."[3] During the
seven years of his presidency, TR's tentative embrace of regulation
turned into a bear hug. Just as he gleefully enhanced the profile of the
United States in the world abroad—traveling to Panama to watch
the construction of the Canal, offering his services as a negotiator to
the French and the Germans, sending American troops to occupy the

Dominican Republic—he urged more active uses of federal power to redress the imbalances caused by the Gilded Age and continued corporate and demographic expansion.

Roosevelt viewed the federal government as an impartial tribunal which would adjudicate between the public good and private profit. The legal hinge for government's growth was the interstate commerce clause of the Constitution, and Roosevelt, among others, used that clause to justify new laws. Speaking at the end of his presidency in 1908, he rather dubiously asserted that, "The chief reason . . . that led to the formation of the National Government [in the 1790s] was the absolute need that the Union, and not the several states, should deal with interstate and foreign commerce. . . . We believe that the administration should be for the benefit of the many; and that greed and rapacity, practiced on a large scale, should be punished . . . relentlessly." For those who worried about the concentration of power in the hands of government administrators, TR had little but scorn. "Democracy is in peril wherever the administration of political power is scattered among a variety of men who work in secret. . . . It is not in peril from any man who derives authority from the people, who exercises it in sight of the people, and who is from time to time compelled to give an account of its exercise to the people."[4]

Because of Teddy Roosevelt, the philosophy of Progressivism was absorbed into the mainstream of American culture. The earlier ethos of expansion wasn't directly repudiated, but the public debate became less warm toward those who had been the champions of the previous stage. Though the aristocratic J. P. Morgan almost singlehandedly bailed out the dollar during the economic collapse of 1907, he was soon made the target of congressional investigations headed by Representative Arsene Pujo that attempted to uncover the abuses of the robber barons. The promise of the Gilded Age was now dismissed by the dominant culture as a self-serving ideology meant to fool the many while the few got rich. The fact that Roosevelt believed it was the responsibility of the national government to punish greed showed just how significantly the prevailing sentiments had shifted.

But there still was only a hazy notion of what government could do in a positive sense. Regulation is inherently reactive. The Progressives focused on curtailing abuses and creating a framework of laws, but slowly, they also started to envision a new world that government could create. By 1912, TR had been out of office for four years, and he disliked his successor, the rotund Howard Taft. Failing to gain the Republican nomination, TR secured the leadership of the Progressive Party. The 1912 election pitted Taft against Roosevelt and both men against the Democratic nominee, Governor Woodrow Wilson of New Jersey. In its platform, the Progressive Party decried "corrupt business and corrupt politics." The Progressives seethed with hostility to the established parties, but the platform also looked ahead to a brighter future. "The new party offers itself as the instrument of the people to sweep away old abuses, to build a new and nobler commonwealth."

The notion that government could help create a better world was a hallmark of Progressivism, and it was a new vision for American society. When the Founding Fathers drafted the Constitution, they saw the government as a limited instrument, necessary to bind the disparate states, but not an instrument of Providence. The Progressives, however, combined a bitter critique of big business with a dream of a paternal national government that would lead the way to an idyllic society.

This better society would protect the weak and defenseless. It would zealously prosecute monopolies. It would honor the efforts of the working men and women who made the industrial age possible. It would make sure that the courts did not interfere with laws that limited child labor, set maximum working hours and minimum wages, and outlawed unsafe working conditions. It would eliminate corruption in government, not just at the local level, but all the way to the inner corridors of Washington. It would make sure that the natural resources of the continent would not be irreparably damaged by logging and mining companies. And it would seek to establish a more stable financial system, overseen by public servants.

The Progressives believed that the product of these efforts would be a stronger, more morally pure, and more equitable nation than any in the world. It would be a United States that realized the dreamiest dreams of the framers. It would also be a society that would more closely approximate a City on a Hill than the Puritans had ever been able to create. A strong strain of religious fervor ran through the Progressives, and it was only fitting that the inadvertent inheritor of the Progressive flame was an austere preacher's son who bitterly fought the Progressive Party in 1912 but who soon coopted most of its plat-form.[5]

Thomas Woodrow Wilson was born and raised in the South, the child of a Presbyterian minister who inculcated a firm sense of right and wrong. The family moved several times, from Virginia to South Carolina and to North Carolina, as Wilson's father looked for better opportunities than the war-devastated South could offer in the 1870s. Tommy, as the future president was then known, went north to college—to Princeton—and then continued his studies at the newly established graduate school of Johns Hopkins in Baltimore. Wilson became a scholar, and his primary focus was the philosophy of the Constitution and the evolution of the national government. He was appointed president of Princeton, and from that elite perch, he ran as a Democrat for governor of New Jersey in 1910, and won.

Wilson developed a reputation as a brilliant but aloof scholar whose expertise on American politics was unsurpassed. Thin-lipped, immaculately dressed, his face drawn tight, Wilson struck no one as fun-loving. In private, he actually could be, and he was known to friends as a marvelous raconteur. Austere persona notwithstanding, he was an effective politician, largely because he navigated between the extremes.

By the time Wilson ran for president in 1912, the Progressive movement overshadowed American politics. There was also a rapidly expanding Socialist party led by Eugene V. Debs, who was a passion-ate advocate of an activist state. Countering these forces were power-ful corporations. Wilson supported the Progressives, but he announced that he would keep their more draconian inclinations in check. With his cool demeanor and his Olympian calm, he was the anti-TR, and the resulting election of 1912 was bitter.

While Roosevelt went on the campaign warpath denouncing cor-porate greed, assailing the Republican Taft for inaction (an unfair charge), and belittling the Democrats, Wilson took pains to distance himself from the excesses of Progressivism. Wilson acknowledged that he lacked TR's charisma. "He appeals to the [voters'] imagina-tion; I do not. He is a real, vivid person, whom they have seen and shouted themselves hoarse over. . . . I am a vague, conjectural per-sonality, more made up of opinions and academic prepossessions than of human traits and red corpuscles." However, he characterized the Progressives as a party that wished to replace one injustice—monopoly—with another—all-powerful government. Wilson believed in some regulation, but not in an ideology of regulation. The Democratic Party, which had only a few years earlier been represented by the fire-breathing William Jennings Bryan denouncing Northeast capitalists for crucifying the American people on a cross of gold, now had as its standard bearer a scholar who declared about his opponents, "Ours is a program of liberty, and theirs is a program of regulation."[6]

In one of the most closely contested elections in American history, Wilson won. He received barely 40 percent of the votes, but he defeated TR by more than two million. He announced at his inauguration that he would usher in a period that was soon described as "the New Freedom." In soaring oratory, he declared, "At last a vision has been vouchsafed us of our life as a whole. We see the bad with the good, the debased and decadent with the sound and vital. With this vision we approach new affairs. Our duty is to cleanse, to reconsider, to restore, to correct the evil without impairing the good, to purify and humanize every process of our common life without weakening or sentimentalizing it." If any of his listeners had closed their eyes for a moment, they could have been forgiven for mistaking the speech for a sermon. Wilson embodied the religious impulses of Progressivism and of the Puritans, and in him coursed all the various currents of the earlier stages.

Intending to navigate a new balance, Wilson eventually became an avatar of government. By the end of his first term, legislation passed by the Democratic Congress increased the scope of antitrust laws. The Federal Reserve Act of 1913 created a banking system that survives to this day. Wilson signed legislation that set up a federal loan program for farmers and legislation that protected workers' rights. Though the banking law did not mean strict federal regulation of big business, it wove the federal government into the national financial system to an unprecedented degree. And though the Clayton Antitrust Act was perverted by the courts to allow for injunctions against unions, the Wilson administration established the primacy of the national government over business.

Even more significant was the growth of federal power during Wilson's second term. After the United States declared war on the Axis powers in the spring of 1917, Wilson crafted an ideology to justify intervention. He declared that the war would be the last world war, and that the United States fought to preserve an enduring peace. He enunciated a vision of collective security that eventually became the basis of the United Nations. Domestically, however, the war led to the involvement of the federal government in every aspect of society. During the Civil War, Lincoln had overseen a significant expansion of the government's powers, but that soon receded. But the Civil War expansion of the government didn't compare to the growth under Wilson, either materially or ideologically.

The war cost the United States more than $30 billion, at a time when the entire annual federal budget barely exceeded $1 billion. The war saw the creation of new government agencies, from the War Industries Board, to the Food Administration, the Fuel Administration, the Railroad Administration, the War Shipping Board, and the infamous propaganda agency, the Committee on Public Information, headed by George Creel. These agencies transformed the relationship between government and business in the space of less than two years. By 1919, when the war ended, business and government were tightly bound, as the needs of war had required a partnership in which government enjoyed seniority. This expanded vision of government often helped big business. No longer so favorable to labor, the Wilson administration passed laws limiting the right to strike. The war years also saw laws restricting the right to speak. The federal government arrested thousands and emerged from the war with its police powers vastly enhanced under the Attorney General, Mitchell Palmer.[7]

Wilson, flush with victory, journeyed to Paris at the end of 1918 to participate in the peace negotiations. He was hailed as a conquering hero. He promised a peace without victory that would see a new age of harmony amongst the nations of the world. Full of utopian fervor, he helped draft a plan for a League of Nations, but at home in the United States, Republicans, led by the senator from Massachusetts, Henry Cabot Lodge, and the rigid William Borah of Idaho, opposed tying the traditionally isolationist Americans to the European state system. Wilson journeyed home to urge the Congress to pass the treaty, but he suffered a stroke in the fall of 1919, and was never the same again. His wife, Edith Bolling Galt, quietly assumed some of his responsibilities, but Wilson's judgment was impaired and he unwisely made the contest an all-or-nothing one. Rather than accept limitations on the treaty, he demanded it be passed as he had drafted it or not at all, and so it was defeated.

That defeat symbolized the recession of government, neatly represented by an actual recession in 1920. The federal government let many of its wartime powers expire, and the high-water mark of government activism appeared to have been reached. As government became less active, the vision of government also stalled. The next decade saw a popular resurgence of the type of laissez-faire attitudes that echoed Van Buren of the 1830s or the robber barons of the Gilded Age. The vision of government was kept alive by the Progressive Party of the 1920s, and by the Socialists, but that vision became more marginal as the Republicans occupied the White House for three successive terms. Farmers ineffectually lobbied for more protection, but the economy boomed and the industrial might of the nation continued to grow at an astonishing pace. The Progressive Party platform of 1924 denounced the tyranny of monopoly and warned that freedom was imperiled, but Calvin Coolidge, dour New England Yankee that he was, coasted to victory in the general election.

Herbert Hoover, the brilliant technocrat who had overseen the Food Administration during World War I, became president in 1929, on a platform of "rugged individualism." In the midst of a thriving economy, as the stock market tripled in value to nearly $70 billion, as Americans eagerly bought new goods—cars, kitchen gadgets, electric lamps, vacuum cleaners, and of course, radios—the government receded from the headlines of the hundreds of newspapers that had popped up. Hoover spoke for many when he described "the American system" as one that was "founded upon a particular conception of self-government in which decentralized local responsibility was the very base. Further than this, it was founded upon the conception that only through ordered liberty, freedom, and equal opportunity to the individual will his initiative and enterprise spur the march of progress."[8] He believed in what commentators at the time called a "trickle-down" theory of prosperity. Like the Republicans who rallied around Ronald Reagan in the 1980s, Hoover was convinced that the wealth of the few would generate wealth for the many.

In 1929, it seemed as if the earlier stages of American culture were reemerging. Instead of an era of government, it appeared to be an age of individualism and economic expansion. The Republicans touted the values of hard work and corporate creativity, and with Prohibition, the country embraced a hybrid of Puritanism and nineteenth-century social reform. In the cities, the Jazz Age and the Harlem Renaissance heralded an age of artistic creativity unfettered by government, and fortunes rose on Wall Street. Then everything changed.

THE NEW DEAL, THE GREAT SOCIETY, AND THE APEX OF GOVERNMENT

The stock market crash of October 1929 was bad enough. The depression that followed in 1930–31 was more painful by far. The paper wealth that evaporated on Black Monday, as the Dow sank, wiped out investors, but the ensuing depression was a slow death for millions of ordinary Americans who lost jobs, farms, and dignity. Part of a worldwide depression that saw the collapse of the rudimentary international financial system, the Great Depression in the United States led to the insolvency of thousands of banks. Their savings wiped out, an army of out-of-work war veterans descended on Washington to demand aid.

Hoover watched, empathizing, his face becoming more lined with each passing month. But he refused to mobilize the federal government. He believed in voluntarism, not federal action. He would no more violate the morality of individualism than he would have taken another person's life. Even as the reality of the times made a mockery out of his laissez-faire philosophy, he clung to it. He took some steps, including a moratorium on debt payments, but in essence, he waited out the storm, assailed by criticism and trusting that the sinking economy would stay afloat.

Finally, the chasm between Hoover's vision for America and what the country was actually suffering became too great to bear. Those who believed that the most the government could do was suspend debt payments and encourage charity were part of a long and honorable tradition. That was the philosophy that guided Martin Van Buren in the 1830s, and it was the stance that congressmen and presidents took during economic crises in the 1870s and 1890s. But the Great Depression rendered that philosophy null and void. Drawing on a legacy of progressive reform that looked to government to play a pivotal role in creating a better world, a new generation of reformers came to Washington and, in a chaotic flurry, began a revolution known as the New Deal.

This revolution found its catalyst in the eclectic enigma of Franklin Delano Roosevelt. Little in Roosevelt's life had suggested what he would do as president. Ambitious, charming, affable, and immensely self-confident, FDR grew up in upstate New York, graced and burdened with an extremely attentive mother. Like his distant cousin Theodore, he went to Harvard, enjoyed the martini-laced luxuries of the upper class, and wended his way to becoming assistant secretary of the navy in the Wilson administration. He married Eleanor, had children, and as the vice-presidential nominee of the Democrats in 1920, lost in a landslide to the thoroughly bland Republican Warren Harding. Roosevelt showed every sign of living a highly successful but unremarkable life, until he was crippled and nearly killed by polio in 1921.

Transformed by his disease, he could no longer walk, though it was years before he conceded that he would be dependent on a wheelchair for the rest of his life. Burning with a need to transcend the limitations of his body, he returned to politics, became governor of New York in 1928, and then the nominee of a suddenly resurgent Democratic Party in 1932. The philosophy of Hoover and the Republicans, which until 1929 was celebrated as the best of the American dream, now struck many as insensitive, harsh, and undemocratic. Whether or not someone else would have done what Franklin Roosevelt did, we will never know. He was a great man in desperate times, and though he clearly was the focal point of the energies and dreams of millions, another person might have galvanized the country had he not. That's the mystery of great men—whether they arise and thrive because of the times or in spite of them.

Personally, Roosevelt could be maddeningly inconsistent, devious with even his closet advisors, and insensitive. There was also a streak of paternalism in his approach to the public, a sense that he and his class knew best what was good for the country. He had been raised to believe in elitism, and his view of government was a product of a conviction that those who could, should help those who couldn't. But whatever his personal foibles, FDR defined the next turn of the cultural wheel, and the age of government which his presidency inaugurated would last for more than half a century.[9]

In a speech he gave while running for election in the fall of 1932, FDR charged that the United States was being run by an economic oligarchy of some six hundred corporations. Instead of a commonwealth of equality, the nation was plagued by imbalance, and now the country was paying the price. The only hope was government. "The day of enlightened administration," he announced, "has come. . . . Our government . . . owes to every one an avenue to possess himself of a portion of that plenty sufficient for his needs through his own work. . . . We know that individual liberty and individual happiness mean nothing unless both are ordered in the sense that one man's meat is not another man's poison."[10] This was a novel conception of government as the instrument to fulfill the American dream. FDR imagined a society that required an active government to achieve the aspirations of its citizens. "We shall fulfill," he concluded, "the obligation of the apparent utopia which Jefferson imagined for us in 1776, and which Jefferson, Roosevelt, and Wilson sought to bring to realization." Faced with the challenge of the Great Depression and the suffering of millions, government would be the vehicle to transport Americans to the promised land.

The frenetic legislation that accompanied Roosevelt's inauguration became known as the "Hundred Days." He asked Congress to give him powers comparable to those of a commander-in-chief during a time of war. The enemy was fear, insecurity, and economic collapse. During these first weeks, the federal government underwent a sea change. Multiple agencies were created, including the National Recovery Administration, and dozens of laws reorganized society. Banking laws such as the Glass-Steagall Act restricted banks by erecting a fire wall between commercial and investment banking. The federal government funded local public works projects to a degree that would have been unimaginable to Henry Clay and other early-nineteenth-century advocates of federal assistance.

As these programs evolved over the next few years, the federal government employed artists, photographers, writers, bricklayers, road workers, foresters, and millions of others. A housing administration meant that Washington would assist average Americans by underwriting mortgages, and a Securities and Exchange Commission meant that the government would be doing the once unthinkable: monitoring the financial transactions of corporations. A youth administration sponsored student education, an electrification administration brought lights to rural America, and the Tennessee Valley Authority built dams and recreational areas.[11]

The New Deal showed just how thinly spread the prosperity of the 1920s actually was. The rhetoric of individualism of that decade successfully masked the fact that tens of millions of Americans had no relationship to the Jazz Age or to the dissolute affluence of F. Scott Fitzgerald's novels and readers of *The New Yorker*. New Deal farm laws and the labor laws were designed to ameliorate the plight of workers and farmers, and in the most constitutionally controversial aspect of the New Deal, the Department of Labor and the Labor Relations Board became involved in all major negotiations between labor and management. As Francis Perkins said in announcing the passage of the Social Security Act of 1935, the goal of the New Deal was to pass "legislation in the interest of national welfare." That entailed laws to raise the standards of living for all Americans, to compensate for unemployment, and to level the field so that labor and business could meet on equal footing.

The advocates of the New Deal believed that government had a responsibility to redress the sufferings of citizens. Hoover was so reviled in these years because he had appeared to be indifferent. The New Deal was a philosophy that demanded government action in times of great need. The Roosevelt administration was not hostile to business. Quite the contrary. The aim was to invigorate business and workers, and to find a harmonious middle ground that would allow all to prosper. Some even criticized the New Deal for being overly warm to corporations.

In retrospect, many have suggested that because Roosevelt and his administration did things ad hoc, the New Deal was too disorganized to constitute a coherent vision. Yet one emerged. In speech after speech, in language used to justify law after law, and implicit in most of the programs were a set of values and a set of assumptions. Embedded in the New Deal was a belief that left to its own devices, society would devolve into haves and have-nots and the economy would founder. The New Dealers applauded the dream of universal prosperity, security, liberty, and happiness. Their question was how to realize it. It wouldn't just happen by itself. Slavery had been abolished, the Union had been secured, wealth had been created by bankers and industrialists, and the dream remained a will-o'-the-wisp. As much as the New Deal was a seat-of-the-pants operation overseen by a president who was often fuzzy in his thinking and who was careless in how he delegated tasks, it was a bold vision of the role of government in society. By its very nature, it said that the American dream could only be realized if the federal government took an active, invasive, and constant role.

With his regular radio addresses beamed into living rooms across the nation, with his bold rhetoric calling for action, FDR described government as a "powerful promoter of society's welfare." He was clear and adamant about this. "Against economic tyranny . . . the American citizen could appeal only to the organized power of Government. . . . Better the occasional faults of a Government that lives in a spirit of charity than the constant omission of a Government frozen in the ice of its own indifference." By the end of Roosevelt's first term, the whole country was "Washington-conscious" in a way that it had never been before.[12]

Roosevelt won reelection, but though he would serve in the White House for a record twelve years, the New Deal was effectively halted in 1938 by congressional conservatives who did not embrace the vision. A combination of Republicans and Southern Democrats mustered enough strength to thwart subsequent legislation, and the Supreme Court found key elements of the earlier initiatives unconstitutional. Though the economy recovered somewhat, there was a second dip in FDR's second term which demonstrated that the Depression wasn't over. The mood of the country improved, but the only ballast that the Roosevelt administration was able to provide after 1937 was through deficit spending. That was a radical departure for the federal government, and it remained a prominent feature in the years to come. By injecting money into the economy, the government offset some of the worst symptoms of the Depression, but the economy only turned around dramatically when the United States entered the war against Germany and Japan at the end of 1941.[13]

The New Deal focused primarily on economic reform, and government in these years attended less to the moral and social causes championed by the Progressives than to the business of business.

World War II both halted the New Deal and expanded it. Once again, in wartime, the powers of the government expanded, and multiple agencies were set up to coordinate the American war effort. After years of championing an ethos of government intervention to secure the economy, the Roosevelt administration now called on Americans to support the government in order to secure freedom against the tyranny of Nazism and Japanese imperialism.

The growth of the government to fight the war proved permanent. Unlike in 1919–1920, there was little retreat back to less power after 1945, though the federal government did shrink, as did expenditures. Wartime price controls were lifted in 1946, and the military rapidly demobilized. But under FDR's successor, Harry Truman, the government retained many of the powers that it had accrued during more than a decade of the New Deal and war.

The Cold War with the Soviet Union provided a reason to maintain a large military establishment during peacetime, and that alone was a break from a century and a half of tradition. The creation of the Department of Defense and the Central Intelligence Agency in 1947 was yet another innovation, and Washington continued its wartime role as protector of the American way of life. Government propaganda implanted that ethos in popular consciousness, as warnings about the Nazis were replaced with warnings about the dangers of Communism. In a seemingly unstable world of nuclear weapons and Communism, Washington became the focus of American society.

These developments were challenged by Republicans and assorted Democrats. The election of 1948 saw several splinter candidates who described the growth of Washington as a dangerous threat to American liberty. Truman had secured the passage of the Employment Act of 1946, which pledged the government "to use all its resources to promote maximum employment, production, and purchasing power," and to use government to protect both business and the larger society from "the dangers of recession and the evils of inflation." The heirs of Hoover blanched, as did latter-day progressive reformers who began to worry the growth of Washington.

As Washington grew, so did the fear of it. Americans have always been uncomfortable with government power, and the Anti-Federalists lived on, now represented by Robert Taft, the dour son of the former president. Taft was as anticharismatic as he was anti-New Deal, and though he excelled at backroom politics, he was utterly unappealing in public. Described as the perfect composite of a post-war Republican, Taft tried to prevent the expansion of the United States role abroad and of the federal sphere at home. He not only saw the Employment Act as a dangerous precedent; he also saw the New Deal as severely flawed, expensive, and inefficient. It had, he felt, created a generation of people who looked to government before they looked to themselves, and for Taft, that was a perversion of American values.[14]

But unlike the second stage, this was not the age for individualism. Taft might have been celebrated two centuries earlier, but in the late 1940s, he lost to those who advocated more government. His success as a senator and party leader was proof that individualism, so prominent during the Revolutionary era, was woven into American society, but his failure to achieve more shows how entrenched the government ethos was becoming. In politics, even though the Republicans won the White House with Dwight Eisenhower in 1952, the federal government became ever more involved in social and cultural life, from health and welfare to education and loyalty oaths. The culture grew more Washington-centric. Television news focused on Congress and the White House, and political conventions attracted a viewing audience of three-quarters of the population in 1956 and 1960. The presidency, enhanced by Eisenhower, assumed levels of pomp and circumstance that would have appalled Thomas Jefferson and raised the blood of Thomas Paine.

The 1960s were the high tide of government. Beginning with the election of John F. Kennedy in 1960, Washington became sexy. A young president, a fashionable wife, and the low hum of good PR transformed the staid White House into the hottest spot in the country. The Kennedy administration became known as "Camelot," as sung by Richard Burton in the popular Broadway musical about King Arthur's court. Kennedy called on all Americans to do something for their country, and the way to do something in those years was to get involved with government. Kennedy not only galvanized the resources of the country to put a man on the moon; he created the Peace Corps, which drew thousands of young, eager, and optimistic men and women to go and help the world. In hindsight, there's something woefully naive about the Peace Corps, and about the belief that helping Africans build bridges or teaching Quechua Indians English would dramatically improve their lives. But Kennedy was idolized, and the shattering grief of the nation when he was assassinated in November 1963 was all too real.

Kennedy's successor was Lyndon Johnson, one of the crudest, toughest, oddest, and most ambiguous men ever to serve as president. His life is one long, colorful anecdote. Johnson is a biographer's paradise. He was a true Texan. As a young politician, he was so ambitious that he risked his life by renting a ramshackle helicopter for campaigning, and he may or may not have stolen the 1948 Senate election against the taciturn Coke Stevenson. Later, he became a Senate majority leader who understood the human face of legislation about as well as any ever have or ever will.

But Johnson tormented himself trying to preserve his reputation, his legacy, and his image. Like the Southerners who dueled to the death in the early nineteenth century, Johnson obsessed over how others saw him. Physically, his face was a gaggle of lines, all jowls, the smiles were deep and full, and the furrows and frowns seemed to cut to the bone. He was a sexual dynamo and a flirt, devoted to his wife Lady Bird, but equally devoted to carousing. He was someone who would sit on the toilet while giving an interview, who could flatter people that they and they alone could make his life better, and who could point his finger in the face of a recalcitrant senator and bark until his listener blanched. He was a loyal New Deal liberal who believed in government activism, and any who felt otherwise . . . well, they ought to go and look some poor old woman in the eye and explain to her why they didn't believe that the government ought to at least make sure that she had a roof over her head and three square meals a day.

On a spring commencement day in May 1964, Johnson addressed a huge audience at the University of Michigan in Ann Arbor. He immediately got to his point. His administration would launch a war on poverty. "We have the opportunity to move not only toward the rich society and the powerful society, but upward to the Great Society. The Great Society rests on abundance and liberty for all. It demands an end to poverty and racial injustice." He said that the fight would involve three fronts: the cities, the countryside, and the classroom. "While our Government has many programs directed at those

issues, I do not pretend that we have the full answer to these problems." Those answers would come with the active partnership of millions of citizens and government. Together, Americans could end
poverty and racism, increase prosperity and education, and achieve
an unprecedented level of material and social security.[15]

The multibillion-dollar effort was coordinated by Sargent
Shriver, the brother-in-law of President Kennedy. The War on
Poverty funded Head Start, the Job Corps, Community Action
groups, the Office of Economic Opportunity, and increased budgets
for the departments of Housing and Health, Education, and Welfare.
In 1965 alone, Congress passed eighty-nine bills, most of which
authorized programs and expenditures to make the Great Society a
reality. The federal government underwent a period of growth rivaled
only by the New Deal thirty years before, and thousands of young
men and women flocked to Washington to be a part of the dream.

With few exceptions, if you wanted to be a part of the zeitgeist in
the 1960s, you either went to Washington or you put pressure on
your elected representatives to pass legislation that would address the
problems you believed needed addressing. This was the golden age of
government. The various strains of reform, public service, and utopianism converged on a few acres of official agencies in a small quad-
rant of the District of Columbia. Americans routinely told pollsters
that they trusted government and looked to it as a source of initiative and answers to pressing social problems. Universities throughout
the country formed public-policy schools to train the future bureaucrats who would staff the new agencies. At the state and local level as
well, government was invigorated. Municipalities devoted money and
manpower to urban planning, believing that if the growth of cities
was rationalized, the problems of race and poverty could be eliminated. Public housing was seen as a way to elevate the standard of
living, and as a way to restore dignity. Welfare programs were designed to help the needy and provide a cushion for those down on
their luck. "Government," Johnson said, "liberates the individual from
the enslaving forces of his environment."[16]

In the heady atmosphere of the mid-1960s, no problem seemed
beyond the reach of government. Earlier reforms, during the Progressive period and during the New Deal, had addressed concrete problems: worker rights, unemployment, banking. The Great Society

didn't simply attack poverty and education but tried to go a step further, and entered the amorphous realm of beliefs and values. Government programs were conceived as a way to change attitudes and inculcate national harmony, racial and sexual respect, and environmental sensitivity.

The courts, in a quiet but consequential fashion, enlarged the scope of rights. This was the age of entitlements and the regulatory state. Americans demanded, and were granted by the courts, multiple new rights: the right of privacy, the right of work, the right not to be offended. Traditionally, constitutional law had focused on "rights from," and not "rights to." The Bill of Rights was designed to protect the people *from* government abuse. But in the second half of the twentieth century, people claimed that they were entitled to certain rights as citizens and demanded that government make efforts to guarantee them. These new rights entailed new regulations and new regulators, and that meant an increase in the size and scope of government.[17]

Certainly, there were exceptions. Millions of Americans never fully embraced the notion of an activist government, as Ronald Reagan's gubernatorial victory in California in 1966 showed. Both the struggle for civil rights and the struggle for women's rights were waged first at the grassroots level, by people who identified what they took to be egregious moral wrongs, and they fought for change. They ultimately demanded that government embrace the validity of their cause, but in the midst of heated struggles, such as the passage of the Civil Rights Act of 1964, the Voting Rights Act of 1965, and the fight over the Equal Rights Amendment, many people saw government as an obstacle, even though they looked to it as an essential component of meaningful reform.

Nonetheless, the vision of what government could do led to government activism in areas of life that had until the mid-1960s been private. Were relationships between men and women strained? Well, people asked, what should government do to help people understand each other? What programs could be set up that would reduce the divorce rate? How could government improve the quality of family life? And if American citizens were unhappy in their social relations, what was government doing wrong that was making life less pleasant, less happy? If factories were polluting the air and the water, why had government permitted that and what should be done to prevent it? If children were not learning to read at the proper age, what programs could the government institute to help children learn?

These questions became so automatic that it was easy to lose sight of just how much the culture had changed during the era of government. Until the twentieth century, no American would have thought of turning to government for the multifarious reasons that people turned to government in the 1960s and 1970s. Government was an all-encompassing vision in these years. That made it difficult to conceive of any other way, and government started to seem like an eternal verity, as omnipresent as the sun.

Fueling the fifth stage expansion of government was a familiar idealism, a conviction that problems could be solved and the world made a better and perhaps even a perfect place. That infected U.S. foreign policy as well as domestic. The Peace Corps was part of a global effort to defeat Communism, even in places where communists were acting independently of the Soviet Union. The war in Vietnam was ostensibly fought to preserve democracy, but the gap between that rationale and the reality of the war soon became too large to overlook.

By 1968, significant groups of Americans were so disillusioned by the war that they took to the streets in large numbers. Their anger at government was the flip side of their expectations of government. Mostly young and middle-class, the protesters imbibed the paternalistic notions of government that had permeated American society. They expected the government to embody the noblest ideals of American culture, and when they were confronted with the harsh and sometimes brutal realities of government as an instrument of violence, they recoiled in anger.

At its apex, the government ideal incorporated the wildest dreams of a bountiful, harmonious society, one that would be characterized not only by material comfort but by emotional well-being. Physical suffering would be eliminated, social tension would be decreased, families would communicate more effectively, and all in all, Americans would enjoy a spectrum of advantages that humans beings have desired for centuries but never quite secured. From Teddy Roosevelt and the Progressive reformers, through the New Deal, and then culminating in the Great Society, the government ideal took form and triumphed. And then, it collapsed.

The Fifth Stage Comes to an End

The vision shone brightly, but like all previous visions, it was weighted with unrealistic expectations, which produced a cascade of confusion, disillusionment, and reaction that brought the fifth stage of this country to a close. Even at its height, government had its critics. The heirs of the 1920s Republicans and of Robert Taft nursed their resentments and disagreements, and they developed an alternate vision of society much as the reformers and critics of the 1880s and 1890s had conceived of alternatives to the Gospel of Wealth.

As the sphere of government increased, some Americans reacted with discomfort. They believed that the scope of government, which had traditionally been narrow, should be limited, and they saw the New Deal and the 1960s regulatory state as dangerous to liberty, inimical to individualism, destructive of economic expansion, and even incompatible with religion and morality. This group of dissenters was no more cohesive than the Progressives had been, and they were frustrated by their apparent powerlessness. Decrying the welfare state in 1968 seemed about as futile as protesting against the robber barons must have seemed in 1880s New York. But the opponents of government were passionate and energetic. In time, they also became organized.

Like attracts like, and those who wanted to put a halt to government expansion found each other and began to plan. In the 1970s, these groups benefitted from a general sense that something had gone terribly wrong. The twin effects of the Vietnam War and the Watergate scandal shattered the faith that millions had put in government. The policies toward Vietnam of Johnson and then his Republican successor, Richard Nixon, gradually lost the support of most Americans. As the rationale for the war became less clear with each passing year and with each returning body bag, the veneer of governmental inviolability eroded. Americans were disgusted with the response of officials to student protesters, and were outraged when the National Guard shot and killed four students at Kent State University in 1970. Of course, many Americans, and probably a majority of them, disliked the protesters. The cumulative effect, however, was a general climate of distrust and hostility that was only exacerbated by Watergate.

The scandal that unfolded in 1973 and 1974 over a minor burglary in June 1972 at the offices of the Democratic National Committee in the Watergate building in downtown Washington was a pivotal event that helped tarnish the image of government. As the story evolved, it became clear that the break-in was organized by the White House to embarrass Nixon's political opponents and ensure his reelection. The public was riveted by the drama that soon played out on television, just as they had been by scenes of the war in Vietnam. The exposure of duplicity, blackmail, and dirty tricks made the government look sordid. People were shaken, and understandably wondered how a Washington composed of people like Richard Nixon, his chief of staff H. R. Haldeman, and advisers like John Ehrlichman and G. Gordon Liddy, could be entrusted with the power that the government had gained in the past decades. Though Watergate and Vietnam forced people to shed their naïveté about the purity of government, these two crises undermined the claims of Franklin Roosevelt and Lyndon Johnson that government was a progressive, moral force. Government, from the vantage point of 1975, was only as good as the people who served in it, and, judging from recent events, that wasn't very good at all.[18]

By the end of the Nixon administration, the government was still growing, and the regulatory state was still expanding. Programs were begetting programs, bureaucracies were giving birth to new bureaucracies, and the courts were steadily expanding the sphere of government activity. The growth was startling at the state and local level as well, though that expansion didn't receive the harsh scrutiny that federal growth did. At the same time, the economy was mired in "stagflation," a noxious mix of low economic growth and rising prices. After Vietnam, the United States was not exactly well liked internationally, and American society was riven internally by the cultural changes in sexual mores and family life that had accompanied the Great Society.

The government vision was in disarray. The partisans of more government had promised a wide range of benefits. Not only could Americans be assured of material security, but they would, by dint of government action, enjoy more inchoate advantages as well. Society would be unified; people would feel part of a larger community; families would be strengthened; and the bonds linking people to one another would be fortified. In short, people would be happier, wealthier, and safer. In the 1970s, however, Americans felt sadder, poorer, and more insecure. Sad at the combined effects of war and scandal, poor because of stagflation, and more insecure because government had become unwieldy and alien, and the world outside more hostile. Even more troubling, government was unable to achieve what the Great Society promised. Yes, the Great Society reduced the number of people living below the poverty line, but not as dramatically or substantially as had been expected. In the 1970s, working-class wages began to flatten and prices rose. Interest rates soared, and it became harder for average Americans to own homes or start small businesses. Divorce became more prevalent; drug use rose; inner cities decayed; and crime rates rocketed alarmingly. Government programs proved incapable of transforming society in the manner envisioned, and millions were left angry and disappointed.

The reasons for government's failure are complicated and debatable. Some believe that the Great Society was undermined by opponents who wished it to fail and who made sure that its programs were never adequately funded. Others feel that the government simply tried to do things that no government can really do, while some think that the real culprit was bad planning and inept bureaucrats. Whatever the cause, by the 1970s, it was hard to deny the fact that government had not succeeded in achieving the aims of the Great Society. It was one thing to regulate banks and put people to work temporarily, as the New Deal had done, but it was another thing entirely to strive for the permanent social and economic improvement of millions of people to educate them, instill them with hope and pride, and have their lives thereafter be better. Government also fell short of creating a national sense of community. People found the world of the 1960s and 1970s unfamiliar and bewildering, and government was largely helpless in providing a mooring.

In this climate of disillusionment, the opponents of more government grew in strength as the 1970s went on. As had happened in the previous stages, the government visionaries overreached and a reaction followed. After the victory of Jimmy Carter in 1976, an antigovernment coalition combined to create a new force in the Republican Party.

In the blockbuster film *Back to the Future*, released in the mid-1980s, the main character played by Michael J. Fox finds himself transported back to the 1950s. Desperate to make his way back to his own time, he tracks down the scientist who invented the time machine and tries to get his help. "So you're from the future," the skeptical inventor says after he's listened to the improbable tale. "Well, who's president in 1985?" "Ronald Reagan," Fox's character answered. "Hah," the scientist says, and slams the door. He can then be heard yelling in the other room. "Ronald Reagan?" he says sarcastically. "The actor?"

Ronald Reagan had been a successful B-movie actor, memorable for appearing frequently on screen and then as the television spokesman for General Electric. In 1964, he became an outspoken advocate for the Republican presidential candidate Barry Goldwater. At the time, Goldwater seemed almost beyond the fringe, and he was successfully parodied by Lyndon Johnson as a dangerous man who might lead the world to nuclear Armageddon. But Goldwater's defeat was also the birth of the new wave of the Republican Party, which would have its first triumph with Reagan and its next, and last, with Newt Gingrich and the Republican Congress of 1994.

Reagan hated what happened in the 1960s. Like many, he watched the growth of government with horror. For him and millions of others, the rhetoric of the Great Society was a betrayal. Reagan and the groups that gathered around him saw the government as a threat, and they inherited a tradition that stretched from the revolutionaries to the Anti-Federalists to the Southern secessionists and to agrarian Populists of the late nineteenth century.[19] Determined to restore "traditional" values, Reagan successfully ran for governor of California in 1966 and then positioned himself in the 1970s as an alternate leader for a Republican Party that had been unable to present a viable ideological alternative to the Great Society and the New Deal.

Rugged, energetic, vacuous, charming, Reagan could project passion, outrage, and humor as well as any politician in recent memory. He seethed with resentment over the course that the country had taken, and he truly believed that unless something was done and done soon, the American dream would be lost forever. He thought that the combined policies of Johnson, Nixon, and Gerald Ford had appeased the Soviet Union and made international Communism an even more formidable threat, and he sensed that the social policies of the government were somehow violating the moral fiber of the country. In this, he was supported by a wide, disparate coalition of voters, which included the "Religious Right," composed of suburban, Southern, and Midwestern conservatives who wanted to halt the march of government into the homes of America.

At a White House Conference on the Family held in 1979, Christian conservatives united to prevent any meaningful resolutions from passing. Led by an aggressive, dynamic young woman from South Carolina named Connie Marshner and backed by conservatives such as Phyllis Schlafly, Paul Weyrich, and Timothy LaHaye, the Religious Right portrayed the Carter administration as trying to legislate what goes on in the bedroom. They ridiculed liberals for believing that it was the responsibility of government to feed the poor and to house the homeless. The conservatives thought it was up to families and churches and local private organizations to care for the poor. They felt that it was wrong for the government to collect high taxes in order to administer a welfare state, and that when it did, its efforts were rife with inefficiency. Reagan took this critique one step further.

Debating Carter during the election of 1980, Reagan answered a question posed by Barbara Walters of ABC News. "Mr. Carter seeks the solution to anything as another opportunity for a Federal Government program," Reagan replied. "I happen to believe that the Federal Government has usurped powers of autonomy and authority that belong back at the state and local level. It has imposed on the individual freedoms of the people, and there are more of these things that could be solved by the people themselves, if they were given a chance. . . ." Relentlessly attacking the principle that government should be part of all major issues, Reagan defeated Carter, and declared triumphantly during his inaugural address, "Government is not the solution to our problems. Government is the problem."[20]

The government paradigm was under assault, but for the 1980s, it continued to exert its hold. Buffeted by public disillusionment, government was no longer Camelot. Eighties pop culture celebrated Wall Street and cowboy corporate raiders like T. Boone Pickens, and an emerging group of "yuppies," those young urban professionals who were transforming life in cities across the country and were the object of bemused fascination. The attention on banks and Wall Street, however, was itself partly a product of the Reagan administration. The culture still followed Washington's lead, and that of the powerful White House. Reagan pointed to Wall Street, to middle America, and to the free market, and the country took the cue. Reagan spoke, and people listened. He said that the best of America was represented by the entrepreneur working with as little interference from government as possible, and tens of millions of people nodded in agreement.

In spite of Reagan's rhetoric, government institutions continued to be involved in every major aspect of life, and social issues such as drug use and divorce, sexual harassment and income disparities were still debated with reference to what government should do about it.

Reagan provided the bridge between the government vision and the market vision. While he and many of those around him began to develop an alternate framework, one that looked to the potential of the market, the very fact that Reagan ran against government and campaigned against government indicated the degree to which government remained the predominant factor in the culture. The 1980s combined disappointment with government with giddy optimism about what society would look like if market mores rather than governmental ones were dominant.

During the late 1970s and 1980s, public confidence in government plummeted, as conservatives waged a relentless campaign to delegitimize it. Bureaucratic inefficiencies were so prevalent that government made an easy target. But as had happened with the previous stages, reaction preceded the evolution of a coherent new vision. Reagan spoke brightly of "morning in America," but under his watch, that antigovernment animus never morphed into a commonly accepted vision for a different type of society. His administration vowed to shrink government, but the reality was otherwise. Government at all levels continued to grow. State and local government escaped the worst condemnation, and the federal government shrank not at all. Military expenditures mushroomed as Reagan championed the "Second Cold War," and the Democratic Congress cut no major social programs. As a result, government deficits exploded.

In many ways, it was the worst of all worlds. Government was everywhere in disrepute, yet it was getting bigger and spending more money than ever. The Reagan years represented the flip side of the fifth stage, but not yet a fully developed new stage.

Phrases like "Reaganomics" and "trickle-down economics" suggested what the new ideology entailed—a society in which the government stood aside and let the free market drive the country. Within a decade of Reagan's presidency, the free market vision would replace the government vision, but in the 1980s, what happened in Washington continued to matter, viscerally and daily. People were emotional and passionate about their distrust of government, and about their support or antagonism for Ronald Reagan. Events in Nicaragua led to a scandal involving senior White House officials, and the country was transfixed in the summer of 1987 by televised hearings of Colonel Oliver North swearing that he had been a loyal Marine and done what his commander in chief wished. Though the stock market crashed in October of 1987, more people were obsessed with the latest developments in the Iran-Contra hearing than they were with the value of the Dow Jones industrial average. Washington remained at the center of national life, for better or for worse, and the vision of a society made better by government lingered, weakened and discredited but not yet supplanted.

By the 1990s, it was clear that the constant rhetorical assault on government was having a lethal effect. Gradually, more and more people lost faith in what government could do. The optimism of the Great Society was in such disrepute that the very word "liberal" became politically toxic. When the governor of Massachusetts, Michael Dukakis, ran against Reagan's vice-president, George Bush, in the 1988 presidential election, he saw his lead evaporate and the election lost in part because he was effectively portrayed as a liberal who would return the country to the dismal days of inflation, stagnation, and social chaos. As president, Bush consolidated the legacy of the far more charismatic and popular Reagan. Under Bush, the federal government was widely perceived as ineffective and plagued by gridlock. With a Republican in the White House and the Congress controlled by Democrats, little meaningful legislation was passed. Bush concentrated on foreign policy. Between the collapse of the Soviet Union, the emergence of Eastern Europe, and the successful war against Iraq in 1991, there was more than enough happening in the world to keep the Bush administration active and occupied.

The frenetic pace of foreign affairs, however, barely masked how moribund the federal government had become. Americans were conflicted in their feelings, and in 1992, the public was presented with three candidates in the general election. William Jefferson Clinton, the young governor of Arkansas with a penchant for extramarital affairs and an ability to outthink, outdebate, and outcharm almost anyone, won the presidency with less than 50 percent of the vote. Given that barely 50 percent of eligible voters voted, that meant that Clinton became president with the support of less than a quarter of the population. The events of Clinton's first term would demonstrate that not only was government in a holding pattern, but its days as the dominant paradigm were coming to an end.

That's not how it seemed when Clinton took the oath of office. Promising a period of vigorous government activism, Clinton plunged into his term. There was a buzz of excitement amongst those who had suffered in the wilderness of the past twelve years of Reagan–Bush. Finally, the lost legacy of government activism, of the Great Society and the New Deal, would be reclaimed. Clinton himself was fuzzy about this. He certainly sounded as if that was his plan, and his initiative to create a universal, government-backed health care system stemmed from the Great Society. But Clinton had also risen to power as a "New Democrat" who repudiated the grandiose schemes of the party in the past. In a sense, Clinton was the obverse of Reagan. Where Reagan had inveighed against government but decreased it hardly at all, Clinton championed government rhetorically but ended up overseeing its demise as the dominant factor in American culture.

The tumultuous debates surrounding national health care marked the beginning of the end. A Democratic president and a Democratic Congress in 1994 were unable to come up with a politically feasible plan to insure the forty million uninsured Americans. Health insurance was the sine qua non of the Great Society, and the inability of the federal government to craft legislation was a potent indication that the philosophy of the Reagan years had had a devastating effect. The Clinton administration was widely criticized for its ineptitude, but it is far from clear whether aptitude would have made a difference. While there was a wide public consensus on the need to insure the uninsured, there was no agreement on how that ought to be accomplished. The idea that government would be intimately involved made a significant portion of the public uncomfortable. In a series of ads, a couple known simply as Harry and Louise talked about their concerns that the government would soon be deciding what doctors they could see, and what medical procedures they were eligible for. Though the ads distorted the facts of the proposed plan, the critique resonated. Most Americans, shaped by the legacy of the 1970s and Reagan, didn't trust that government would or could be a responsible intermediary. Whatever the partisan politics, that simple fact remained. Government had ceased to command the respect necessary for a national health care system to be viable.[21]

If there was any doubt, the results of the fall mid-term elections of 1994 sealed the fate of government. Led by Newt Gingrich, Congressional Republicans stoked the flames of antigovernment sentiment and marshaled support throughout the South and the midwest. As a result, Republicans captured both houses of Congress for the first time in decades. Committed to shrinking the role and the size of the government, the "Republican Revolution" swept into Washington, with a grinning Gingrich at the helm. Congress was now controlled by an ardent group of mostly white conservative men who were dedicated to making the antigovernment rhetoric of Reagan a reality. They promised to slash the budget and to eliminate departments and hundreds of "wasteful" programs. And they swore that never again would government dominate the American scene.

Four years later, the so-called revolution flamed out, with most of its goals unmet. Clinton stymied the more extreme proposals by threatening to veto the legislation, and Republicans in power found it harder to get rid of programs than they had thought. Each program represented federal dollars being spent in someone's district, and cutting the program meant cutting those dollars. No congressional representative wanted to go back to his or her constituents to try to explain why there was now less money flowing to them. Furthermore, faced with the reality of what eliminating programs might mean, many Americans had second thoughts. As it stood, most people in most places wanted the federal government to make sure that prescription drugs are safe, that planes land and take off without exploding or crashing, that highways are built and repaired, that students have access to college loans, that borders are patrolled, and above all, that the elderly have an income and health care. That is what most of the money is spent on, and bloated though the bureaucracy may be, there is little public support for cutting Social Security and Medicare, or for drastically cutting the Defense Department and dozens of regulatory agencies.

However, though government as a series of institutions survived the attacks of the Republican Revolution, government as a paradigm did not. Addressing the nation in his State of the Union address in January 1996, Clinton conceded: "We know that big government does not have all the answers," he said. "We know there's not a program for every problem. We have worked to give the American people a smaller, less bureaucratic government in Washington. And we have tried to give the American people one that lives within its means. The era of big government is over." He called on people to work together and with government to face whatever challenges arise, but the game was over. Later that year, running for reelection and faced with a bill to phase out government welfare programs, Clinton signed the bill into law, thereby ending welfare as it had been established during the 1960s. Though federal welfare spending was never as large as the attention focused on it would have suggested, the fact that a Democratic president agreed to its termination was the crossing of a cultural Rubicon.

The concession of Clinton was the proverbial final straw. So long as there were powerful advocates of the government paradigm, the vision continued to exert a strong pull on American society. But when the most prominent representative of those advocates announced, in effect, that the vision was no longer viable, that consigned the government stage to the past.

The events of Clinton's second term, which for more than a year displayed all the elements of theater of the absurd, only cemented what he had declared in January 1996. The impeachment and trial of William Jefferson Clinton, on the charge that he perjured himself about whether or not he had had sexual relations with a White House intern, was a daily soap opera throughout 1998 and into the first months of 1999. While an overwhelming majority of people believed that the president had lied about his conduct, an equally overwhelming majority felt that he was doing a good job as president and that he should not be removed from office. That did not prevent the Republican Congress from pursuing Clinton, and the hatred that characterized these months was divisive and depressing. The soap-opera hysteria, however, only served to mask the fact that government had ceased to be that important. The very pettiness of the crisis indicated that government no longer mattered in the way that it had. Instead of widespread clamor that official Washington cease its self-consuming passion for the scandal, the public reaction was one of bemused apathy tinged with voyeurism. Everyone watched, and everyone eagerly gobbled up the details of the president's sexual peccadillos, but for the most part, people cared the way they care about a sports event. Passions were intense but also selective and contained. It was all very salacious and intriguing, but it gradually became clear that it wasn't all that important.

Of course not everyone sees it that way. On each side partisans claimed that the events surrounding Clinton's impeachment struck at the very foundation of American society, but those claims rested on a dated assumption. The impeachment could only strike at the core of society if government defined the core of society. For much of the twentieth century, there was truth in that assumption, but by the time of Clinton's impeachment, it no longer was. A century and a half earlier, the impeachment of President Andrew Johnson had been traumatic but not overly consequential because government was not the dominant factor in society in the late 1860s. By the end of the twentieth century, that again was the case. Clinton's impeachment trial faded from public consciousness as rapidly as the other tabloid events of the 1990s. Monica Lewinsky, Kenneth Starr, and the dress lost their resonance and joined the village of forgotten obsessions alongside O. J. Simpson, Rodney King, Princess Diana, and JonBenet Ramsey.

The opposition to Clinton did demonstrate that the earlier stages of American culture continue to resonate. The Religious Right came out strongly against the president. Some people who defined themselves as Christian conservatives not only interpreted Clinton's actions—from the murky Whitewater affair to the Lewinsky scandal—as immoral but as evil. In the eyes of some, Clinton was doing the work of the devil, just as the dissenters from Massachusetts Bay were seen as heretical in the mid-1600s. Clinton's prosecutors also seemed to be driven by a religious morality reminiscent of the Puritans. The pull of religion remains strong, as does the suspicion of government. For some, Clinton became the embodiment of tyranny. The destruction of the Branch Davidian compound in Waco, Texas, in 1993 was lauded in many quarters, but others interpreted it as proof that the Clinton administration intended to strip the American people of their liberty. The sense of utter peril that the government posed to liberty, typical of the partisans of the Revolutionary Era, was in evidence in the motives of those who bombed a federal building in Oklahoma City in 1995. Though few Americans are part of the Religious Right, and only a very small number share the paranoid suspicions of the Oklahoma City bombers, the currents that characterized the previous stages still percolate.

But the previous stages do not exert the cultural influence they once did, and now, neither does government. In the midst of the trial of Clinton by the Senate in February 1999, one Republican senator bitterly attacked the public for not caring. He claimed that people were too busy tracking their stock portfolios to care about what was happening in Washington. Underneath the noise of the scandals in Washington and the acrimonious debates between Republicans and Democrats, the attention and energy of the culture had shifted elsewhere. The process of detachment from government had been going on for decades, at least since the mid-1970s. But only with the Clinton administration did it become evident that the air had gone out of this particular balloon. For all of the hullabaloo, there was little sense of crisis. Certainly, people throughout the country were distraught, and in some areas there was outrage, either at the Republican Congress for its efforts to remove Clinton or at Clinton for his lies. But that outrage was more smoke than fire. The Clinton scandals were a sideshow to the New Economy, tolerable only because a new set of visionaries had successfully made the case that the market would secure a better future.

The end of the fifth stage shouldn't be confused with the end of government as a force in American life.[22] The federal government continues to extract more than a trillion and a half dollars in revenue each year, and it employs millions of people in the military and in assorted departments and agencies, from the post office to the Immigration and Naturalization Service. Government programs and regulations still influence key aspects of public life, and many areas of private life. Just as religion and individualism are firmly rooted in

American culture, just as the values of expansion and unity still have a hold on the collective conscience, government remains embedded in society. Americans at the turn of the twenty-first century believe in many aspects of the regulatory state to a degree that would have been alien a century earlier. The reaction against government halted the extension of government beyond the point that it had reached circa 1965, but those who believed that government was imperative to the American dream of wealth and happiness transformed the United States, and there is no going back.

The government vision arose in reaction to the dislocations caused by expansion, and then in the 1930s, in response to problems that were not being solved without government. The vision for what government could do was based on what the previous framework had failed to do. The idealism that surrounded government was cut from the same cloth as the utopianism of the City on a Hill and the Declaration of Independence. It took visionaries—the Progressives, the New Dealers, Teddy Roosevelt, Wilson, F D R, and Lyndon Johnson—to envision roles for government that it had never played before. Their belief that government could change the material and social conditions of life for the better created those agencies and programs and laws. The fact that their vision fell short, that government was unable to achieve as much as the Great Society or the New Deal promised, set in motion a reaction. That reaction, itself part of a long tradition of antigovernment sentiment, undermined the vision, and that in turn opened the door to a new vision, to a next stage, to our present and the market.

PART TWO

THE PRESENT

SIX

THE MARKET

It's an early spring day, midweek, and James Young, thirty-nine years old, wakes to the sound of his alarm clock going off at 6:30 A.M. He has to go the airport to make a 9:00 A.M. flight for New York City. He stumbles groggily to the bathroom, and turns on the radio while his wife gets up to make breakfast. "Well, it's a beautiful day in the neighborhood," says the voice on the radio. "The sun's about to rise, and if we're lucky, so will the Dow."

He brushes his teeth, showers, and catches a hurried bite in the kitchen. His wife barely glances up from the financial pages, where she notices that the couple's mutual funds went down yesterday. She mentions this to her husband, who furrows his brow, remembers that they're still up for the year, and that even with the recent declines, they've done better than they would have in bonds. They've also been paying into a college fund for their daughter, and he glances at the charts to see how it's doing. The rest of the paper sits unopened on the counter, the front page festooned with news about the presidential election underway. Mr. Young grabs the sports page, tells his wife not to worry, and heads out the door for the airport. Mrs. Young, who isn't at all worried, makes a note to log on to her computer at 9:30 in order to check the Morningside rating for a global equity fund that a friend in her book group told her about the night before. But first, she goes upstairs to help her fifteen-year-old daughter prepare a report on the difference between stocks and bonds for one of her classes.

In the car to the airport, Mr. Young listens to more news radio. Two analysts are arguing about which direction the market is going, and neither is fully convincing. There's a brief tidbit about the Senate race, and Mr. Young flips the channel to Howard Stern, who's talking about what to do with his money once his divorce is finalized.

In the lounge, before he catches his shuttle, he performs his usual ritual and grabs a handful of the free magazines: *Smart Money, Inc. Magazine, Worth Magazine, The Economist, Fast Company, Money*, and of course, *The Wall Street Journal* and *The Financial Times*. He takes a few minutes to gulp down a burnt cup of Starbucks coffee, peruses the headlines ("Alan Greenspan Speaks About the New Economy," "Your Business? Are You Ready for the Future?" "How to Maximize Your Portfolio and Minimize Your Risk: Ten Tips for the Wise Investor"). He briefly registers the titles in the window of the bookstore: *Die Rich, The Roaring 2000s, Irrational Exuberance, Die Rich 2, The Long Boom, The Coming Crash*. Well, which one is it, he says to himself in annoyance. If only he knew. He zips past the Internet kiosks, which tout FREE STOCK QUOTES with each connection fee, flashes his driver's license for his e-ticket, and gets on the plane.

Just before he lands, he makes a call, reaching over the person sitting in the middle seat to retract the GTE Airfone embedded in the seat back. The LCD display on the phone shows the latest Dow and Nasdaq figures (prices delayed twenty minutes, of course). He makes a quick mental note that the technology-laden Nasdaq is down and tries to figure out what this means for his funds. The handset also offers Bloomberg business news for $1.99 per minute, which seems excessive to him, even if his company is going to pay. He swipes his credit card and places the call to confirm the address of his first appointment. He's meeting a team that his company has hired to design the e-commerce site that he's hoping to have ready for launch in the fall.

He checks into his hotel, and, before unpacking, plugs the phone wire into his computer and logs on to check his e-mail. Interspersed between his personal messages are two pieces of spam, one from MultiPlex Investor with the subject line "Internet Stocks—Why the Bubble Burst," and another from Ameritrade blaring new rates for bulk trades. His wife sent a quick message with the precis on the global fund as a file attachment. A colleague at work forwarded him an e-mail making the rounds with a spoof news announcement. "Microsoft to Acquire U.S. Government. . . . It's actually a logical extension of our planned growth, said Microsoft chairman Bill Gates." Not likely, Young thinks; with the antitrust action, it's more like "U.S. government to acquire Microsoft."

Then it's to the meeting, in an industrial loft space in lower Manhattan with exposed brick, insulated exhaust tubing, work stations divided into pods, computers everywhere, and a Nerf basketball court. Everyone appears to be twenty-four years old. The meeting takes place in a conference room dappled with light funneling in at odd angles from the skylights above, with seven people seated around a raw steel table.

Listening to the presentation, he realizes that he needs to get up to speed on the latest B2B developments. His company is focused primarily on consumer business, but he knows that the greatest potential for growth lies in the business-to-business sector. He needs to come up with some viable ideas soon, because the architecture of the web page will need to include features for business applications. If not, it will be more work and more expense to alter the design at a later date. He knows that the curve of e-commerce will head sharply upward in the coming years, but his company hasn't fully figured out how to make the transition to web-based business. The design group has some suggestions based on other projects they've done, and he jots down the better ideas.

That evening, he takes the group to a baseball game, on his company's nickel, of course. Box seats on the first-base line. It's not a snazzy new ballpark built from local taxes and bond issues, but there are plenty of luxury suites and amenities. In the middle of the third inning, the diamond screen flashes the nightly Nasdaq report, with the lithesome Willow Bay, former model turned stock maven, narrating the latest news from the street. He shakes his head slightly. "A stock report? In the middle of a baseball game? Things really have changed." Two of the young guys are talking heatedly about the arty movie *Hamlet*, with Ethan Hawke, that they'd seen the night before. Hamlet is now the child of the slain CEO of the Denmark Corporation, the main action is set in boardrooms and swank hotels, and the tortured young man roams the streets against a backdrop of stock tickers and Times Square neon. After Willow Bay disappears, it's back to the game, random conversation, an inordinate number of home runs ("It's the juiced-up ball," one of the other guys tells him. "The owners think that home runs bring in the crowds, so the more the merrier"), and the unsettling feeling of too many hot dogs.

THE MARKET IDEAL

James Young is the New Economy's Everyman. He is a composite who lives in a world ruled by the cadence of the stock market, by the buzz of corporate leaders, appointed officials, magazines, newspapers, web pages, television, radio, movies, and sports events, all of which weave the sixth stage of American culture.

Very few real, flesh-and-blood people resemble James Young. Most of us don't share all of the values of the market ideal. We disagree with some of them, and we simply do not focus on others. We may not buy into the vision of the ads we read, hear, or watch; we may be skeptical of the claims of web designers that the future lies on the Net; and we may not think about the stock market any more than earlier generations thought about savings bonds. But a vision of the market and the Internet permeates our lives, just as religion did in the 1640s and government did in the 1960s. The New Economy is both a specific economic concept and a utopian grab bag. It is where the current version of American idealism lives.

The signs are all around us. By the year 2000, the market as the dominant cultural force had so infiltrated society that it is increasingly difficult to remember any other reality. Running for president in 1992, Bill Clinton and his campaign team came up with a simple slogan, IT'S THE ECONOMY, STUPID! At the end of his administration, that was truer than ever. In his State of the Union address in January of 2000, Clinton told the country, "We have built a new economy. Our economic revolution has been matched by the revival of the American spirit. . . . In the best traditions of our nation, Americans determined to set things right. We restored the vital center, replacing outdated ideologies with a new vision." Clinton may have been a questionable president, but no one ever accused him of misreading the prevailing public spirit. In the space of a few years, he declared the end of big government and the beginning of the New Economy, and whether or not he can fairly take credit for either, he accurately mirrored the transformations that took place in his second term.[1]

The market may be omnipresent, but it is also amorphous. As any first-year business school student learns, the market is simply a place where goods and information are exchanged. Ideally, people have full information, and no one person or group can skew the market, either by setting arbitrary prices or controlling supply and demand. As conceived by philosophers and economists, the perfect market is free of outside intervention, and it works seamlessly. Perfect market theory envisions a process by which buyers are informed and virtuous, sellers rationally try to maximize profit, and transactions cost neither more nor less than they should. Because no one can control any aspect of the market, there is also perfect competition. Sellers and buyers compete, but the result of their competition is better products and more satisfied buyers. In short, the ideal market is efficient and satisfies the needs of all involved.

As any first-year business student also learns, the market in reality often bears little resemblance to the market in theory, just as Massachusetts Bay bore little relation to the City on a Hill, and the Great Society was neither great nor a society. But the proponents of the New Economy believe that the perfect market can be created, and with it, the ideal society. Energized by technology and the stock market, these visionaries see the New Economy not only as a source of material affluence, but as the foundation for a better world. Traditionally, the potential of the market was thought to have been stunted by human failings, imperfect information, and political mistakes. Now, by the grace of the Information Revolution, the New Economy visionaries are convinced that the dreams of the market are on the verge of becoming real.

"It's been dubbed the 'new economy' for the simple reason that no one has ever seen anything like it," began an article posted on CNNfn.com. "An era in which growth and innovation have created jobs that never existed, boosted productivity to new heights, and driven the economy forward for such an extended length of time. . . . It's an era when everything seems to be on the cusp of getting better, faster, cheaper, more accessible and more profitable."[2] These messages are everywhere. The New Economy promises unimaginable wealth, individual fulfillment, and a world of perfect information and perfect connectivity. It imagines a society in which inequalities are offset by universal prosperity. It suggests a future in which poverty, disease, isolation, and alienation are no more. It sees a world in which everyone has access to the goods and services they want and need. At the center of the New Economy ideal is a belief that, finally, human beings have the capacity to end the cycles of boom and bust, security and insecurity, war and peace, and that finally, most of us, most of the time, will live happy, fulfilled lives.

The New Economy consists of two parts: a vision of the market and a vision of the Internet. These two parts are intimately woven together. In fact, without the rise of the Internet in the 1990s, the market paradigm would probably not have taken hold. This chapter and the next consider each part separately, but keep in mind that the New Economy represents a fusion of the two.

By itself, the market archetype is the ancient Greek agora where citizens congregated to exchange goods and information. In one respect, the Internet is a twenty-first-century update of the agora. It allows people to "gather" in a way that hasn't been possible since the demographic explosions that began to change the world two centuries ago. There are just too many of us to gather physically in one place, but the Internet allows people to assemble electronically. The Internet also facilitates commerce on an unprecedented scale.

The adoption of the market paradigm stems from the economic prosperity of the 1990s. First, there was the incredible rise in the stock market from under 4,000 in 1990 to more than 10,000 a decade later, and the even more startling explosion in the value of stocks traded on the Nasdaq exchange from 500 in 1990 to more than 4,000 at the end of 1999. By most counts, nearly 100 million Americans owned stocks as of the year 2000. Most own them indirectly, through mutual funds and pension plans. Millions of others purchase stocks directly. Between 1996 and 2000, the gross national product (GNP) grew at an average rate of more than 4 percent a year, and for the first time since the early 1970s, there were dramatic gains in productivity. Stock ownership, rising equity prices, and economic growth led to a rapid rise in consumer confidence. This was not just an urban phenomenon. Nor was it confined to a small percentage of the population.

Never before have so many people prospered. The trend shows

no long-term signs of abating. Four percent of American households now have a net worth of more than $1 million. In the 1990s alone, the number of families with more than $1 million in assets doubled. By the year 2000, more than 10 percent of households had a declared income of $120,000 or more. In short, more people than ever have more money than ever.[3]

In the glare of this wealth creation, government as a paradigm has been eclipsed. Today, the days when the visionary idealism of society found its purest expression in institutions such as the Peace Corps seem as quaint and distant as frozen figures in nineteenth-century daguerreotypes. During the election of 2000, public interest flared at various moments, especially during the surreal weeks of indecision after Election Day, but equally striking was how utterly disinterested most people were for most of the year. In the months before the summer conventions that coronated George W. Bush and Al Gore as candidates for president, voters surveyed by Harvard University actually forgot what little information they had acquired about the candidates in the spring. In April and May, months that on the calendar should have been taken up with the presidential primaries, public attention was consumed by two things: the melodramatic saga of Elian Gonzalez, a six-year-old Cuban boy at the center of an international custody battle, and the whiplash gyrations of the Nasdaq index. Dips in the stock market were the focus of more cultural concern than who would be the next president of the United States.[4]

The degree to which the economy in general, the stock market in particular, and the Internet have moved to the center of cultural life is obvious. Public opinion surveys show that the majority of Americans give little thought to government, and low voter turnout indicates that fewer and fewer people see government as a high priority worthy of their attentions. In every significant area of culture, the market, both as a general idea and in the specific form of the stock market, is central. Whether you overhear conversations on cell phones, own mutual funds, tune into business channels such as CNBC, MSNBC, CNNfn, and Bloomberg, buy the plethora of books and magazines devoted to the New Economy, or just subliminally register the vision presented in ads or infomercials, it is impossible to be out of earshot of the market for long.

At the same time, because the sixth stage is a description of the present, it has a different resonance than the previous stages. Those were descriptions of the past, and hence, static. The sixth stage is a picture of the present, and as such, it lacks the past's sharp reductive simplicity. Impossible as it is to view the present in hindsight, it's also impossible to pin it down. The present is a moving target, and writing about the sixth stage while in the midst of it is a bit like writing about a dream while you're having it.

Describing the sixth stage as the era of the market and the New Economy triggers at least one immediate objection. What about the people whose lives haven't been improved by the New Economy? Are they also living in a world colored by the sixth stage? At least a fifth of the population, or more than 50 million people, live near or beneath the poverty level of $17,000 a year for a family of four, and millions of others have no access to computers, no money to invest, no health insurance, and no resources.[5] Many people have been left out of the economic expansion of the 1990s and derive no direct benefit from the stock market, the Internet, or the values and obsessions that accompany them. In this age of the market, the gap between the rich and the poor is greater than at any time since the Gilded Age.

Nonetheless, the inequities do not alter the degree to which the market and its values are the predominant vision. There is no other alternate vision at the center of the culture. The sixth stage, like the previous ones, is the prevailing paradigm, whether or not one agrees with its values and whether or not one benefits from it. As we've seen, utopian visions are not malleable; they are not kind. They are dreams for a perfect world, and people can be harmed in the process of trying to realize them.

Another objection to the notion of a sixth stage is that few people internalize all of the values of the New Economy. The complexities of how people internalize a utopian vision are easy to gloss over when we look at the past. Even Andrew Carnegie may not have, at all times of the day, believed his own vision of the Gospel of Wealth, and people who knew him personally or had impressions of him would have been quick to point that out. It's even easier to see the immense variety of experiences during the sixth stage, our present. Furthermore, the utopianism surrounding the New Economy is less coherent than Puritan theology, and it is defined by far more people than articulated the philosophy of the Revolution or the New Deal. But as with each previous stage, the vision of the few dictates the culture of the many. In manifold ways, James Young's personal worldview may be quirky, individualistic, unpredictable, and impervious to generalizations. But every day, James Young interacts with the New Economy, and in that sense his entire life is influenced by the sixth stage.

Because we live in the age of the New Economy, it is both easier to agree on the simple fact that we do and easier to disagree with any particular picture that might be presented of this cultural moment. None of us has any direct experience of the Puritans, and so, few of us have formed strong impressions one way or the other. All of us live right now and have our own particular perspective on what matters, what's important, and what's happening. No picture of the present will look precisely the way we think it ought to. Talk to most people in most parts of the country, and most of the time, there will be general agreement that computers and the financial markets occupy a more central place than government, but beyond that, perspectives vary widely. For some people, religion and matters of the spirit may be foremost in their minds, and the prevalence of market mores may trouble them deeply. For others, career and office politics may occupy their conscious thoughts. And for a majority, now as in the past, family and personal relationships probably consume the lion's share of energy. In short, describing a cultural moment is not the same as describing individual experiences.

All that being said, the New Economy and its values have come to occupy a particular space, a space loosely defined by the information and entertainment that almost all of us are exposed to on a daily basis. Some of us are acutely attuned to the various signals transmitted, others of us less so. Some of us are powerfully influenced and driven to act by the signals that we receive from radio, television, newspapers, magazines, books, movies, web pages, advertising, political speeches, business retreats, office gossip, and bits and pieces of conversation overheard. Others feel compelled to remove themselves from that mainstream and dissent from those signals. Yet, whether we act or react, embrace or reject it, the market and its values are all around us, influencing us, making their way into our lives in ways welcome and unwelcome.

The Origins of the Sixth Stage

Market values have evolved over centuries, and many of the ideas now ascendant have percolated through European and American societies since the Middle Ages. Markets as places where goods are exchanged extend back beyond recorded history and have existed in every culture for as long as we can identify. But the market as a utopian paradigm is a more recent phenomenon. Though the eighteenth-century Scottish philosopher Adam Smith elaborated on theories of the market, he concentrated mainly on describing how markets worked. The same could be said for the English philosopher David Ricardo and for the nineteenth-century proponents of free trade known as the "Manchester School." Some of the English thinkers conceived of the market as a vehicle to a better society, but it would take the events of the twentieth century for that ideal to develop fully.

The current market utopianism did not simply supplant government; it also emerged as a reaction to it. The Great Depression and the New Deal led the U.S. government to embrace Keynesian economics, named after the English economist John Maynard Keynes. Keynes didn't have much faith in "efficient markets." Rather, he saw events such as the Great Depression as inevitable consequences of leaving markets to regulate themselves, and he proposed that governments could intervene in the economy to prevent drastic cycles of boom and bust. By employing various devices, including public works projects and deficit spending, Keynes suggested, a national government could limit economic depressions. After World War II, John Kenneth Galbraith expanded on Keynes. Galbraith explained the need for government oversight by arguing that though markets require competition, many American corporations are so large and powerful that they disturb the natural balance of the market. Only the national government possesses the power to act as a countervailing force and maintain the needed balance.[6]

Keynesian economics provided the initial framework for economic regulation. Even with the waning popularity of Keynes and the eclipse of government as a paradigm, the federal government continues to manage the economy, though it now favors monetary policy over deficit spending. The Federal Reserve Board, an agency created in 1913 by the Wilson administration, uses its power today to determine interest rates as a lever to control inflation.

By the mid-1970s, however, the same chorus who questioned the Great Society and the New Deal also began to cast a skeptical eye on government manipulation of the economy. The economic slump of the 1970s, combined with the international oil crisis, led Americans to doubt the capacity of Washington to manage the economy effectively. Big hair and disco notwithstanding, the decade was one of economic malaise which saw a deep depression in stock prices, double-digit interest rates, and stagnant growth in wages and productivity. Suddenly, ideas that had been dismissed as crankily irrelevant were seen in a new light, and theorists who had been treated as Cassandras were looked to as sages.

Henry Hazlitt, Friedrich Hayek, and Milton Friedman were no one's dream dinner guests in 1970; ten years later, they were viewed as visionaries. The Austrian-born Hayek did much of his most important work in the 1940s in reaction to Nazi Germany, and he developed a scathing critique of state control and government meddling in the natural workings of the economy. His books were read by a small, devoted circle, which included a college dropout named Henry Hazlitt, who left City College in New York after a year and a half and proceeded to demolish the arguments of Lord Keynes with a stylistic brilliance that belied his absence of formal education. Hazlitt had no patience for Josef Schumpeter's idea that capitalism survives on creative destruction, and he honored the dictum that the market would regulate itself perfectly if only the government, in its infinite stupidity, left it alone.

Those ideas received an academic imprimatur from a curmudgeonly University of Chicago professor named Milton Friedman, who thundered against the idiocy of Washington and those Americans who seemed to think that the economy could be tamed and society improved by bureaucrats. Only pure capitalism, Friedman asserted, could guarantee prosperity and freedom, and the greatest threat to universal prosperity was not the workings of the market and corporations but the ill-conceived ideas of people like Keynes and their acolytes in the corridors of governmental power.[7]

There were other thinkers and writers who spoke from the cultural wilderness against the prevailing norms, but for the most part, the idea that the market ought to be left alone to work its magic stayed on the margins of society until the 1970s. Though there remained a core of the Republican Party that tried to keep the memory of the 1920s alive, even most mainstream Republicans would have squirmed had they been forced to listen to a Milton Friedman lecture in the 1960s. But with the various developments of the 1970s, these views received new attention, and other voices were added. Peter Drucker, the dean of modern management, wrote voluminously about the inefficiencies of government, and conservatives drawn to the quirky charisma of William Buckley developed a sophisticated vision that posited a free-market alternative to government.

In a less partisan fashion, a new generation of economists in the 1980s saw the potential of international free trade and less government intervention. Academics such as Jeffrey Sachs, Paul Krugman, and future secretary of the treasury Lawrence Summers approached the market as an essentially benign force that is, unfortunately, often plagued by "imperfections." Rather than seeing the market as a threat to be managed by government, they started with the axiom that a better understanding of how the market works would allow for a better working of the market. The answers to market quandaries, these new economists believed, lie in market mechanics, not government programs.[8]

In tandem with its ideological assault on government, the Reagan revolution also celebrated the market and its potential. Of course, some of the Reaganites were deeply hypocritical. While denouncing big government, certain social conservatives who supported Reagan tried to use government to advance their agenda on everything from school prayer to abortion to immigration. But true free-market idealists are libertarians. They believe in minimal government and prefer the widest possible extension of the market into all walks of life. During the Reagan years, they, unlike some of the social conservatives, urged a full-scale retreat of government from the public sphere and predicted that in a free-market era, everyone would prosper.

The collapse of the Soviet Union and the end of the Cold War in 1989 gave the market ideology an additional boost. The fall of Communism in the Soviet Union and Eastern Europe was greeted in the United States as proof that the free market is the best economic system known to man. In the eyes of many, capitalism had gone head to head with Communism and won. This post–Cold War capitalist triumphalism blended nicely with the market vision of the Reagan years.

By the late 1990s, the proponents of the market had won the ideological debate. The size of government, at both state and federal levels, is still immense, and in that sense the free-market ideologues believe that the war is not yet over. But though Friedman still decries the degree to which the government follows the beat of turn-of-the century Progressives, more has changed than he can bring himself to admit. In both 1992 and 1994, voters seemed to be angry at government, angry that the promises of the fifth stage had not been fulfilled and that the expectations raised by government had not been met. Running for president in 1992, Ross Perot, the archetypal self-made millionaire, lampooned Washington for overspending by comparing the bureaucracy to a normal family maxing out on its credit cards. With this one devastating analogy, he reduced government to an irresponsible consumer, and twenty million voters agreed.

Americans have always wanted to get rich.[9] But never before has the market assumed such prominence as the promised vehicle to a better future. Not only has the New Economy rushed in to fill the vacuum left by government's ideological retreat; it has also entered realms where government feared to tread.

THE SIXTH STAGE

"Are you ready for a revolution?" asked an ad for the consulting firm Arthur Andersen. "Two hundred years ago, New Yorkers thought they had just finished one." The brochure went on to compare the American Revolution to the present day. Then, the cause was liberty. Today, it is new technologies, electronic commerce, and the New Economy. "Hold on to your hats. Here we go again."[10]

Every day, millions of people play a daily game on their computers. They have spent some time setting it up, having entered into their browsers purchase prices and ticker symbols, so that when they log on in the morning the information is there, personalized and ready for them. And then, at 10:00 A.M., they begin to track their investments, watching their portfolios rise and fall, and monitoring the ups and downs of Wall Street. In New York City, pedestrians can play the same game just by walking through Times Square, where the Nasdaq exchange has erected an immense curved screen several stories high, gleaming diaphanously, with the prices of the stocks floating by. When the Nasdaq crashed in April 2000, *The New York Times* printed pictures of angst-ridden faces staring up at the prices as if watching doomsday.[11] One irony is that the Nasdaq display is attached to the Condé Nast building, which owns some of the leading magazines in the country. The juxtaposition of *The New Yorker* scribes, *Vanity Fair* glitterati, *GQ* fashion mavens, and *Glamour* women with the ebb and flow of stock prices is the perfect symbol of the symbiotic relationship between culture, the media, and the market.

"Everyone's Getting Rich But Me!" screams the cover of *Newsweek*, next to a Keith Haring-like picture of a worried-looking man. The mantra of the New Economy? That's what the editors of the popular news magazine wryly wanted to suggest. And indeed, for a while it seemed as if not a day went by without some story about the latest twenty-something to strike it rich on some initial public offering. Even though the mania surrounding new technology companies cooled in 2000, many people are still plagued by a pervading sense that other people are getting vastly rich. Books like *The Millionaire Next Door* suggest that it's easy to become wealthy if you only figure out which stock to pick or which company to join. Online brokers such as Ameritrade, Schwab, and Prudential promise that they'll help you navigate the shoals and find financial security. And everywhere you turn, someone is offering some advice or admonition about how to profit from the New Economy.

There's a reason why the culture is filled with these messages. The people who generate culture—the advertising agencies, the journalists and writers who pen stories such as these, the editors who commission them, the publishers and authors of the books about the market, the professors who teach college and graduate students, and the newscasters and producers who generate content on television and the Web—are part of the same class as the twenty- and thirty-somethings who have gotten rich as the market boomed. Though New Economy multimillionaires are a tiny portion of the population, they have received an inordinate amount of attention, in part because wealth always fascinates and in part because the people who produce culture all know someone who found windfall profits in the New Economy. For the same reason, the tens of millions who are left out of the new prosperity are culturally almost invisible. Every journalist and every producer of every news or entertainment program knows people that they went to school with or met socially who have gotten rich, and they themselves may have made some money from stocks or from their own media companies going public. But they probably don't know farmers or low-wage workers or millions of others who live in trailer parks and eke out a marginal living. The culture they produce reflects the world they know.[12]

But that culture extends well beyond the world they know and informs the lives of millions who have no direct part in it. Whether you have any direct stake in the New Economy or not, you have been influenced by it. The simple act of watching television exposes you to its values, as advertisers riff on the Internet revolution and television presents young, affluent faces. During the Super Bowl, in both 1999 and 2000, seventy million viewers were treated to a nearly unbroken strain of ads from "dot.com" companies that hoped to use the huge audience as a way to improve their corporate fortunes. A company called Monster.com spent nearly half its assets in 1999 to air a commercial touting its virtues as a job-hunting site, and the ploy succeeded in establishing Monster.com as a viable company. The very act of airing this commercial, and dozens of others like it, brought a large portion of the country in contact with the vision of the New Economy, as well as to the idea that other people have profited while you have been being left out.

In one sense, money is the object. But the vision of the market is more complex than pure profit. Money is simply the currency. The goal is fulfillment, and the market visionaries hold out the promise that the market will solve the eternal conundrums and generate both material security and spiritual contentment, both income and happiness. Skeptics of market values (and there are many) are quick to point out that marketers have always sold a vision of the good life. The trend, these skeptics say, is a familiar one. The goal of advertising is to generate a demand for goods and to convince consumers that certain products and services are necessary. In the 1950s, *The Saturday Evening Post* ran a cover that said, "Soon the Good Life will be yours, along with all the good things of your dreams." The notion that a product or a service will make the buyer happy is hardly particular to the sixth stage. In some respects, the hype surrounding the Internet and the new technologies is just the latest turn of the wheel. Today's computers are yesterday's General Electric dishwasher.[13]

In the past, however, the vision of the market was circumscribed. Businesses during the Gilded Age touted the promise of new products, and ads in publications like *Collier's* sounded much like similar ads today. But during the previous stages, there were other messages buzzing through the culture, whether these were the values of Progressivism or the ideological struggles that marked the Cold War. In other periods, the values of the market were prominent, but not dominant. The sixth stage, however, enshrines those values as fully as the earlier stages enshrined theirs.

"Yes! You Can Have It All!" That motto, which was used in 1999 to plug a beautiful new home in Scroggins, Texas, is the creed of the New Economy.[14] The market is suffused with the notion that it's possible to have all that we dream of, from the Perfect Information of Ask Jeeves to the good life that has always seemed beyond our reach. As described by Robert Samuelson, "the New Capitalism [means] social justice without Big Government." It means a world where "good corporations" harness the energies of free enterprise to provide secure jobs, ethnic harmony, and general well-being.[15] It is the same dream of the Declaration of Independence, the same vision of the Great Society, except now the means to the end is the market.

There is something peculiarly American about the conceit that you can have it all. It's hard to picture a French company successfully advertising a product with a similar motto, or a Chinese bureaucrat rhapsodizing about the limitless, painless future that the market and the Internet portend. In most traditional societies, stability and safety are the primary objective, and if people are able to have enough, that's something to be thankful for. Held together by history, ethnicity, race, language, or religion, many societies can look to shared experiences or common roots as a binding force. Granted, those "shared" experiences are sometimes invented and sometimes imagined, and there is often a good deal of violence that comes with creating a nation.[16]

The United States is atypical, however, because one of the few things that has bound people together, that has united them, is a shared vision. And that vision has often been articulated by a small, dynamic group of visionaries, people who conceive of the world in a new way, who see a better future, and who are relentless in their ambition to achieve it: the Puritans, the Founding Fathers, the Great Triumvirate, the robber barons, the Progressives, and now, in the sixth stage, a potent mix of financial elites, politicians, Silicon Valley entrepreneurs, and the media. For better and for worse, the United States is fueled by visionaries. They characterize the cultural moment; they set the agenda.

Today, American society is noisier than it has ever been. More outlets of expression in the form of cable, the Web, and other avenues of communication mean that there is more information than ever. It also means that culture is fragmented. There are tens of millions who pay attention to baseball, but a hundred million don't. There are tens of millions of political junkies who follow every permutation of Congressional and presidential politics, but many more do not. There is a group of devoted market watchers, who tune in every day to business channels such as CNBC and CNNfn and listen to the endless speculation and prognostications about the market; but most people can't distinguish between Willow Bay and Massachusetts Bay. There are few events that most of us pay attention to. Yet each of us, in our way, lives in a universe that is shaped by a market vision.

One manifestation of that vision is how the language of government has changed. During Clinton's first term, Vice-President Al Gore launched an initiative to make the government more efficient, to "re-invent" it so that it responds to its "consumers" along the lines of a smoothly functioning business. During Clinton's second term, Congress passed legislation whose import was not fully reflected in the amount of coverage it received. In November 1999, one of the pivotal laws of the New Deal was repealed. By an overwhelming vote, both houses of Congress put an end to the Glass-Steagall Act of 1933. Glass-Steagall had kept commercial banks, investment banks, and insurance companies from entering one another's businesses. After more than 10,000 banks failed in the early years of the Great Depression, the federal government believed that the cause was unsound banking practices. Glass-Steagall was designed to keep banks in check. But as free-market economists revised the history of that period, more people came to believe that the legislation was based on a faulty premise that the link between banks and the stock market caused the Depression. Instead, the free marketers believe that the Depression was the result of wrong-headed decisions by the Federal Reserve. In their view, Glass-Steagall, far from guarding against future depressions, had added an unnecessary and costly layer of bureaucracy and kept a lid on the economy. With its repeal, law makers declared, American banks would be more internationally competitive and consumers would save as much as $15 billion a year.[17]

Not only has the legislative agenda tilted, but the federal government is now epitomized by those involved in economic issues. The market vision has infiltrated government itself. During the Cold War, the president, the national security adviser, and the secretary of state were the focus of attention. In the 1970s, Henry Kissinger bestrode the national stage like a German-Jewish colossus. In the 1990s, the focus shifted, largely toward two men: the chairman of the Federal Reserve and the secretary of the treasury. One of the beneficiaries of the Glass-Steagall repeal was the financial conglomerate Citigroup, which was formed by the merger between the banking giant Citicorp and the insurance titan Travelers Group. Without the change in banking laws, Citigroup would have had to divest itself of its insurance business. And one of the three most important figures at Citigroup is Robert Rubin, who was until 1999 the secretary of the treasury.

In the 1920s, financiers such as Andrew Mellon and Thomas Lamont had steered the economic policy of Republican administrations, but Rubin was cut from different cloth. Modest, passionate about government, and piercingly though self-effacingly intelligent, Rubin was initially Clinton's chairman of the National Economic Council and then appointed to be the secretary of the treasury after Lloyd Bentsen retired. No one could ever accuse Rubin of being a media hound, but as the Clinton administration became mired in scandal and stymied by the president's flamboyant knack for self-immolation, Rubin's unprepossessing qualities were a strength. He was looked to as the proverbial calm in the storm, as someone who would quietly, firmly, and patiently explain the rationale for the administration's economic policies not only to reporters but to Congress and to others in the White House. He was at once a liberal Democrat and a conservative financial man who believed that the

Clinton administration and American society would be best served by trimming the national debt and honoring the demands of Wall Street.

Unlike the secretaries of the treasury of the 1920s, Rubin somehow escaped the opprobrium of seeming to pander to Wall Street. In the mainstream media, he was rarely accused of ignoring the inequalities that the New Economy was aggravating. Rather, he was widely admired because he appeared to have the interests of all Americans at heart, and his philosophy of debt reduction and free trade seemed to be connected to a progressive vision for the larger society. Though the Republican Congress led by Newt Gingrich in 1995 refused to sanction Rubin's proposal to bail out Mexico (which was then in the midst of an economic collapse), Rubin found emergency discretionary funds to the tune of nearly $20 billion and propped up the peso. In 1997, as several of the Asian "Tigers" were reeling, Rubin crafted a plan that kept Korea, Malaysia, and Japan from the potential disaster of a total financial meltdown. And for these actions, as well as for advocating fiscal conservatism in the Clinton administration, Rubin received universal accolades.[18]

Or at least, that's all that most people heard. Because Rubin represented the kindest, gentlest, and most intelligent face of the New Economy in Washington, he was lionized by a culture that was itself in the midst of celebrating the market and the New Economy. Those who weren't as gung ho about the New Economy—from the freshman Republican congressmen of 1994 to the Reform Party of Ross Perot to Pat Buchanan and others—weren't quite so gung ho about Rubin either, but their voices were drowned out in the market-driven culture. It was almost as difficult to make a critique of Rubin in the late 1990s as it would have been to speak out against the vision of a City on a Hill in mid-seventeenth-century Massachusetts.

When Rubin retired in May 1999, the other person who had come to symbolize the new Washington became even more prominent. Alan Greenspan is as unlikely an icon as Kissinger was. A somber academic, fond of heavy framed black glasses, jowly, and dour, Greenspan is the Kissinger of the financial world. Though he was an important figure in the waning years of the Nixon administration, and though he was appointed chairman of the Federal Reserve by Reagan in 1987, his name would have been recognized by few

Americans outside of Washington until the mid-1990s. Only with the emergence of the New Economy did Greenspan burst into public consciousness. Whether measured by the number of times his name appeared in articles, was mentioned on television, or was invoked by politicians, Greenspan grew more famous and more influential as the 1990s progressed.

Eschewing on-the-record interviews, Greenspan cultivates an aura of mystery. He testifies regularly in front of Congress, makes frequent public speeches, and of course, presides over the regular meetings of the Federal Reserve Board. His public pronouncements have carried even greater weight because they are unmitigated by other quotable conversation. The combination of a visible public persona and an impenetrable private one lends Greenspan the aura of an oracular figure. Though he clearly believes in the role of the Federal Reserve, he has exercised extreme caution about predicting future trends in the economy. A favorite parlor game in Washington and Wall Street has been to try to parse Greenspan's prose to figure out just what he thinks about the New Economy. He seems to be for economic growth and against inflation, but the rest of his views remain shrouded in opacity.

Greenspan's name is frequently juxtaposed to words like "icon" and "almighty." "The greatest central banker in the history of the world," quipped Senator Phil Gramm of Texas. He has achieved "cult status," according to *The Economist*, as "the patron saint of the New Economy." A news article in 1999 began, "Alan Greenspan revealed last week, in an almost unnoticed comment in his testimony to Congress, that he is indeed King of the World." During a presidential primary debate in late 1999, Senator John McCain was asked if he would reappoint Greenspan as chairman if he became president. McCain replied that his respect for the head of the Federal Reserve was such that if Greenspan died, he would prop up the chairman's corpse and keep him on the job.[19]

Greenspan is not without his eccentricities. For many years, he was closely involved with Ayn Rand, the author of several best-selling books in the 1940s and 1950s. Just how close they were remains a hotly debated question, but Greenspan has always acknowledged his intellectual debt to Rand. She is often remembered for celebrating the free market, and that is certainly true for Greenspan and most of contemporary American culture. But Rand also posited the notion of exceptional individuals who imagine the future and make it real. These people, modern American versions of Nietzsche's Superman, see possibilities that others do not. Blessed with a vision for what could be, they also have the strength of character, the force of will, and the intellect to see their vision through. In short, Rand believed that the select few, the visionaries, can change the world.

Many have noted the dangers of Rand's thinking and the degree to which it could be used to justify totalitarian fascist visions just as easily as it could be used to buttress democratic, capitalist ones. But that is a danger inherent in all visions. They are potentially totalitarian in that they reduce reality to a simple set of values. Not usually known for their humility, visionaries often reject nuance and try to silence dissent.

Greenspan is something of a post-modern Rand hero. He doesn't preen, and he doesn't make a grand entrance. But he has been willing to use his power to steer the country in the direction that he sees fit. He believes in the infinite capacity of the market. Heroes are only exaggerated reflections of a society's dreams. Judging from the enraptured response to Greenspan's economic stewardship, he is not alone in his beliefs.[20]

The visionaries of the sixth stage are the people who have created the philosophy of the New Economy. Many of these have founded companies, such as Larry Ellison of Oracle, Jim Clark of Netscape, Jeff Bezos of Amazon, Scott McNealy of Sun, and Steve Jobs of Apple; others have reinvented old, traditional corporations, such as Lou Gerstner of IBM, Jack Welch of General Electric, and Jacques Nasser, head of Ford Motors. Some are Wall Street mavens, who work at places like Goldman Sachs (where Robert Rubin was once a partner) or Morgan Stanley. Some are venture capitalists who have funded the companies that define the New Economy, epitomized by Vinod Khosla and other partners of the Bay Area firm Kleiner Perkins. Some are writers, economists, or academics who give intellectual form to the New Economy, people like Thomas Friedman of *The New York Times* or Lester Thurow of MIT. And some are the commentators who cover the world of business and the market, like Maria Bartiromo on CNBC, James Cramer in all of his many incarnations, and Neil Cavuto of Fox.

The New Economy mavens are the latest in a long lineage of visionaries. Their ancestors are Revolutionary leaders like Paine and Jefferson, Gilded Age figures like J. P. Morgan and Carnegie and Rockefeller, and government-era stalwarts like Sargent Shriver and John F. Kennedy and Franklin Roosevelt. The new visionaries both embody and articulate the amorphous mores of the market: entrepreneurship, self-confidence, a disdain for rules, an emphasis on maverick behavior and taking risks, and a flair for dramatic leaps. They are lauded for an intangible ability to think outside of the box, and they are dismissive of those who don't share their vision.

One of the things that is said to make the New Economy new is the nature of its advocates. At a conference organized by the White House in April 2000, Kim Polese, cofounder of a high-tech company called Marimba, observed that "the new economy is less about a revolution in technology or economic policies or accounting principles. It's really more about a change in attitude." This is just another way of saying that the New Economy depends on the creative imaginings of countless people. For that reason, people in the business of generating words and stories and ideas, people, that is, in the media, are a more central part of the culture than they have been in the past. They are an integral part of the collective imagination that makes the New Economy real. They will also be an integral part of the collective imagination that brings the New Economy to an end.[21]

Not everyone agrees about the New Economy. Greenspan may be the poster boy for Wall Street, but he appears to be wary of extrapolating too much from the recent boom. Others feel that there is nothing particularly new going on, and that we are simply in a prolonged period of growth that has led to hyperbole. Almost everyone recognizes that the technology of the computer age has transformed the material world and continues to do so. But some prominent dissenters question whether the laws of the New Economy are any different from the laws of the old. They assume that eventually the economy will cool off, as it has ever since the maturation of the modern economic system centuries ago. They are certain that the cyclical nature of capitalism is not so easily altered by a few boom years, and that claims to the contrary are sure evidence not of a new economy but of speculative bubbles, which have been forming and bursting ever since humans ventured into the marketplace.[22]

There is a heated debate going on between economists, business-men, stock analysts, and government officials about the New Econ-omy. This debate revolves around whether or not the stock market is overvalued. Because so much of the New Economy is financed by the stock market, the fate of the Dow and Nasdaq appear intimately linked to the fate of the New Economy. The unprecedented growth of the stock market in the 1990s, and the even more meteoric rise in the technology-laden Nasdaq from 1997 through early 2000, led to a novel form of financing new companies. Companies have always gone public as a way to raise cash and alter the financial structure of the corporation. But traditionally, companies first relied on investors, or on bonds, in order to establish themselves as profitable ventures. With the booming stock market, and with millions of Americans par-ticipating in it, companies began to use Initial Public Offerings as the primary cash-raising device. They sought just enough investors, including angels and venture capitalists, to fund operations for a year or two in order to set up the skeleton of a business. Then they filed for an IPO, and used the millions, or even billions, raised as a way to forge ahead and create a viable business.

This trend was most prevalent in the high-tech area, and in Inter-net companies in particular. When the Nasdaq shed almost 40 per-cent of its value in the spring of 2000, the fever for IPOs cooled, but a new pattern had been established, one that linked the stock market to economic growth. That link has troubled many economists who believe that the investment of so much excess capital in stocks, and especially in highly speculative stocks, is dangerous and shows all the signs of what Yale economist Robert Schiller termed "irrational exu-berance."[23]

Rational or irrational, new or not new, wise or foolish, the con-temporary template is the New Economy, and, as Robert Samuelson pithily said, "The dirty secret of today's economy is that no one truly understands it. Not Alan Greenspan. Not Larry Summers. Not Abby Joseph Cohen [of Goldman Sachs]. We listen to these and other ora-cles, examining their every utterance for enlightenment. They're the experts. They know more than we do. But what they don't know may well be more important than what they do."[24] Economists and politi-cians and stock analysts interpret the world based on models, and these models are derived from a careful study of what has happened in the past. Models for how the economy behaves are therefore only as accurate as history can be. They may perfectly describe how events will unfold in the future, provided that nothing happens that hasn't happened before.

That is the conundrum of the New Economy: is it part of a traditional economic cycle or is it revolutionary? Will we come to understand its workings in terms of productivity, price-earnings ratios, supply and demand, interest rates and money supply, employment data and housing starts—that is, in terms of the economic indicators and tools and metrics that have helped us grasp the nature of the economy until the present? Or will the New Economy break the mold, set new rules, and force a dramatic rethinking of the laws of economics?

Take a step back from the debate over whether the Dow will reach 36,000 by 2005 or 40,000 by 2007 or crash to 5,000 before then, and something else becomes clear. Muffle the noise over whether companies are overvalued, whether or not productivity is rising enough to justify the giddy optimism, and whether or not the economic boom in the United States is sustained only by a strong dollar internationally which, once the Euro establishes itself, will be drastically undermined, and something else reveals itself. The focus of public discussion is the market. Whether or not the New Economy proves to be a new *economy*, it is unquestionably a new utopian vision.

THE MARKET VISION REACHES FAR

Human needs exist on a spectrum, from the most material needs and desires at one end to the most ephemeral, nonmaterial needs on the other. The need for shelter, or the desire for a new pair of shoes, hovers on the material end of that spectrum, while the desire for happiness and the yearning to comprehend love and death reside in the nonmaterial realm. Of course, in real life, these get blended. An awful lot of happiness can get attached to buying that new pair of shoes, and the urge to find a mate and have children is a delightful muddle of the material and the nonmaterial. The market is primarily a function of the material world, but as we plunge deeper into the sixth stage, it is starting to occupy a larger percentage of the entire spectrum.

The "you can have it all" mentality extends beyond the goods you can have and the houses you can buy. It extends beyond the conspicuous consumption that the current affluence makes possible (at least for those who are profiting). The market promises not just material wealth. It suggests that other desires, more intangible, less material, but no less real, can also be satisfied by the market. Just as the Founding Fathers believed, erroneously, that independence and individualism could secure life, liberty, and the pursuit of happiness, the market ideal promises the same.

Take Social Security. The cornerstone of the government era, Social Security offers a cushion to the elderly, though not an overly plump one. Social Security, if not antithetical to the free market, exists in a realm of values that the free marketers have never been comfortable with. Underwritten and administered by the government, Social Security takes money from taxpayers and redistributes it to retirees. Though the United States provides less support than the countries of the European Union, Social Security is sustained by the premise that care of the elderly and infirm is a public good that should not be assessed in terms of profit and loss, and not be exposed to the unpredictable currents of the open market.

Until recently, that is. As the stock market boomed and more individuals invested in equities, people started to talk about privatizing Social Security. If Social Security were to be "privatized," it would cease to be a government program, and would become indistinguishable from long-term savings for retirement. Yet social security was created because millions of people can't save for retirement, as they hardly have enough to live on day to day. Others, for reasons both sound and foolish, do not save for retirement and will need to be cared for. Recognizing that government involvement is inevitable, proponents of Social Security reform talk about "nudging Social Security in a free-market direction." The alternatives range from permitting individuals to invest for themselves some of the money they would have paid in Social Security tax to authorizing government administrators to invest a portion of the fund in low-risk stocks and bonds.[25]

In health care as well, the market is perceived as more dynamic and effective than government. When the attempts of the Clinton administration to craft a national health insurance system foundered in 1994, the country's health care was left largely in the control of insurance companies and HMOs. These are for-profit entities, and they manage health care as a business. In order to do so, they attempt to translate health into a product. But health for most of us is an amorphous thing, and a relative one. Yes, most people agree on a broad middle ground of what constitutes health and what constitutes illness. But there is also a substantial gray area. HMOs, however, have shareholders, a board of directors, and all the accoutrements of a corporation. In conceiving of health as a product that they are in the business of delivering, they look for ways to deliver the most amount of health to the greatest number of people at the least cost to the company and for the largest profit.

There is nothing inherently pernicious about these attitudes, nor anything inherently good. Rather, they reflect a value system and a language that derives from the market, and not from medicine or from public service. Market mores can make health care more efficient, doctors more productive, and people healthier. Conversely, market values sometimes conflict with "health." Why should my cousin be denied drugs to ease the psychic pain of his manic depression even though an HMO has determined that "psychic pain" is too subjective to be eligible for coverage? Why should I not be allowed to have an expensive optional test done if it will ease my fear that something is terribly wrong with me? Why should I not ask the hospital to take heroic measures to save my ninety-four-year-old grandmother, even at great cost of time, money, and resources? These are all valid questions, and the answers differ depending on the standards one uses. The market is one set of values, religions offer another, and social mores might offer still another. All of these are present in health care today, but as anyone involved in the health care "industry" will attest, market values are front and center.

The same trend is transforming education, from grade school through graduate school. What goes on in a classroom is often mysterious and difficult to quantify. Education in the United States has been seen as a way to socialize the young, impart values of citizenship, imbue students with respect for the individual, and teach skills from home economics to reading, writing, and 'rithmetic. Education has been the touchstone of disagreements over identity, religion, and secular society. Parents and educators have agonized over how to measure the success of schools and colleges, and testing services have flourished as a result. But the goal has usually been to teach students, to make them knowledgeable. During the sixth stage, however, the language is changing, and education is becoming "marketized."

It begins with grade school. In 1995, Milton Friedman wrote an article in *The Washington Post* calling for privatizing education. He said that "only for-profit industry" could improve the quality of education in the United States. As if on cue, a company called the Edison Schools began operation that same year. Responding to the perception that public education is ineffective, the Edison Schools operate more than seventy-nine schools nationwide, with a total student enrollment of nearly 40,000. While students enroll as if at a public school, the Edison Schools is a for-profit, publicly held company. Its schools answer to local school boards, like normal public schools, and are often authorized as "charter schools," which many districts have set up as a way to encourage innovations. But the schools also answer to corporate executives. Like any corporation, Edison has shareholders, a board of directors, and executives. It has a research and development department, a public relations office, and annual shareholder meetings. Edison's goal is to provide expert management of public schools at prices that school districts can afford. The company promises districts that Edison students will do better on state assessment tests than comparable students at publicly managed institutions. They have developed what they call a "Quarterly Learning Contract," which consists of goals mutually set by the student, the family, and an adviser. This contract is signed by all parties, and the company prides itself on the results.[26]

The trend is more dramatic at the college level. In the 1990s, hundreds of new community colleges were funded by state legislatures in response to the demands of businesses and individuals who needed skills and credentials for the new workplace. Students and parents have started to think of themselves as consumers who are purchasing a product called education. As a result, students feel increasingly comfortable demanding that they pass the courses they take and that professors help them do so. Competing with other schools for students, administrators take these demands to heart and put pressure on faculty not to give failing grades. In the 1990s, the federal government expanded its guaranteed student loan programs by billions of dollars a year, which was a boon for banks and loan agencies who were able to make millions of loans without risk of default. Whether or not the students repaid, the federal government would. Degrees have become, more than ever, the prerequisite to thriving in the New Economy. Less attention has been given to what these degrees actually mean than to the credential itself. Any desirable job requires a college degree, and as more people seek a share of the New Economy, more people than ever seek degrees as commodities that will allow them to access jobs that will in turn allow them to purchase other commodities.

"Boola, Boola: E-Commerce Comes to the Quad," ran the headline for a *New York Times* story in February 2000. "Welcome to the ivory tower in the dot.com age," the article continued, "where commerce and competition have set up shop." The article spoke of the sudden rise of "distance learning," a mode of "education delivery" that the Internet has made possible. Instead of paying tuition dollars to enroll in a college, students can now pay a per-course fee for "on-demand" learning.[27] And these students are no longer the eighteen-to-twenty-one-year-olds who have defined higher education for generations. They are consumers of any age who want knowledge, whether for personal growth or for a job.

A rash of new companies try to tap into the expanding "education market." Universities such as Harvard, Stanford, and Columbia look for ways to utilize their "brand" in order to profit from distance learning, and professors look to offer their intellectual property, in the form of course curriculum and books, for sale. Says SCT, one of these new companies, "The wants of learners of twenty years ago have evolved to needs, and now they've become insistent demands. To be competitive, institutions must be in tune with students' changing demands and deliver services and learning methods to meet their expectations. SCT's vision for higher education revolves around a Relationship Leverage strategy: leveraging the relationships with students, faculty, alumni, and other constituents for breakthrough results." The company promises university administrators a menu of "new business processes, tools, and approaches."

Meanwhile, the history of higher education is quietly being rewritten. Until early in the twentieth century, higher education was more entwined with religion and the liberal arts than with secular society, and few would have thought to use business methods or apply business principles or language. Professors and university presidents were more likely to talk of molding character and serving society than of bottom lines and maximizing productivity. Today, those involved in higher education treat it as business with a special set of goals, and they demur that it has always been this way. "Higher education has always been market driven," said one speaker at a conference on "Market-Driven Higher Education." It is, the speaker continued, "a niche market, with 3,000-plus nonprofit institutions and several thousand more for-profit institutions, particularly because this is so segmented an industry and so segmented a marketplace." Deans can be heard lamenting the outmoded "delivery system" that requires a professor to stand physically in front of a class at great expense in terms of inflexible hours and a rigid schedule. Now, with online distance learning, the product can be molded to suit the needs of knowledge consumers (formerly known as students) and the needs of knowledge purveyors (formerly known as professors).[28]

Perhaps the most important shift in education is from knowledge to information. Knowledge is far too complex to be reduced to a product. What, exactly, is knowledge? At the very least, it is the ability to process and utilize information. Knowledge has always been the alchemic goal of education, and for good reason, it has proven to be a challenge. But knowledge cannot be easily packaged and sold. It isn't a commodity, any more than companionship or love is. At best, marketers can use the word "knowledge" to sell some product or experience. Today, "knowledge" is being used to sell something valuable but more prosaic: information.

Information can be packaged. It is an "it," and has form and substance. As part of the transformation of higher education during the sixth stage, universities are marketing themselves as information providers. Higher education has suddenly become an "information delivery industry." One of the hallmarks of the New Economy is that it is said to represent the Information Age. In myriad ways, the cultural message is that only those able to process and obtain the information they need will find success in the New Economy. Those who have the skills to manipulate information are in demand. High-tech companies in Silicon Valley, Silicon Alley, and Route 128, and in Austin, Seattle, and Portland recruit college graduates who have demonstrated an ability to think. And because the word "information" has cachet, educators and distance learning companies harness the word to a product that they can sell to consumers.

That is where branding comes in. If information is generic, information from Harvard has a distinct advantage in a competitive information delivery industry. MIT and Caltech can use their brand to position themselves as market leaders in the delivery of high-quality technical information. Business schools such as Wharton and Columbia University can piggyback on their brand by offering distance learning courses in accounting and entrepreneurship. Of course, actually setting up a viable business consists of many factors, only one of which is information. Creativity, the willingness to take risks, leadership, and management skills are also essential, but they are much more difficult to quantify. They are less easily transferred than information from someone who possesses them to someone who doesn't, though that hasn't stopped distance-learning ventures from claiming that they will and can.

The sixth stage reaches even farther. Areas of life that were once considered "market externalities" are now seen as obeying market forces and responding to market rules. At that conference on market-driven higher education, the president of a successful academic management firm was asked whether or not there are limits to what can be made into a product and sold as a commodity. He replied, reasonably enough, that the market isn't just about the exchange of goods, but also about the exchange of information. In that respect, he continued, information is a commodity, and most significant aspects of life fall within the market's purview. That includes religion. "After all," he concluded, "the Apostles were the first marketers. They had a tough message to sell and an even tougher product. But they did it."

Describing the New Testament as an exercise in marketing may be going a bit far, but the culture of the sixth stage encourages such thinking. If you define markets as places of exchange, then almost any human activity can be folded into the market paradigm. If the goal is to maximize market share, then even the Apostles are market mavens. Some contemporary churches would agree. In suburban Chicago, the Willow Creek Community Church has an elaborate, welcoming web site that touts the virtues of the congregation and describes the origins of the church in the mid-1970s. "Using contemporary music, drama, and Bible teaching that was highly relevant to the lives of high school students, the services grew from a handful of teenagers to one thousand students a night." The site is a bundle of different motifs. At one point, the goal is described as building community and encouraging spiritual development. But the site also highlights "services for Generation X," the size of the buildings, and the planned expansion. The church uses techniques familiar to test marketers in order to hone its message and approach. Surveys were sent out to some of the 1.5 million people within a twenty-minute drive, asking them what they'd like to hear at a sermon and what activities they'd be interested in attending if Willow Creek offered them. The ministry pays attention to its local "market share" (formerly known as parishioners), and makes assessments of its success based in part on how many people it draws.

Churches have always looked to their audience, and successful pastors, priests, and rabbis frequently conduct informal surveys to make sure that the congregants are getting their needs met. The difference is that market language and corporate behavior are now explicit components of many churches, coexisting with matters of the spirit and community. Few people would say that the market supercedes God, no more than most Americans believed that government did during the fifth stage. But increasingly, even the most godly people conceive of the world in market terms.

The market vision reaches farther still. The 1987 film *Robocop* depicted a futuristic Detroit that is lawless, crime-ridden, and anarchic. Incapable of keeping order, city hall outsources its police power to a private company. One of the keys of the Progressive Era was urban policing, and government bore the responsibility. Policing was a public good that people considered separate from the profit/loss mores of the business world. But in an era that celebrates the self-correcting efficiencies of the market, it follows that all areas of life can benefit from applying market principles. During the sixth stage, functions as vital as education and, in the future perhaps, policing, are considered too important to be left to government.

No major city has yet gone as far as *Robocop*, but many states and the federal government have started to privatize prisons. Incarceration is a boom industry in the United States, topping $20 billion a year. Funding the construction of prisons and paying for their operation is a significant burden for local and state governments, and the task is made harder by the constraints imposed on government bureaucracies. Contracting can be awarded only after bids have been solicited, and it usually must go to the lowest qualified bidder. Government agencies rarely perform these functions as efficiently as the private sector, and so prison corporations are now muscling their way into the "prison market."

Firms like Wackenhut and the Corrections Corporation of America operate hundreds of prisons, and the number is growing. They hire the guards, manage the properties, and act as subcontractors for prison construction. In hiring these firms, state and local governments save money by eliminating much of the bureaucratic red tape. The prison corporation makes a profit. It seems like an ideal solution, but as some critical studies have shown, states don't save that much money. More troubling, these companies have at best a spotty record when it comes to corruption, abusive guards, and lax security. Contracts are often valued by assigning a dollar value to inmates. Yet even some critics of the way these companies manage prisons argue that the application of market principles improves the situation.

Prisons are a public issue, and a societal challenge. While incarcerating millions of citizens is no one's idea of a good society, even here, the market is looked to for amelioration. If crime is a product of poverty, as many people believe, then the more affluent we become, the less need there will be for all those prisons. And in the meantime, says the market vision, the best way to manage the problems is to let the market work its magic.[29]

THOSE LEFT OUT

For many, however, the promise of the market is hollow and the vision feels like a cruel hoax. If it were just a matter of a few thousand "day traders" losing their shirts, that wouldn't do much to puncture the mystique. But for every washed-out day trader there are hundreds of working families whose lives bear little resemblance to the James Youngs of the world. The 34 million Americans who live below the poverty line swim in the same cultural waters as the 5 million Americans who have a net worth of greater than $1 million. And they watch the same television programs, listen to the same music, see the same ads and the same movies, and are influenced by the same signals as the Internet billionaires. The median household income in 1997 was about $38,000, which was actually less than what it was in 1990. In the age of the market, a significant portion of the population isn't benefitting from it.[30]

Millions struggle just to stay in place. "Middle-class" families, who comprise the majority of the United States, find that they are working as hard as ever, but they don't have the sense that their economic situation is improving. Economic data support these impressions. The heady language of the New Economy relates only marginally to their lives, but in thousands of interviews and surveys, these families confess to feelings of confusion and inadequacy that they aren't doing better. They hear the drone of the New Economy vision, and they feel pressure. Why aren't their lives reflecting this brave new world? Why, if everything is so wonderful and promising, do they still have to struggle with mortgage payments, car payments, and monthly expenses? If the New Economy is supposed to liberate their energies, why do so many feel so enervated?

Some of these issues predate the rise of the New Economy. Americans have long had a fear of failing, a sense that there's a party going on somewhere and they weren't invited. Middle-class angst was pronounced in the 1970s and the 1980s. The eighties were notable not just for Reaganism but for images of Wall Street raiders, rampant greed, and image-conscious yuppies. Many people confessed that they felt pressured by the consumerism of those years, and that their lives were colored by the fear that good fortune was at best fleeting. In the late 1980s and early 1990s, as the country experienced a steep recession, millions of middle-class and white-collar workers were "downsized," and the major industries that had sustained workers in the past—steel, automobiles, mills—closed factory after factory. The phrase "downward mobility" entered common parlance, and stories of broken families and disappointed lives were prevalent.[31]

Today, there is a gap between the elevated rhetoric of the New Economy and the reality of many people's lives. The United States is so big that it's possible for tens of millions to be doing extraordinarily well and tens of millions of others to be standing in place. No single picture can accurately reflect the whole. But one of the distortions of the sixth stage is the elision of contrasting perspectives. Judging from appearances, it's all one big happy family getting richer and feeling happier. The people who produce culture have seen their standard of living rise, and the cultural artifacts that they produce mirror their world. Hence the friends on *Friends*, who are unexceptional professionally, act as if they live on a minimal income, yet live in apartments that only people with incomes in excess of $150,000 could afford. The culture is awash in the vision, but there is a wide gap between those profiting from it and those still seeking to.

The eclipse of government may have enjoyed widespread support, but the rise of the market has left many people feeling utterly helpless. During the Gilded Age, most farmers and workers believed that the country was being run by the rich for the benefit of the few. That conviction gave rise to the Progressive movement, which included reforms that made government more accountable to the electorate. Critics of the current situation claim that "the larger events now rocking the world are being addressed by people largely hidden from public view, unaccountable to the democratic process." These words were written by the former secretary of labor, Robert Reich. In his opinion, unelected officials such as Alan Greenspan, the whole Federal Reserve Board, the World Trade Organization, and the International Monetary Fund have more power than the country's elected representatives. The fact that economists and businesspeople and bankers have unparalleled influence over the country's direction may be inevitable in the age of the market, but it is a development that many people do not welcome.[32]

The sixth stage has opponents, but they are given short shrift in the news and in the culture. The opponents aren't unified, and they often make strange bedfellows. They share an animus but little else. Some are writers and intellectuals who are quick to point out the self-serving nature of New Economy rhetoric.[33] Others are less systematic in their animosity. They see the rise of the market paradigm as a threat to their way of life, and in myriad ways, they are trying to halt its spread. Each stage begets its own reaction, its own disappointments, and its own discontent. But until these coalesce, they appear atomized and incoherent.

Pat Buchanan, onetime Republican turned independent, has seized some of Ross Perot's mantle and tries to speak for those who feel that they have no voice in the nation's present or its future. He rails against the Wall Street brokers and their allies in Washington who seem to be calling the shots. Ralph Nader, who once seemed as far to the left as Pat Buchanan was to the right, rallies the discarded pieces of the old Great Society Democratic coalition and raises his voice against the onslaught of free trade. The AFL-CIO, its membership greatly reduced from its heyday at mid-century, galvanizes its members to contest the World Trade Organization, the North American Free Trade Agreement (NAFTA), and the crumbling of trade tariffs that they fear will mean the loss of millions of American jobs. Meanwhile, fundamentalist Christians look for ways to opt out of the mainstream. Defeated time and again in their political agenda, they turn away from engaging the society. Using home-schooling, separate television stations, or no television at all, they try to create a world with mores of their choosing.

Free trade became a lightning rod for the opposition. It is an axiom of the New Economy that growth is both imperative and potentially limitless. In the eyes of the New Economy boosters, national boundaries are an inconvenience because they add a layer of bureaucracy, taxes, and hence, cost to the exchange of goods. The end of the Cold War invigorated the free-trade movement, and leading Democrats, Republicans, and businesspeople looked to reform the international system. The governments of other nations, eager to participate in the booming American economy, pushed in the same direction. The ideas had been percolating for years, but only in the 1990s did they become real. First came the collapse of the Soviet Union and the end of Communism in Eastern Europe. That was followed in 1992 by the formal creation of the European Union, which was the culmination of forty years of work. Then, in 1994, the North American Free Trade Association was established, which removed numerous trade barriers between Canada, the United States, and Mexico. A short time later, the 135-nation World Trade Organization came into being.

The World Trade Organization (WTO) became the focus of protest. As a prominent advocate of economic globalization, the WTO tapped into deep currents of mistrust and suspicion that the rhetoric of the market was just a smokescreen for robbery. In late November 1999, the WTO met in Seattle to negotiate the latest round of international tariff reforms. Catching the Seattle police off guard, thousands of demonstrators descended on downtown and disrupted the meetings. Some of these protests were ad hoc, while some were orchestrated by labor unions, the Reform Party, and other organizations that had tried to prevent passage of NAFTA a few years before.

The Seattle demonstrations were so sudden and so effective that the WTO could not finish its planned meetings. The vehemence of the opposition took many by surprise. The anger of the protesters was tied to economics. In national polls, those who earned over $75,000 a year supported globalization by a two-to-one margin, while two-thirds of those who earned less than $50,000 saw globalization as a threat. The protesters were the voice of that considerable portion of the population that viewed the goals of the WTO with alarm. Not everyone understood what these goals were, of course. In fact, many of the protesters probably would have been surprised had they known how little power the WTO actually has. The WTO is only a coordinating body for international trade policies, but whatever its actual role, in the minds of the protesters, it symbolized the dangers and inequities of globalization.[34]

The protests may have appeared random and confused, but they reflected widely held attitudes. You wouldn't have known that, however, if you had read or listened to the news reports. Though most of the protests were peaceful, a handful of groups was determined to make their mark violently. Loosely described as anarchists, several hundred people came to Seattle from Portland and elsewhere, intent on creating chaos. Wearing black balaclavas, they smashed store windows, threw homemade explosives, and goaded the police to attack. Their presence made it easier for the protests to be dismissed as the work of marginal groups who were violent as well as ignorant. As commentators noted at the time, the WTO had fewer decision-making powers than the World Bank or the International Monetary Fund (IMF), and the protesters were ridiculed for not realizing that the WTO was an advisory body that didn't have the authority to do what the protesters feared it would.

In almost every major publication, and on almost every television station, the events in Seattle were derided as the work of a lunatic fringe. Brushing aside the concerns of the protesters, *The New Republic* ran a piece with the headline, "World Government is Coming. Deal with It," as though the protesters had some cognitive deficiency and simply failed to grasp reality. *The New York Times* columnist Thomas Friedman, who is one of the many cheerleaders of the New Economy, skewered the naiveté of the protesters with his usual combination of pithy aphorisms and puns. The dockworkers who marched in Seattle, he said, were like a "milkmen's union coming out against cows. No trade, no dockworkers. No milk, no milkmen." He lambasted the protesters for their ignorance about free trade, and many others shared his sentiments.

The protesters may have been ignorant. A handful of them might have been thuggish, alienated young men who wanted nothing but to see Seattle burn. They may have been naive about the economics of free trade, and they may have unwittingly carried the sputtering torch of American isolationism, distrust of the world outside, and fear of Washington. But they also reflected the disconnect between the New Economy as an idea and the New Economy as an economic reality. Regardless of the biased tone of the coverage, Seattle, even more than the debates over NAFTA several years before, showed that globalization reaches deep. In the 1960s, people took to the streets to protest war. Now, they take to the streets to protest economic policies.

The Seattle demonstrators also showed that in the process of pursuing a utopian vision, the proponents of the sixth stage dismiss evidence that all might not be so well with the world. Like visionaries before them, those who espouse the New Economy can be blind to the harm done by their vision.

The statistics about the relationship between one's income and support for globalization are telling. If you're in the upper tier economically, and hence profiting from the New Economy, you tend to support globalization because you believe it will benefit you. If you fear globalization, you probably have not benefitted from the New Economy and so, understandably, distrust it. Those who are currently left out of the material benefits of the New Economy are also left out of public discussion. They are largely absent from television, from magazines, from movies, from policy discussions in Washington, and from the Internet mainstream. Where are the dockworkers in an American society that lauds Silicon Valley? In a world that pays so much attention to Bill Gates, where are those who are just getting by? At every turn, globalization is celebrated, and those who dissent or criticize are likely to be ignored or denigrated.

The point here is not that the protesters are right. Globalization is an economic reality. But the protests represent the first stumbling attempts to reject the market paradigm. Said one of the leaders, a young woman who had previously worked for Ralph Nader, "I think a lot of people in my generation—not a majority, maybe, but a lot—feel this void. We feel like capitalism and buying things are just not fulfilling." Haltingly, she and others talk about something missing.[35] For the protesters, lack of fulfillment isn't just a passive sorrow but an active grievance. They may be misguided about the costs and benefits of globalization, but are they equally wrong about the need for community? Like the Progressive critics in the 1880s and 1890s, like the conservatives who tried to halt the Great Society and the New Deal, the different groups that combined in Seattle were inconsistent, incoherent, and ineffective. Their vision, at present, amounts to little more than an antivision, a resounding no. But the impulse to question the prevailing norm is a familiar one, and it is a product of disappointment with the excesses of the current stage. The New Economy promises all of these wonders, yet for so many, it isn't satisfying.

This isn't a question of right and wrong. In time, the New Economy might do much of what its most fervent articulators claim, but even if all of us become rich beyond our wildest dreams, it will still fall short. All utopian visions have, and all such visions must. As manifested in the Internet, the New Economy holds out the hope not just of material prosperity, but of spiritual and societal harmony. The attempt of some groups to step back and question the sixth stage stems as much from skepticism that the promised utopia will not include them as from fear that the material, economic rewards will be unevenly distributed.

Because we are still in the midst of the sixth stage, questions about the paradigm tend to be coldly rejected. Anne Hutchinson and the Antinomians were hardly embraced by the authorities in Massachusetts Bay, and the drafters of the Constitution in 1787 had an uphill battle in a world that glorified the individual's liberties. While a vision is ascendant, it's almost impossible for alternate views to get a fair hearing. Some of the current voices of protest against the New Economy may amount to nothing, but they indicate that the same wheels are still turning, that no vision goes uncontested, and that the days of each vision are numbered.

The several hundred anarchists who descended on Seattle managed to coordinate their activities by using a technology that didn't exist just a few years before. Leaving aside the oxymoron of organized anarchists, there was the notable irony that the same vehicle that was supposed to transport us to the golden age of the New Economy could also be used to fight the New Economy. That tool, of course, is the Internet, and it is there that the vision of the sixth stage is fully realized. In fact, the Internet contains elements of all the previous stages and brings the disparate threads of American culture together in one wonderful, chaotic cybermosaic. The Internet is where the promise of utopia shines most brightly, and it will be the bridge between the sixth stage and what lies ahead.

SEVEN

THE INTERNET

At present, we are so obsessed with the Internet that it's difficult to recognize just how obsessed we are. It is an idea, and a technology. It is a business tool, and a hobby. It is mysterious and uncharted. It is a place of hopes, dreams, and fears.

Businesses view the Internet as nothing short of revolutionary. For the high-tech companies defining the New Economy—for Ask Jeeves, for Yahoo!, for Amazon.com, Microsoft, and thousands of others—the Internet is first and foremost about information, and information is the glue that holds the New Economy together. Business books put the word "information" in bold letters and exhort readers that unless they start thinking of it first and last, their company will be left in the dust. Once, land was power, natural resources were power, men were power. Now, information opens doors, liberates those who possess it, and creates opportunities for those who know how to harness it. For that reason, the New Economy has been labeled "the Information Age."

Like the printed word, the book, the telephone and the telegraph, the Internet conveys information from source A to source B. What makes the New Economy "new" is that until recently, market transactions were slowed down by the difficulty of obtaining information. Consumers struggled to find the products they wanted and then struggled to obtain those products at a reasonable price. Sellers wasted time, energy, and money to communicate to buyers, to inform buyers about the existence of their products. The Internet, however, expands the amount of information available and speeds up the process of obtaining it.

Though we are still at the beginning of this "revolution," there is an emerging conventional wisdom about its effects. The spread of information is altering traditional business models and forcing a rethinking of strategies. This affects everything, from marketing to sales to hiring to management. Businesses must focus on networks which are composed of groups linked by common data and shared interests. These groups then form their own communities and their own markets. "The Internet," according to two respected business writers, "is a powerful platform for connecting people or businesses with each other, enriched and enhanced by relevant information. . . . Ultimately, information about people may be the most important information collected on the Internet—precisely because it helps connect people in a timely and relevant fashion." Messages such as these are increasingly ubiquitous.[1]

Information and ideas have always been part of the market, but in evolutionary terms, markets began as physical places where material goods were exchanged. Now, says the new conventional wisdom, markets are conversations. They are about networks and access instead of physical goods. There has been some clever rewriting of history to suggest that it has always been this way, even if people hundreds of years ago didn't fully see it. Others warn that our world has broken so radically from the past that traditional conceptions of markets are now invalid, and a complete rethinking of all business and social transactions is necessary. In short, there is a wide consensus that now and for the foreseeable future, information is the name of the game.[2]

It's remarkable that even the most pragmatic companies and the driest economists discuss the Internet in grandiose terms. The same language that was once reserved for the Declaration of Independence, the Gettysburg Address, and the Gospel of Wealth now gets used for the Internet. One young entrepreneur after another states in interviews that at heart, their true motivation is to enjoy themselves and "to change the world." Presumably, the technologies of the New Economy will enable people to do just that. "Idealism and utopianism," one corporate CEO told me, "are the fuel rods of the Internet." You don't have to delve too deeply into the culture to notice this.

Hardly a day goes by without some ad, article, book, or show declaring that "[t]he Internet will change everything about the way you live."[3] *Money* magazine offers to explain "how a dream . . . changed everything." The Internet is all about vision.

> Here's to the crazy ones, the misfits, the rebels, the trouble-makers, the round pegs in the square hole, the ones who see things differently. They're not fond of rules, and they have no respect for the status quo. You can quote them, disagree with them, glorify them or vilify them. About the only thing you can't do is ignore them, because they change things. They push the human race forward, and while many see them as the crazy ones, we see genius, because the people who are crazy enough to think they can change the world, are the ones who'll do it.

So ran an ad for Apple Computer. What are they selling? Computers, yes, but the company is also issuing a manifesto for the New Economy, a statement of philosophy, and a vision for a new world that reaches into every nook and cranny of society.[4]

The people involved in high-tech businesses conceive of themselves as both carrying on a long tradition of entrepreneurship and forging ahead into uncharted waters. They think that they can create successful, thriving companies and also reinvent reality. It is the City on a Hill all over again, except that this time, the hill is virtual and so is the city. They foresee a time when there will be total connectivity, multiple interlocking networks, and sophisticated information exchanges that will make the longstanding dream of the efficient market real. In short, the Internet will transform the academic theory of the perfect market into a daily reality.

In this brave new world, prices will be lower because it will be easier for buyers and sellers to find each other. The transition from physical retail spaces to virtual ones will cut costs. Companies will no longer need to employ a substantial sales force, and the savings will be passed on to the consumer. Lower prices will mean that goods can be more widely purchased, which will raise everyone's standard of living.

But this only scratches the surface of Internet utopianism.

Though the Internet vision continues to be developed by business-people, the wider culture has embraced it as well, sometimes in wildly speculative directions. "The beauty of Internet time," ran a December 1999 article in *The Industry Standard*, is that "we can cover the big events of the past 1,000 years by looking at the events of the last few months." Following this reasoning, the Internet doesn't just define the present; it encapsulates the millennium, and all of human experience. Almost every aspect of people's lives supposedly finds expression on the Internet.

Are you worried about your health? The Internet can help you learn about diet and nutrition. The information that various web pages contain brings doctors together with academics in research communities. Knowledge flows freely between different groups working on various questions about the body, aging, diet, and disease. E-mail creates a channel for direct communication. Search engines make it possible to collate vast amounts of data.

Are you a fly-fisherman? You can go to Amazon.com and type in "fly-fishing." You will be offered more than 1,000 books that tell you how, where, and even why. You can purchase *The Caddisfly Handbook*, which will help you identify "one of the most crucial and misunderstood trout-stream insects." The Amazon auction site will helpfully guide you to the caddis fly currently up for bid (two dozen starting at $16.97). In videos, you can purchase *Fly Fishing Basics* on VHS and DVD. In software, Mindscape offers a program called "Fly: Logic Fly Fishing," available for Windows 2000 or Windows NT on CD-ROM, which takes you on a 3-D tour of the Green River in Utah. In merchandise, you can purchase the Cortland Fly Fishing outfit for $159.95. Go to Ask Jeeves and ask about prime fly-fishing spots, and you will be directed to several sites that report on the pros and cons of various regions. You can then click through to Preview Travel or Cheap Tickets.com, or any number of other travel sites, and price out tickets and lodging for your vacation.

Until I did this search, I had never thought about fly-fishing, but it took me a total of eight minutes to compile the information for the paragraph above. Ten years ago, you would have had to go to a bookstore and search for fly-fishing books in the "sports and recreation" section. If you were lucky, you might have found two or three books. Or, if you had been connected to a university, you could have accessed the library card catalog and found more books, if the school had bothered to add such books to its permanent collection. You would have gone to a sporting-goods store for gear, and probably not have been able to find everything you needed. For best spots, you could have asked around and put out the word among friends that you were looking for ideas. Eventually, in days or weeks, you might have heard that Sam, whom your friend's sister used to date, had once gone on a fly-fishing trip, but when you finally got Sam's number and called him, he told you that it wasn't fly-fishing, it was deep-sea fishing, and he had gotten sick the first day and so missed the rest of the trip, and furthermore, he didn't really "date" your friend's sister; they had gone out a few times, and he thought it was just casual.

Fly-fishing may seem of secondary importance in the greater scheme of things, but the ability to learn so much so quickly applies to almost everything. Researchers trying to find a cure for AIDS or Alzheimer's disease in the 1980s were connected through trade journals and conferences, but they had a difficult time coordinating information and pooling resources. Even now, of course, discoveries are not always put online and made available. The proprietary interest in obtaining patents for potentially lucrative drugs precludes that. But far more information is now available to far more people. This expands the pool of people who might meaningfully contribute to or benefit from the knowledge. Knowing the epidemiology of AIDS might help a parent care for her child, and the information she obtains on the Web might alert her to experimental treatments that her son's doctor didn't mention.

But what, precisely, does all of this mean? In short, so what? People still die. They still work. They still have to eat and sleep, and the fish still won't catch themselves. The bells and whistles of this new technology change none of that. Those simple facts get obscured in the heady culture of technological utopianism, but they are such basic truths that they can only be denied for so long. Will that be the Achilles' heel of the current stage? Will the wide-eyed tendency to overlook the unchanging essentials be the vision's fatal flaw that leads to disappointment and reaction? Will the current stage be undermined not by another technology, or a new vision, but by old realities and basic facts?

The vision may be exaggerated, just as the visions of earlier stages were, but the fact that we can do more and learn more with less effort and cost will have a host of unforeseen consequences. The curve of potential is exponential, not linear.

That then leads to speculation about what lies ahead. If the Internet has already had such a dramatic effect, what will happen when everyone is using it? Access to the Web is almost as unevenly distributed as income, and in the United States, there is a significant "digital divide" between the Internet-haves and the Internet-have-nots. That divide is even more pronounced internationally. But what will happen in ten years when the Internet becomes a utility, at least in the United States and the European Union, available at low cost and universally used because it will be impossible to live without it? What will happen when the Internet becomes as common as television and the telephone?

Scott McNealy, the forty-something, energetic, hockey-playing chairman and CEO of Sun Microsystems, has been one of the most vocal boosters of the Internet revolution. Aware that some people are skeptical of the Internet's potential, he frequently reminds audiences and interviewers that because we're in the midst of the revolution, it's difficult to see where it's leading. McNealy claims that the very ubiquity of the Internet is what makes it revolutionary, but he gets ahead of himself. The Internet is only commonplace for a portion of the population, albeit a portion that is growing daily and already includes tens of millions in the United States and hundreds more worldwide. The Internet, McNealy says, makes "the off-line lives we lead easier." How this technological revolution will unfold, McNealy concludes, "is ours to define."[5]

Speculation about the implications of the Internet gallops far ahead of present reality. Robert Wrubel, being driven from the airport to downtown New York to negotiate for another round of financing for Ask Jeeves right before the Nasdaq "correction" in April 2000, let his imagination run rampant. "Models for the future . . ." he mused, and then went off on a riff that had more in common with jazz improvisation than boardroom presentation. "There's the access question. We will have more and more access points, wireless, phones, which will enable constant web-based organization. . . . You'll have personal buying programs and locator services. You will control an intelligent compilation of data. And then there's the wild part," as if what he's saying isn't wild enough, "Jeeves today lives in the old-world metaphor of personal service. Tomorrow, on the twenty-four-hour Web, he or others like him will be your intelligent personal servant, and he will have an identity particular to you. He'll make reservations, find a babysitter, get your wife a gift, and invite your friends. He'll give you options and help you spend more time away from the Web. Jeeves will free you from the Web, not tether you to it, unless you want to be tethered."

And many do want that. Lives lived on the Web? That evokes visions of Huxley's *Brave New World* or the film *The Matrix*, and conjures an image of people connected to the Web via virtual-reality devices that permit them to design their own universe. Some forecast that within a decade, most commerce will be Web-based. Stores will close, malls will be shuttered, and people will become increasingly isolated as work becomes virtual. Instead of going to an office, people will connect to a virtual company from their homes. Instead of going out to be entertained, people can summon entertainment to their homes. Television will be transmitted via the Web, and games, movies, shows, and music will then be downloaded and ordered at whim. If you're so inclined, you will hardly need to exit the hermetic bubble that you call home.

This picture of the New Economy future, which suggests isolation and disconnection, is offset by the prospect of increasing connection that the Web will make possible. Instead of the dystopia of atomized individuals in separate rooms living on the Web, the utopian vision looks at that fly-fishing expedition and sees a world in which it's easy to find people who share your interests, first via the Web, and then in person. We will be more integrated into national life because the Web will allow direct democracy. We will be able to vote online both for candidates and issues, instantaneously, thereby making our elected officials accountable and responsible. We will be able to contact people to talk about issues that interest us, problems that trouble us, and challenges that face us. We will be able to meet more people and find romance based on shared passions. The visionaries keep sprinting ahead. Who knows? Maybe we will even learn more about the spirit and the body, as the Web allows us to probe the mysteries of meditation and trances, using sound waves or virtual reality. Maybe we will push beyond the physical world into some sort of global soul.

It sounds fantastic and surreal, but the very phrase "cyberspace" came from a gritty science fiction writer named William Gibson, who imagined a world in the not-too-distant future that was anarchic and dangerous and overpopulated, but which was linked by computers. The culture of the Internet, as created by businesses and individuals, is the child of science fiction and shares a similar spirit of pie-in-the-sky dreams.

The Net, for the moment, is tied to the market, and, as anyone who started spending time on the Web in the mid-1990s will attest, the culture of the Internet is rapidly moving away from the anarchy and libertarianism that characterized Internet culture in its infancy, toward buying and selling. Market forces are shaping the Internet just as they shape every other aspect of life during the sixth stage. The Internet is more complicated than a glorified supermarket, but it does makes it possible for market mores to flourish, with a breadth and reach that are truly extraordinary.

Cyberspace contains unexplored regions that will, in all probability, help supplant the market and pave the way for the seventh stage of this country. In order to understand how the sixth stage has evolved to date and how it will unfold in the future, we need to look more closely at an eclectic group of visionaries who helped create the technology of the New Economy in the first place.

THE WEB MAKERS

One spring day in 1994, I was staying with some friends on the far west side of Manhattan below 23rd Street, between 10th and 11th avenues. Relics from the days when central New York was a freight terminus, old elevated train tracks lie abandoned and rusting between the gentrified warehouses. In the past few years, these warehouses have been bustling with art galleries fleeing SoHo and with start-up Internet companies seeking low rents. On that day in 1994, affixed to the tracks, in the middle of one of the streets, was a billboard, and on it was an entirely white background with some letters in the middle. They began "WWW." I have no idea what came after, but at the time, all that I could think of was, "What the hell does that mean?"

Seven years later, those three letters are as familiar as a telephone area code. The Internet in general, and the World Wide Web in particular, have rushed into American culture at breathtaking speed. In 1994, the Net had more than 25 million users in more than 130 countries, but less than 5 percent of all traffic on the Net occurred over the World Wide Web. Today, by some estimates, there are as many as half a billion people with access to the Internet, 110 million in the United States alone, with a billion worldwide forecasted for as early as 2005. And almost all of these people use the Web.[6]

The Internet and the Web burst into the culture unexpectedly. The Internet itself was developed in the 1960s by the Defense Department to preserve the nation's computer data against nuclear attack. By dispersing information between independent but linked "servers," the chance of U.S. missiles and communications being crippled by a Soviet attack was significantly reduced. But the adoption of the Internet and the Web as tools utilized by hundreds of millions of people stemmed from the personal computer revolution of the 1980s. It was also aided by innovations in networking software. The technology of the Web and the technology of the PC are distinct, and it's easy to conceive of a Web that doesn't depend at all on PCs. But the development of the Web is linked historically to the development of the PC, and the Web as we know it, the Web as an integral part of popular culture and mass consumerism, only flourished because of the personal computer.

In the early 1980s, the personal computer was just starting to shift the way business was conducted and the way people organized their lives. Before the PC, the computer industry focused on mainframes—bulky, powerful, and very expensive machines that made it possible for large organizations such as the Defense Department and Fortune 500 corporations to organize and innovate. The mainframe business was controlled by a few players, because although computers were essential, the market for them was high-end and narrow. There was also a subculture of enthusiasts who fiddled with smaller computers that companies like Wang and Commodore and Tandy developed in the late 1970s. This culture was composed mostly of young, socially awkward white men. Uncomfortable outside the neon-lit, windowless rooms at university campuses where the computers were housed, they developed an ethos that rewarded individual genius, stubbornness, mathematical or engineering brilliance, and vision. Some of them became known as hackers; most of them didn't care what they were called. They just sat and wrote endless lines of software code and thought of applications for computer power.

It took a maverick company called Apple to make the next leap. Introducing the Apple PCs in the early 1980s, and then, most dramatically, the Macintosh in 1984, Apple Computers changed the image of the computer. Suddenly, owning a personal computer was not only possible, it was cool. IBM had a far larger share of the PC market in the mid-1980s, but Apple set the tone with ads like the one introducing the Macintosh during the 1984 Superbowl. The legendary commercial was only aired once, and it showed a grim black-and-white industrial future of drones watching a Big Brother figure speak on a screen that hovered above them ominously. Then, a woman, in color, ran up and hurled a sledgehammer into the screen, shattering it, and a voice announced that the Macintosh was on its way.

Even so, it wasn't until the late 1980s that the demographics of computer ownership started to be substantial. In those years, prognosticators focused on how the PC would be integrated into every aspect of life, and the leaders of the PC industry, such as Apple and IBM on the hardware side and Microsoft, Lotus, and WordPerfect on the software side, received the lion's share of attention. The hacker culture of the 1970s was uneasily integrated into the corporate culture of Silicon Valley in the 1980s. This valley, stretching south from San Francisco to Palo Alto and Stanford University, was a flat, dull expanse that was home to Hewlett-Packard, which was a product of the 1930s but which had survived and thrived. HP became a magnet for other companies, such as the research arm of Xerox (known as Xerox PARC), Apple, and Sun Microsystems, which was created by a group of engineers and scientists from Stanford.

The programmers of the late 1970s and early 1980s who produced software for computers scorned hierarchy and traditional corporations, though they grudgingly admired the authority of brilliance. They also dreamed of creating new worlds through the magic of computer codes. Given their affinity for overturning the old order, it's surprising that anyone could get them to work in a company. But individuals like Bill Gates and Steve Jobs did.

The cherubic, geeky looking Bill Gates is one of the giants of this era. With his clunky eyeglasses that seemed to constantly slide off his nose, he became a familiar figure in the mid-1980s. Today, other than an upgrade in wardrobe, he hardly seems to have aged. He's worth tens of billions of dollars. His biography is hardly a mystery: grew up in Seattle with a best friend named Paul Allen; went to Harvard with Paul Allen; spent all his time in the computer room; was not particularly social; met a programmer named Steve Ballmer; founded a company called Microsoft (short for microcomputer software) in 1975; dropped out of Harvard; worked on various programs in the late 1970s before selling IBM an operating system designed by another company but adapted by Microsoft; cornered the market on operating systems with MS-DOS; and became a billionaire in 1987, a year after the company went public.

Gates never went out of his way to cultivate an appealing public persona. Ill at ease with the attention he receives, he rarely strikes people as likable. His fame and fortune make him an easy target for others who envy his success. He was not a brilliant programmer, and Microsoft has developed software that few informed observers laud. Yet Microsoft came to dominate the PC software market, in part because Gates was driven by an omnipresent sense that failure always loomed over the horizon. Lacking public polish, he has been characterized as a man obsessed with control and power, for whom computers and software are just the means.

In the 1990s, Microsoft became even more powerful, and as the stock price soared, so did the wealth of Chairman Gates, even though Microsoft developed programs and systems that others had developed first and better. Windows was a derivative of Apple's graphic interface; Word was a pale alternative to WordPerfect; Excel was a less compelling option to Lotus 1-2-3; and Explorer was an attempt to undercut the more fluid Netscape browser. But in each of these categories, Microsoft and Gates prevailed. Unable to defeat Gates in the arena of the market, the remaining competitors—men like Sun's Scott McNealy and Oracle's Larry Ellison—mounted a campaign to use government regulation to weaken Microsoft. Government as utopian vision may be dead, but its powers to regulate monopolies live on. In early 2000, after years of investigation by the Department of Justice, Microsoft was declared a monopoly by a federal judge and condemned for violating antitrust laws that had been on the books since the Progressive Era.

The preferred image of Gates is that he is a paranoid mogul who has dominated an industry by a few fair means, and mostly foul ones. Yet Gates does have a vision for the future. In his first book, *The Road Ahead*, he painted a picture of a wired world, connected by an information highway that uses multiple devices and intricate networks of computers. Glaringly, he hardly mentioned the Web, but soon after he wrote the book in 1995, he recognized that the Web would wash over the computer industry like a "tidal wave," and he shifted the strategy of Microsoft to focus on the Web. He had already forecast a world of connectivity and networks, and the World Wide Web was a logical, if somewhat surprising, extension of that vision.[7]

Like the robber barons during the Gilded Age, Bill Gates has been described as someone who simply craves control and wealth. The same can be said of all the towering figures of Silicon Valley, from the CEOs of the major high-tech companies to the financiers who make them possible. Intel's Andy Grove, who transformed that company into the dominant computer chip maker, strikes most people as a truculent, suspicious Austrian immigrant of great will, acumen, and paranoia, who could just as easily have led a widget company. But the fact that these men (and nearly all of the most powerful people in the industry are men) may not be primarily driven by an altruistic desire for a better world doesn't mean that what they say about the future, or about how their products are altering the way we live, can be dismissed as clever marketing. Thomas Jefferson was fervent about liberty, yet he owned slaves; Ronald Reagan believed in shrinking government even as it expanded under his watch. Human beings are contradictory and hypocritical, even the most idealistic visionary among us. There's no inherent contradiction between a lust for wealth and a noble vision for improving the world. Megalomania and utopianism can coexist quite easily.

That's no news to anyone who has encountered Steve Jobs, a man who has invented Apple twice, the second time more astoundingly than the first. With his penchant for sandals and shorts and a perpetual smirk on his face, Jobs was so countercultural that he couldn't deal with Oregon's Reed College in the 1970s and dropped out, which is like leaving New York City because there aren't enough people. After working at an orchard and then for Atari games, he hooked up with another twenty-something eccentric named Steve Wozniak, and they founded the Apple computer company. Jobs understood better than anyone that computers are not just a piece of hardware; they are ideas and images. Under his watch, Apple masterfully marketed itself as a company run by visionaries making products for visionaries. At the height of Apple's success in the mid-1980s, Jobs left the company, only to return in 1997 when Apple appeared on the verge of extinction. No one accused Jobs of being a particularly good businessman, at least not in the traditional sense of containing costs and setting up a smoothly functioning corporate bureaucracy. But no one accused Jobs of lacking in imagination, either. His genius—more than almost anyone else's in the computer industry—was to see the computer as a physical manifestation of the hopes and dreams of businesses and individuals.

When he returned to Apple, the company was nearly bankrupt and rapidly losing market share. Jobs managed what even his detractors admitted was a stunning turnaround. He did it with a new computer, the iMac, and a new ad campaign, created by the same agency that had designed that Macintosh ad in 1984. The iMac and Apple were sold with a simple slogan, "Think Different," and it worked. Apple still has only a small share of the PC market, but it has reclaimed its role as an industry trendsetter.

Under Jobs, Apple markets a vision to consumers. The Apple strategy begins with the assumption that the PC is how most individuals access the Web. The more vital the Web becomes for commerce and communication, the more people will be unable to live without PCs in their homes. In Apple's view, as the PC and the Web become an intimate part of people's lives, they should be treated as more than appliances. The PC, as the physical tool for connecting to the Web, should be an extension of people's personalities. In order to market a computer, therefore, Apple markets an identity, or rather, a maverick personality that it thinks its customers want to cultivate. That was why the quirky, multicolored iMac was an unequivocal success. The response to the iMac's marketing was yet another example of how skillfully Jobs and the people at Apple tapped into a zeitgeist. They are only able to do this, however, because they believe their own press. Sure, Jobs wants to get rich, but he also believes in the utopian power of what he is selling.[8]

Jobs spins a vision of a world of self-realized individuals using computers to liberate themselves from the humdrum rules of society so that they can make their own. This is what underlies Apple's marketing strategy, and it has become a central element of many Internet companies, except instead of computers transforming reality, now it's the Web. Gates and Jobs helped define the personal computer, and the personal computer in turn made the Web possible. It's no surprise, therefore, that the vision of today's Internet companies picks up where Jobs left off.

The idea that the world will be linked and then transformed for the better by the Web is the product of many people working in different arenas. Key groups have received less attention than the PC companies and the consumer Internet companies like Amazon, even though they merit just as much. In addition to the PC makers and the pure Internet companies, there are companies that make the software for networks and who make the hardware that runs the Web. Some of these, like JDS Uniphase, receive most of their attention in the business press, while others, such as Oracle and Sun, have dynamic CEOs who draw personal press wherever they go, even though the specifics of their business get glossed over. The vision of the Web is a product of thousands of visionaries.

Some of the most visible champions of the Web, and the most prominent exponents of the new gospel, include:

- Jeff Bezos, the founder of Amazon.com. With his baby face, his wide eyes twinkling with a four-year-old's glee, and a perpetual, "Oh, my gosh, I don't believe it" attitude, Bezos believes that he can change how Americans get the products they need as fundamentally as the invention of the department store did a century ago.

- Pierre Omidyar, the thirty-something American-French-Iranian with improbably thick hair who founded eBay. His simple idea was to create an auction house on the Web which allowed buyers and sellers to find each other in one great democratic mishmash of four million products at any one time.

- Larry Ellison, chairman of Oracle. The bad boy of Silicon Valley, zealous opponent of Microsoft, and promoter of network computers, Ellison attracts attention as much for his social exploits and conspicuous consumption as for his vision of a wired world.

- Jeff Yang and David Filo, the creators of Yahoo! The two dropped out of graduate school in order to devote themselves to refining a Web search engine and directory that morphed into a Web portal that they named in an act of inspired silliness. Yahoo! is one of the few Internet companies that actually makes money, and Filo and Yang have managed to position Yahoo! as a popular guide to the tangled maze of the Web.

- Jim Clark, celebrated by Michael Lewis as the archetype of Silicon Valley visionaries (first with Silicon Graphics, then with Netscape, then Healtheon, and now MyCFO). Clark seems to relate to whatever he is currently doing as just an interim step along the path to what he will be doing, and spends what to most people appears to be an inordinate amount of energy trying to build a fully automated yacht.

- John Chambers, head of Cisco Systems. A traditional corporate CEO who used to be an IBM salesman, Chambers led his company to a dominant position in manufacturing and developing the routers that carry the traffic of the Net.

- Nicholas Negroponte, founder of the Media Lab at MIT in the 1980s. Negroponte started preaching the virtues of a digital world before there actually was a digital world.

- Esther Dyson, publisher of an influential Internet newsletter called Release 1.0. Dyson is an idea woman who brings people together through her publications and conferences. She spends her waking (and probably sleeping) hours jumping one step ahead to see where the present might lead.

- Kevin Kelly, the excitable cofounder of *Wired* magazine. Kelly left *Wired*, wrote a few books, gets quoted constantly, and has emerged as one of the more hyperbolic boosters of an already overboosted Web culture.

- George Gilder, author, speaker, and maverick. As the publisher of the *Gilder Technology Report*, Gilder forecasts industry trends. He predicted the computer and microchip revolution, and now he predicts a future of wireless, light-based communications. Few know what to make of his quasi-religious approach to the market and the New Economy, and few care to bet against him.

- Michael Dell, founder of Dell Computers. By seeing the potential of the Internet to sell computers, Dell brought the PC industry onto the Web and was soon selling more computers than his more powerful competitors.

- John Doerr, venture capitalist. Doerr is the original cowboy king of Kleiner Perkins, who underwrote companies such as Sun Microsystems, Compaq Computers, and Amazon. He epitomizes the venture capitalists of Sand Hill Road.

- James Cramer, financial analyst-cum-investor, money manager, columnist, and tech guru. Cramer's shouting face and bald head have graced numerous television shows. In addition to writing for magazines and business newspapers, with his company, TheStreet.com, he managed to briefly carve out a niche as a high-profile cheerleader for the New Economy.

- Steve Case, founder of America Online. Case went from working for a pizza company to creating the most popular "service provider" in the United States. Case looks so nondescript and sounds so much like your next-door neighbor that it would have surprised no one to learn that he was actually a computer composite of an average guy. Having captured a large share of cyberspace, Case switched gears and engineered a merger with Time-Warner, the largest media conglomerate in the world.[9]

While it would be hard to overemphasize the influence that these men and women have, listing them like this can be misleading. Like the founding fathers, these individuals have become famous for a reason, but their fame reinforces what some have called "the myth of the front runner." There are hundreds of companies and thousands of players in Silicon Valley, and they form one large, complicated matrix. Some business analysts have described Silicon Valley not as a place where hundreds of companies compete but as one decentralized corporation. Job turnover is high, and people move from company to company. Each company and each person shares a passion for new technologies, a desire to get rich, and a belief that they are improving society.

The culture of Silicon Valley extends well beyond its geographical limits. These companies (and their equivalents in lower Manhattan's Silicon Alley, Route 128 in Boston, and the booming area around Austin, Texas) have created hundreds of thousands of Web pages. They have spent more than a hundred million dollars on advertising during the Superbowl alone. They have attracted publicity in the media. And they have been the hottest stocks on Wall Street, ever. Even with the dramatic cooling of Internet fever in the financial markets in 2000, high-tech companies continue to drive the New Economy.[10]

In addition to the denizens of Silicon Valley and their cousins in Silicon Alley and elsewhere, there is one other Web maker: the stock market. Without the financial markets, the Web could never have exploded. And as we've seen, without the Web, the market, as we know it, would never have existed. Day by day, the feedback loop linking the Web and the market becomes more powerful, encompassing the culture in its vortex. Like the principle of atomic fusion, the collision between these two forces released a vast amount of energy, which has made the New Economy incredibly dynamic and occasionally unstable.

Here's how it has worked. After the recession at the beginning of the 1990s, the United States economy began a prolonged period of growth. In those years, the Gross National Product (GNP) has risen on average between 3.5 and 4 percent a year, and unemployment plummeted below 5 percent. Unlike previous economic expansions, this one was marked by very little inflation, a conundrum that continues to puzzle economists and policy makers. As mentioned earlier, in this period, the stock market ballooned, more than tripling in value. That, too, has puzzled and troubled academic economists, a fair number of whom believe that money produced by a booming economy was unwisely invested in speculative equities. As more people invested in the market and mutual fund and pension companies poured more assets into stocks, we created a situation where an excessive amount of money chased a limited number of stocks. The result: the price of stocks soared. In the process, the traditional measure of stock valuation—the ratio between the price of a share and the earnings it produces was disregarded by many investors.

Technology stocks have been in the highest demand. These include computer companies such as Dell, software companies like Microsoft, chip companies like Intel, cellular phone companies (Nokia, Motorola), Internet routers (Cisco), and hundreds of Internet companies such as Yahoo!, Amazon, AOL, Broadcomm, and eBay. Many new Internet companies shot up precipitously on the day of their initial public offering, and it was not uncommon for companies that could not foresee making any money at any point in the near future to find themselves with a paper-worth of hundreds of millions of dollars. These companies received intense publicity on the financial television channels, in the business press, and in the Internet press that emerged in the mid-1990s, including magazines such as *The Industry Standard, Red Herring, Business 2.0, Fast Company*, and *Upside*. The price of these stocks substantially exceeded what any traditional valuation would have considered a rational price, and companies that showed no possibility of profits in the near term suddenly had a market capitalization of billions of dollars.

Rational or not, investor dollars made it possible for hundreds of companies to raise money by going public. This, in turn, enhanced the role of venture capital firms (VCs) in the high-tech area. VC firms stand to make immense profits if the company they finance then goes public, and with the economy awash in money, more venture capital money than ever was looking for investments that would yield high profits. Not only could high-tech companies strike gold in the stock market; they also found it easier to get financing on what would have been considered flimsy business plans just a few years before.

Most "old economy" participants, in the process of starting companies, arranging financing, and bringing them to the public, viewed these developments with a mixture of bemusement and dismay. The New Economy companies weren't following traditional rules, and venture capital firms were becoming ever more carefree in their choices, and many of the new companies were extremely unlikely to survive and profit.

But there has also been territorial tension. The changing dynamics of corporate financing in the high-tech Internet era marginalized the power and influence of traditional financial elites. Stock brokers have lost influence. Individuals have become less likely to turn to stock brokers for advice and assistance because they feel that they can obtain and analyze information themselves and invest their own money. Wall Street firms and investment banks have also lost some power. Companies with an idea were seen as hot commodities, and that gave them greater leverage than old-shoe Wall Street firms. In short, the people and institutions that used to set the rules have been supplanted in this age of the Internet.

The traditional gatekeepers to the world of finance and investment have labeled the new investors "naive" and "irrational." True, the stock market has a herd mentality, but that has always been the case. Even granting the presence of thousands of truly naive day traders who have no sense of market fundamentals and are engaged in nothing more than a novel form of gambling, the behavior of the New Economy can't be so easily dismissed. Investors have always looked for high-yield investments, and high-yield investments are almost always high-risk. In the late 1970s, Michael Milken of Drexel Burnham perfected the art of the "junk bond." Junk bonds were mechanisms to fund companies that could not get a good credit rating, such as casinos. They were called "junk" because the companies were thought to be so risky that there was a good chance that any money invested would go down the drain. Investors who bought junk bonds weren't necessarily irrational. They were willing to take risks, and those who took risks with Milken were well rewarded.

In the late 1990s, the booming stock market created a new financing device in the form of highly speculative IPOs. Investors who purchased the stock of an Internet company were doing so because the returns could be astronomical, and as the ebbs and flows of the market in 2000 showed, so could the losses. But with all the excess money being generated by a growing economy, people could afford to wager their money. If the risks paid off, they'd be that much richer. If not, not.

As a result, dollars flowed into New Economy companies, and these companies then used the money to expand their businesses. They took the millions, or billions, raised from the IPO and channeled it into research on new technologies. Or they used the stock to acquire companies whose products or tools could enhance their businesses. If you give tens of thousands of smart, aggressive young people access to billions of dollars, there's a good chance that a few of them will not only create viable companies but incredible technologies as well. That is precisely what has happened. Many of these companies will not survive, but a few have and a few more will.[11]

And then there is that feedback loop. The technology that these companies develop enhances productivity. Even now, economists have difficulty measuring how the new technologies have improved productivity. The widespread adoption of computers did not correlate with growth in productivity in the 1980s and into the early 1990s because economic measures do not factor in time saving. If it takes average workers less time to do their tasks, how do you know that they used the time saved for more work? Maybe it was used to play solitaire on the computer, or to take a more leisurely coffee break. But in the late 1990s, the economy did show productivity gains, and though it is still difficult to attribute these directly to the computer, the correlation is strong. The new technologies led to gains in productivity, which in turn are part of the reason for the prolonged growth.

Technology keeps the economy humming along, and through venture capital and the stock market, the vibrant economy finances technological innovation, which keeps invigorating the economy. Sooner or later, this loop will lose steam, either because it ceases to work economically or because it ceases to satisfy the utopian yearnings of American culture. In the meantime, however, the promise of the New Economy remains seductive and its visionaries occupy a central place in our collective consciousness.

A LAYER CAKE OF STAGES

The sixth stage of America not only reflects a new utopian formula; it also brings together elements of the previous five stages and adds them to the cultural mix. In its specifics, much of the vision is new and hence a departure from the past. Yet it's also an amalgam of what came before. It's not just the top tier of a six-tier wedding cake; it's the whole cake.

Since the 1600s, religion has been a central aspect of American identity. While the first stage was eclipsed, religion never went away. And as the example of the Willow Creek Church in Illinois showed, religion is finding a home on the Internet with such sites as TheBible Source.com, which does a booming business in church paraphernalia. Content sites such as Beliefnet.com offer a smorgasbord of articles on topics from every faith. Askapastor.org lets you get in touch with a minister of your choosing for advice and guidance. You can e-mail your spiritual questions or set up a live chat. Through Yahoo!, you can go to "Ask the Amish," and get your queries about the famously technology-shy sect answered at fiber-optic speed. For other faiths, there's "Ask the Imam," for issues pertaining to Islam, and "Ask the Rabbi" for Jews. You can access New Age teachings and philosophies, from reincarnation to crystal healing, to Theosophy online and seminars on the teaching of Madame Blavatsky and Krishnamurti.

Spirituality and mysticism are one melody in the cacophony of the Internet, but not a discordant one. Given that many of the people who initially created the Net and the Web emerged from a hippie culture that (among other things) shunned authority, celebrated the individual, and took as gospel that only courageous seekers could find the truth, the mysticism of the Web isn't surprising. The mystical melody of the Web says that the more wired we become, the closer we get to crafting a universal consciousness. Some people dream that the Web will even alter consciousness. The ethereal connectivity of the Net, often likened to a neural network, holds the promise, for some, of a global soul composed of self-defined individuals linked by multiple channels of information and communication.

The individualism of the sixth stage is the great-great-great-grandchild of the individualism of the second stage, though today's individualism is far more expansive than the individualism conceived by the Founding Fathers. The market ethos incorporates many of the values of individualism. It rewards those who set off on their own course, who carve a path of their own making, and who are self-possessed enough to utilize their liberty and the opportunities that come with it. The New Economy celebrates the individual CEO, the inventor, and the investor who sees an opportunity that no one else does. The culture is full of reminders that talented individuals can achieve great things and make their visions a reality. The stories of start-up companies all read like Greek myths where a hero finds his destiny, sets off on a great quest, hooks up with other heroes, and together they achieve their goal. A young Marc Andreessen sits in his college computer lab and invents Mosaic, the precursor to the Netscape Web browser. A young Finn named Linus Torvalds, alone in front of his terminal, dreams of challenging Microsoft; he writes an operating system called Linux that gets distributed for free and gives the world an alternative to Bill Gates's operating systems. In these stories, the lone inventor or entrepreneur creates a start-up company that goes where no company has gone before. They become a symbol of the market ideal, a perfect marriage of individualism and vision.[12]

Internet culture prizes individualism. The anarchic hacker mentality has yet to be displaced. Many in the business of the Web believe that cyberspace should be a self-regulating collective. At conferences on issues of law and cyberspace, "net heads" are as vehement as the American revolutionaries in their distrust of government. The "open source" software movement is characterized by people who see the attempts of both businesses to profit from software and government to regulate cyberspace as threats to liberty. According to the proponents of open-source software, "most Americans will be affected by these issues. The plan [of government and big business] is to take away freedoms before people realize what they lost."[13]

A related development is that the Web has made possible all sorts of disintermediation. Individuals no longer rely as heavily on middlemen, on people and companies whose job it is to steer consumers to products. Instead, these individuals obtain information, goods, and services for themselves, and that has changed the status of stock brokers, book publishers, record companies, media elites, travel agents, universities, and car salesmen, to name just a few.

The sixth stage is suffused with the idea that the new technology can liberate people from that which they find burdensome, including how they acquire the goods they want or need. Instead of having to pay what some company has determined a product is worth, eBay and Priceline.com let people determine what *they* are willing to pay for goods. This shifts the power away from the producer of the goods or the provider of the service and toward the purchaser. For market theorists, it also holds out the possibility of a market in which the price of goods and services perfectly reflects the demand. In other ways as well, individuals are said to gain greater autonomy. They can shun the workplace and work at home. They can ignore and block news and ideas they find troublesome. They can choose communities that interest them and avoid the ones that don't. In short, the sixth stage offers the promise that each of us can design the world of our choosing.

But just as the third stage grew out of a reaction against the extremes of individualism, the sixth stage also says that we will be bound together more closely. There are two sides to this coin, one optimistic, one not. For those who believed that societies everywhere were collapsing in the 1970s in the wake of international turmoil— the Cold War, Third World revolution, oil shocks, and social upheaval amongst students, from Latin America to Europe—the New Economy is greeted as manna from heaven. Instead of collapse, there is a new cohesion. The market and the Web are said to be bringing people together into communities united by shared interests. Like-minded souls can access each other on the Web. New businesses can create alliances with other businesses with far more ease. New technologies remove the geographical boundaries that separated us in the past. Others believe that the new technology could also lead to the creation of a digital public commons and an electronic town hall. The desire to strengthen national unity thrives in the New Economy.[14]

That is the most positive spin. There are other less sanguine perspectives. Where some see a wonderful marketplace of goods and ideas bringing us all together in a bundle of energy and creativity, others see the stifling of variety and individualism. They see a market that tends to reward the preeminent players and drive out competitors. The result is that the spectrum of ideas and options narrows. Instead of true unity, we have cultural homogenization. Some people feel that the closer we are bound together by the culture of the sixth stage, the fewer options we have. It may seem like we can buy anything and access any information. It may look as though individual opportunity is enhanced, but in fact, the market is a totalitarian force. In that view, the market and its boosters are like the North, Abraham Lincoln, and the Republican Party as seen by the South on the eve of the Civil War.

The struggles over union and what it would look like unleashed the expansion of the late nineteenth century; today, the New Economy bubbles with images of expansion into new realms. *The Industry Standard* devoted a Spring 2000 issue to a special report on "Startups: Life on the Internet Frontier." One article was entitled, "Panning for Gold in the Valley," and various CEOs were pictured in kitschy sepia-toned photographs, with handlebar mustaches and six-shooters. In an article on Tim Cahill, head of Homepage.com (a Web page provider) he is pictured with a bandanna over his face, guns pointed up, as if he were some latter-day Butch Cassidy. Cahill is the product of Bill Gross's Idealab, which has been one of the more successful "incubator" companies staking out territory on that particular Internet frontier. Idealab fills the same function as the general supply store in the Old West. Instead of credit, mining equipment, salted beef, and maps, Idealab provides new companies with some seed money, office space, equipment, and advice. At the time the article was written, Cahill was hoping to "strike gold" any day and secure a new round of financing.[15]

The Internet has been described as a virgin land, a digital world of unexplored potential. The men and women who leave their jobs in the "old economy" are likened to the prospectors who pulled up their roots and set off into the West. The unregulated Internet has been frequently analogized to the lawless West, where different communities crafted their own rules and formed their own norms of social and political organization. Granted, some of the images of the West that the Internet recalls have little to do with the actual West of the late nineteenth century and more to do with the West of Hollywood. But the idea of staking homesteads on a new frontier has been integrated into the New Economy vision.

In books and articles, television interviews and profiles, in characterizations in movies, and especially in the bits and pieces of conversation overheard on planes, trains, and in restaurants, the moguls of the New Economy arouse the same fascination as the robber barons of the fourth stage. We gossip about them. What really drives Bill Gates? What is his psychological makeup? Did Larry Ellison really say that to Scott McNealy? What actually went on at the superselective retreat organized each year by investor Herbert Allen at the ranch in Sun Valley? Are Filo and Yang just decent grad students at heart, or does something dark and dangerous lurk beneath those innocent faces?

People want to unlock the secrets of these New Economy mavens because they want the same success. The culture alternately reveres and despises the winners of the New Economy lottery. The moral purity of the early Progressives (which itself stemmed from the Puritans) is evident today in the moral opprobrium of the profligate new millionaires and billionaires. How could Steve Jobs have succeeded? Well, there must be something seedy and morally dubious going on. How is it that a few are profiting while others are left out? It must be because there's a cabal making decisions behind closed doors, circumventing the will of the people and the promise of democracy, justice, equality. The critique of the moguls emerges from the same vein as did the critique of the robber barons. So does the lust to be like them. Because they represent the apex of the sixth-stage pyramid, their lives are dissected for clues, as if understanding them will reveal the path to becoming them.

And just as the fourth stage bustled with concern about the consequences of the country's expansion, the culture of the New Economy echoes with the cries of danger ahead. As the cities expanded in the 1880s and 1890s, reformers worried about the future, convinced that society was on the brink of destroying itself. Today, even the most adamant backers of the technological revolution worry about where it might lead. Sheep get cloned, and visions of automatons controlled by a cadre of evil scientists dance through people's heads. Year by year, computers become more powerful, and more miniaturized. Robotics and artificial intelligence loom on the horizon, and some wonder when it will all turn terribly wrong.

Bill Joy, the chief scientist and cofounder of Sun Microsystems, believes that there is great peril in the network age. At a forum at Stanford University, he spoke on a panel entitled "Will Spiritual Robots Replace Humanity by 2100," a topic seemingly inspired by the dystopian vision conjured up by Isaac Asimov at the dawn of the computer age. Joy called for a temporary halt on further research into biotechnology and robotics, claiming that too many dangers lay ahead and too little thinking had been done about how to steer clear of them. "I've become more troubled," Joy said in an interview. While he recognizes the benefits of wealth creation and applauds the good done by technological innovation, he also fears that no one has adequately considered the downsides.[16] In Joy's lament, you can hear the echo of Lincoln Steffens muckraking about the perils of urban growth and the plaint of William Jennings Bryan as he thundered against how the expansion of capital was destroying too many lives. The more we expand, it seems, the more fear there is that we are headed for destruction.

Finally, the expectations of the fifth stage still linger. Some believe that the Web will make it possible to reinvent government. Though the fifth stage is over, many think that the New Economy will allow the best of government to blossom. With so many people logging on to their computers, using e-mail, and surfing the Web, political parties and nonprofit organizations have begun to use e-mail to spread their ideas and disseminate their messages. During the 2000 presidential election, a consortium of foundations and news organizations banded together to form "Web White & Blue 2000," based on the conviction that "the emerging information technologies can fundamentally enhance the electoral process . . . and revitalize American democracy." After years of public disengagement from the political process, the Web is envisioned as the road to a new civic spirit. Al Gore frequently propounded the notion that the Internet will allow for a more responsive bureaucracy, one which will interact far more rapidly and thoroughly with individuals who need help or information. Have a question about your Social Security payments? Log on to the agency's Web page, e-mail your question, and get a response.

In addition, say the boosters of a new era of e-government, people will be able to communicate more directly with elected officials. They will be able to e-mail petitions and voice their concerns through devices such as the "interactive platform" that the Democratic Party created during the 2000 election. The intimacy of democracy will be restored, as the anonymity of the industrial age is replaced by the empowerment of the Information Age.

To a remarkable extent, therefore, the sixth stage is composed of bits and pieces of the previous stages. That makes the current culture layered, bewildering, and difficult to characterize. The market-Net hybrid that constitutes the New Economy is more amorphous, unwieldy, and futuristic than earlier utopian visions. Given the complexity of contemporary society, that makes sense. We live in a world with many people, many ideas, and many layers. The utopianism of the New Economy is more complicated and more textured than earlier stages. More people add their voices, and the result is a mosaic that is continually in flux. Instead of a few hundred Puritans or a few Founding Fathers, the sixth stage is defined by hundreds of thousands of people making related decisions, and millions more who have a similar set of sensibilities.

Virtual Communities and the Future of the Current Vision

The Internet and the Web, as tools, are not only here to stay; they will become far more prominent. That means that when the New Economy glow fades and disillusionment sets in, not with the Net and the high tech per se but with the vision and its more far-fetched promises, it will be communicated on the Web. And that means that the notes of disappointment will be disseminated throughout the culture with the same efficiency, reach, and range that the current messages about the New Economy are. That might make the cyclical change from this stage to next far more evident than the earlier shifts.

Regardless of the tone of the shift, the question posed at the beginning of the book remains. Are we doomed to an endless cycle of utopian dynamism followed by disappointment and repudiation which gives rise to the next stage? Or is it possible that in recognizing this dialectic in the present we might evolve in a less jarring, more harmonious way?

For the moment, the New Economy continues to unfold. So does the vision. People continue to wonder, as one editorial writer put it, whether "The Internet is capitalist, utopian, Communist, or anarchist." Others speculate about how the next generation—the children now growing up with computers beside their beds and AOL accounts in their cribs—will be shaped by the information age and how they will shape it. The underlying assumption is, as Malcolm Gladwell remarked in a *New Yorker* article, "that this new way of exchanging information must be at the root of the changes now sweeping through our economy and culture."[17]

The hope that keeps the sixth stage churning remains simple. It is the same hope that propelled the Puritans, the same drive that fueled the American Revolution and generated the tensions that led to the Civil War, the same spirit that animated the Progressives and the determined young men and women of the Great Society. It is the belief that the needs that drive human beings can be satisfied if only we figure out how. It is a faith that society's difficulties are the product of human failings, that pain, suffering, poverty, alienation, death, disease, political chaos, and whatever else gets in the way of the ideal society can be removed if only the right formula is discovered. For the visionaries, the only thing that stands in the way is a lack of vision or the inability to have the courage of one's convictions.

It's a heady time. The problem, of course, is that the New Economy vision, like previous visions, is unrealizable. The problem is that to varying degrees, many of the visionaries of the New Economy believe their own PR. And so we live in a culture that is primed for a severe letdown, and we always have.

As in the previous stages, the first glimmers of disappointment with the prevailing vision often take years to coalesce. In hindsight, it's easy to identify the patterns that eventually gelled into the next paradigm. But at the time, it would have been nearly impossible to know that. Watching the trial of Anne Hutchinson, you would have been hard-pressed to guess that individualism was on the way, and listening to William Buckley or Milton Friedman in 1965 would not have led you to put money on the emergence of the sixth stage. Trying to guess which elements of contemporary culture are harbingers, therefore, is tricky business at best.

One way to predict what lies ahead is to look at the needs that the present paradigm doesn't adequately fulfill. When the Web and the Internet first made their entrance into mainstream society, they were accompanied by talk of community. For a while, it seemed as if these new technologies would restore what many people felt had been lost in the modern world: a sense of place and belonging. Initially, people used the Internet mostly for e-mail and usenet message boards. Services such as Prodigy, America Online, and Compuserve allowed people to interact with one another digitally, and chat groups proliferated. As a result, the Internet seemed to be a new arena of community, rather than the commercial, entertainment, and service industry space that it has become.

In the mid-1990s, the phrase "virtual community" was everywhere. It had prominent boosters and academic conferences. Studies were done about lives lived on the Web, about the changing nature of identity in cyberspace. Psychologists theorized that these virtual communities would alter how we understand consciousness and force a rethinking of traditional categories. On the Net, it was said, one person could have multiple personalities. While the ability of people to shift identities might have disturbing psychological consequences, it was seen as a boon for community development. The same person could be a physical member of a suburban community, a virtual member of a MUD (Multiple User Domain), and also a virtual member, with a completely different persona, of a usenet group devoted to fly-fishing.

The proponents of the virtual communities depicted them as offering everything that was good about the real world, with few of the drawbacks. As Howard Rheingold remarked, "People in virtual communities use words on the screen to exchange pleasantries and argue, engage in intellectual discourse, conduct commerce, exchange knowledge, share emotional support, make plans, brainstorm, gossip, feud, fall in love, find friends and lose them, play games, flirt, create a little high art and a lot of idle talk. People in virtual communities do just about everything that people do in real life but we leave our bodies behind."

Furthermore, the Internet, it was said, enabled people to reclaim the local bar, the town square, and the communal belonging that had been all but lost in the bustling late-twentieth-century world. A related idea was the "electronic village," which would give its netizens a sense of place and belonging. What allowed these communities to form and what kept them together, some observers said, was "a feeling of connectedness that confers a sense of belonging." In a world that many people experienced as increasingly impersonal, the Internet was seen as a way back to the basic American values of town and community. These new online communities would not only satisfy the same needs as the lost communities; they would be better. In the real-life towns of the past, you couldn't avoid interacting with people you didn't like, but in the virtual world you could handpick the inhabitants and easily move on if you or they came to an impasse. Virtual communities, their boosters claimed, provided the best of what community has to offer without the traditional costs.[18]

Meanwhile, high-tech companies were expanding their reach and rewriting their business models to utilize the Internet. In the process, the idea of community faded, though it survived as a marketing ploy. The ethos of the New Economy includes the idea of community, but it is a muted theme. However, the need for it hasn't disappeared.

One company took advantage of the yearning for community. In the early 1990s, Steve Case, the chairman and founder of America Online, wasn't taken too seriously. He was perceived not just as a dweeb (that was an asset in the computer world), but as a bumbling dweeb (that wasn't). As of 1992, almost anyone in the know expected his company to fail or be purchased by the serious players. The next few years did little to change that impression, as AOL consistently made PR blunders even while increasing its customer base. At one point, AOL kept adding new accounts, knowing that its system couldn't handle the traffic. The result was that millions of people could not log on, and the incessant busy signals became a nationwide joke (leading to the biting nickname "America On-Hold").

But Steve Case identified something about the Web that had little to do with the mores of the market, though being the aggressive, ambitious businessman he was, he intuitively understood the commercial potential. He saw that in the midst of startling changes in technology and culture, Americans yearned for the small town.

Every month during AOL's first years, Case sent out an electronic letter to the "community," in which he informed America Online subscribers of the growing numbers of users, the technical challenges, new features, and things that the company was working on. He sounded like a genial, not overly bright, mayor. Soon, however, it became clear that Steve Case was closer to the pulse of America than those condescending cognoscenti of Silicon Valley and Wall Street. Perhaps because it was located in suburban Virginia, and not in Silicon Valley, AOL was acutely sensitive to the needs and desires of the average American. While Case may have been cloying, his approach set the tone for the company, and millions of people flocked to it. America Online is now the preeminent Internet service provider, and it thrives on the ease with which its members can communicate with one another online by engaging in "instant message" conversations with a circle of "buddies" that can include more than one hundred people.

Because it took the idea of community seriously, AOL made sure to establish rules and regulations. Just as the American town circa 1920 had codes about what could be said in public and what was not permitted, AOL has "terms of service" that lay out what is acceptable and what isn't. But, unlike that archetypal town, cyberspace gives users the freedom to pick their names, their sex, and their identities. You can't curse or make lewd comments in AOL public spaces, but you can pose as a completely different person. AOL, in turn, acts in loco parentis, and makes liberal use of its power to enforce public morality, just as the small-town justice of the peace could arrest someone for public drunkenness, vagrancy, or any other behavior that disturbed the harmony of the community.[19]

The triumph of AOL may not seem like an indication of things to come. After all, it is a publicly traded company that has reached the economic stratosphere and purchased the largest "old economy" media company in the world, Time-Warner. AOL itself is firmly rooted in the sixth stage, but juxtaposed to other trends percolating through the culture, the reasons for its success say as much about where we are heading as they do about where we are.

Trying to emulate AOL, other companies have used the notion of community to market themselves. Some, like iVillage and Oxygen Media, base their entire business plan on the notion that people yearn for community, and that women are especially concerned about finding communities. "We're in this together and we're here for each other," says Nancy Evans, cofounder of iVillage on the company's Web page. In Evanston, Illinois, a prosperous Chicago suburb, a project called Technopolis Evanston plans to wire every one of the town's 28,000 homes in order to encourage residents to participate in communal life online through a network called the Evanston Electronic City. And companies as diverse as online brokers, Web portals, and phone companies have figured out that community is a buzzword that people respond to.[20]

For the moment, the urge for community has been channeled by the New Economy visionaries into commercial ventures. Critics of the New Economy skewer the hypocrisy, and they see the rhetoric as the self-serving words of an elite group of wealthy businessmen and financial backers. Slowly, the vision of what the market and the Net can do is being challenged. Critics of the New Economy are not united. They work at cross purposes and are motivated by different concerns, save one. They do not accept the proposition that the New Economy can provide for the nonmaterial needs that are imperative to individual happiness and societal cohesion. They do not believe that the New Economy will produce utopia. In fact, they fear that it will lead to a dystopia, in which we are all simultaneously plugged-in and alienated from that which is most important and most vital to the human experience.

In response to these murmurings of dissent, the visionaries claim that the sixth stage will be able to address our essential needs, but then, visionaries in every period have made such claims. They scoff at evidence that some people are being harmed, or that many find the current vision a cold place. They reject other perspectives, and their intolerance creates an adversarial relationship. Having been rudely dismissed, those who suggest alternatives become embittered, angry, and outraged. And if and when they eventually triumph and replace the current vision with the next, they will have little tolerance for the New Economy visionaries that they have displaced.

Meanwhile, the Information Age and the vision underlying it are as dominant at the beginning of the new millennium as any of the previous cultural stages were at their height. We are so in the grip of the sixth stage that, whether we like it or not, its end seems remote. The economy keeps humming, and aside from slower growth in 2001 and continued stock market gyrations, there are few signs that the New Economy as an economic reality will soon collapse. But the old cycle has not ended. We are simply in the midst of a stage, and no matter how unlikely it seems, it will not last.

PART THREE

THE
FUTURE?

EIGHT

CONNECTEDNESS

Only connect! That was the whole of her sermon. Only connect the prose and the passion, and both will be exalted, and human love will be seen at its height.

E. M. FORSTER, HOWARD'S END

For centuries, people have wondered what the future will hold.

Some of the great works of art and literature have been animated by a deep curiosity about what the world will look like a year, a decade, a century hence. Those imagined futures rarely hit the mark. H. G. Wells thought there would be a time machine; Robert Heinlein portrayed a late twentieth century with bases on the moon; and *Blade Runner*, Ridley Scott's grand film depiction of a Philip K. Dick story, had an early-twenty-first-century Los Angeles teeming with androids. These pictures of the future might tell us little about where we are headed, but they do reveal something about where we are. The grimmer the contemporary world seems to be, the more likely it is that people will imagine a future that is worse. When the present seems exciting and secure, the future beckons in all of its fantastic promise. Images of the future are always portraits of the present.

For decades, people looked toward the year 1984 with trepidation and curiosity. George Orwell's awesome portrayal of a totalitarian world stemmed from the heart of the Cold War, and the idea that state thought-control would be welded to high-tech surveillance struck many as credible and terrifying. When 1984 finally arrived, it was clear that the worst of Orwell's vision hadn't come to pass. But then again, some of its more disturbing features had. Surveillance techniques had progressed to the point where the thought-control that imprisoned the pathetic Winston Smith could be implemented by a crafty dictator. The ideological war between the superpowers combined with the evidence that government officials had been lying with impunity during Vietnam and Watergate signaled to many that the dystopia of Orwell wasn't far away. And in one other respect, Orwell was eerily prescient. 1984 was the symbolic beginning of the personal computer age, when Apple aired the Superbowl commercial that so seized popular imagination.

Orwell's pessimistic vision of the future emerged from the political and social climate of his day. What's remarkable is that he succeeded, not in accurately predicting what 1984 in fact turned out to look like, but in accurately highlighting the moral and ideological struggles that dominated the world for decades after he wrote. What was remarkable about the Apple commercial was that it heralded the beginning of a new age, an age that Steve Jobs and his team in Cupertino believed in, but which only a small part of American society was even aware of.

It's fun to speculate about which technologies will transform life, and which gadgets now in development will become the ubiquitous products of tomorrow. Magazines and television shows regularly run features about the world in 2010 or America in 2050, which forecast handheld Web phones, instant interactivity, wireless integrated communication devices, global locator chips, smart kitchens (haven't these been around for years?), self-cleaning fabrics, automated cars, digital navigation, robotic nannies. Some of these will prove to be as impractical as the nuclear-powered dishwasher forecast in the late 1940s. Others will be readily adopted, but when they are, the world will not feel like science fiction. By the time these fanciful things become everyday products, we will have adjusted to them being normal and natural, just as so many of us now log on and surf the Web as if it were second nature.

Similarly, when the seventh stage finally emerges, it will seem organic and natural. Several of the previous stages were punctuated by dramatic events—the Revolution, the Civil War—but cultural shifts tend to occur gradually over the course of years and become visible more in hindsight than at the time. With one possible exception, the same will be true for the seventh stage. It will develop slowly, in fits and starts, not fully understood or recognized until later. Only in retrospect will the turning point be apparent, and only years from now will it be evident which of the alternatives to the sixth stage actually coalesced to form the seventh.

There are at least three possible scenarios for the future of the New Economy. One is that more wealth will continue to be generated for more people throughout the country, and then throughout the world. In twenty or thirty years, the rewards will be diffused throughout society. Instead of a minority gaining immensely and the rest stagnating, everyone will become richer and more secure. The quality of life will improve for the tens of millions who are currently left out, in a rising-tide-lifts-all-boats scenario. No one will be without the Internet or lack the ability to utilize what the Information Age has to offer. The democratic process will be revitalized, and the pace of technological development will continue to accelerate as larger amounts of money are channeled into research. As poverty finally becomes extinct, the traditional tension between those who have more and those who have less will fade, if not to oblivion, than to social insignificance. The wealth effect will also lead to startling advances in health care, genetic research, and environmental science. People will be able to determine the contours of their lives to a degree that is difficult to imagine even now. Work will be more fluid and responsive to the needs of family, and there will be no more cycles of boom and bust, inflation, recession, hard times. Instead, the economy will grow steadily, the market will come ever closer to self-correcting, and innovation will continue to reshape the world every decade.

A second possibility is that the stock market will collapse, either in a matter of days, or slowly, bleeding to death over the course of several months. Trillions of dollars in savings will be wiped out; pension plans will lose a majority of their assets; demand for new goods will shrivel; and the economy will be plunged into a protracted recession. Banks will call in loans. Firms will go bankrupt. Land, purchased at overvalued prices, will take decades to recover its value, and the entire economy will be mired in what is currently called the "Japan syndrome," named after the Japanese economic meltdown of the 1990s.

A variant of this scenario is that the rise of the Euro as a substitute currency for the U.S. dollar will lead international businesses and government to stop using the dollar as the international standard. That will in turn erode the ability of the United States to run its enormous trade deficits. Combined with the perilously low U.S. savings rate, the growth of the Euro in the next decade will trigger an economic meltdown in the United States. Faced with the evaporation of paper profits and the decline of the dollar, the New Economy will become a joke. The dreams of the sixth stage will seem ridiculously overblown, and they will be rejected.

The third scenario is that the New Economy doesn't collapse but also doesn't fulfill its incredible promise. In this case, the upper tier continues to thrive, but the gap between rich and poor continues to grow. The millions at the top live in a world without lethal diseases, with bountiful distractions and amusements, and more than enough like-minded souls to keep the economy of goods and ideas vibrant and humming. Technological advances continue to expand the amount of information available; those who know how to obtain it and manipulate it thrive.

But life is radically different for the millions who are not integrated into the New Economy, and that begins to erode the credibility of the sixth stage as an ethos. Increasing numbers of people lose jobs, never to find permanent employment again. Families get displaced from homes and communities, and hover on the fringes of the economy, managing to subsist, but just barely. From time to time, the frustration and despair of those left out erupts into violence, ranging from shooting sprees to bombing. The regular outbreaks of violence demonstrate that all is not well with the world, though the response of most people is to isolate themselves in privately guarded communities and buffer themselves with creature comforts that only money can buy. In addition, environmental degradation worsens as government loses its capacity to coerce companies to abide by regulations, and as population growth continues its steady acceleration in the United States. The Northeast, the Pacific Coast, from San Francisco to San Diego, the corridor from

Dallas to Houston, all become areas of unbroken sprawl, and the expansion of the Web as a utility leads to greater isolation and less national cohesion.

WHY THE NEW ECONOMY WILL BE REPLACED

No matter which of these scenarios comes to pass, each undermines the vision of the sixth stage. Given that the New Economy is as much a cultural mind-set as it is an economic reality, they will all fatally weaken the New Economy as the dominant vision.

As has happened in each prior stage, the discrepancy between the utopia promised and the reality delivered will eventually become too great, and the paradigm will collapse under the weight of its own expectations. No matter how encompassing the current stage appears to be, it can never live up to its aspirations. The dream of the market and the promise of the Internet may transform life as magnificently and as completely as the first scenario envisions. But even in the first scenario, there are needs that will not be met. As usual, the Achilles' heel of the cultural vision is overweening and unrealistic expectations.

If either of the last two scenarios is correct, it's easy to see why the sixth stage will be discredited. Economic collapse would quickly corrode the vision, and skeptics would have a field day. In the case of the third scenario, the neither-feast-nor-famine outcome, disillusionment would slowly set in. That was how the government paradigm came to an end. But, say that the first scenario is correct, and the material goals of the market and the Internet are realized and even exceeded. What then?

The weakness of the New Economy vision is not that it makes grandiose material promises, but that it offers the hope that nonmaterial needs will also be satisfied. In short, its visionaries and their vision intimate that people will be happy as well as rich.

To some extent, that has been true of the earlier stages. Each was an attempt to construct the perfect world, and though the specifics have changed, the desire has remained. The Puritans were pessimistic about human nature, but they trusted in God's power and believed that a City on a Hill would not just be a spiritual society but a materially affluent one as well. The Founding Fathers blurred individual liberty and happiness, and their language suggested that independence was a prelude not just to a more powerful and productive nation, but also a more enlightened, contended citizenry. For those who struggled over Union, national cohesion was the key to both economic growth and a noble society in which the good of the many triumphed and the needs of all were provided for. The Gospel of Wealth was about money but also about fulfillment—about not just the clothes on one's back and a roof over one's head—but also a sense of purpose, place, and mission. And the fifth stage, the era of government, was a vision for a nation in which all citizens could flourish in whatever way they chose.

For most of our history, we have nurtured the illusion that the answers to our needs and desires are attainable and that it is possible that, one day, we will have it all. That is what gives the New Economy, like each previous stage, such dynamism. Unfettered by cynicism, its visionaries undertake to change the world, and they do. The culture echoes that vision. The problem lies with what we expect. The disappointment is usually a product not of failure but of the absence of success commensurate with the goals in mind.

The culture of the New Economy seems to recognize that people yearn for more than wealth, and that there are a range of needs that wealth can barely address. But in their giddiness, the proponents of the New Economy seem to believe that the gizmos and gazmos of the coming decades, combined with economic growth, will not only alter the material world but will also make it possible to fulfill the injunction of E. M. Forster: "Only connect."

As we've seen, the Internet and the Web do allow for the development of virtual communities. Many predict that as technology improves, as the Web and cell phones and related devices proliferate, people will feel more connected to each other than ever before and more in command of their lives.[1] But it's not just virtual connectedness that the New Economy promises. It's connectedness to our bodies and to actual people. One of the touted aspects of the sixth stage is that the advances of technology will lead to breakthroughs in health care. Early in the twentieth century, people imagined that science would soon push back the frontiers of mortality, but those dreams were unrealistic in a precomputer age. Now, because computers have made it possible to collate and process the immensely complicated data of DNA, those dreams are said to be on the verge of realization. Serious research is underway in areas such as gene therapy, nanotechnology, and synthetic drugs. Genetic manipulation may make it possible to replace decaying organs, revitalize neural networks, and halt, if not reverse, the process of growing old. Though these techniques will initially be prohibitively expensive, they will eventually become as common as aspirin or vaccinations. The result will be a substantial extension of the normal life span.

Another hope is that the exchange of information which the Web makes possible will make it easier for people to meet one another, particularly romantically. Finding that right person will be simplified by online databases. You create a profile of yourself and post it on a dating service, complete with streaming video. Then, via e-mail, you get to talk to people who interest you, and that then allows for a further narrowing until the right person is identified. The chances of locating an appropriate mate are greatly enhanced, and as more and more people turn to the Web for dating assistance, they will find what they are looking for more easily.

But in both of these cases, the potential is limited to the material world. Even if the average life span is expanded, we will still die, if not at eighty then at one hundred, and if not at one hundred, then at one hundred and twenty. And even if you can reduce the possibility that you'll waste time and energy on utterly unsuitable people, you will still have to deal with a flesh-and-blood other person, and the elusive path to intimacy will still be elusive. The sixth stage can do many things, but it cannot obviate the fear of death. It cannot banish those uncomfortable silences on a bad date. And it cannot get parents to stop fearing for their children, nor children to stop raging about the frustrations of childhood. It cannot teach people how to love one another, how to live with one another, and how to listen to their bodies. It cannot solve the mysteries of human relationships, nor remove the need for them. The New Economy can make it possible for more people to acquire more things than ever before, to learn more than they ever have, and to change the world for the better. But it cannot alter the challenges of being alive. Money can't buy love, or happiness, and the New Economy won't change that.

Few of us, of course, explicitly think that the sixth stage can do any of that. At the same time, however, the culture is not subtle. It may not promise these things explicitly, but it doesn't rule them out, either. It insinuates that it's just possible for the intangible challenges that have confronted humans for as long as they've had consciousness to be settled, once and for all. That, after all, is what it means to be driven by a utopian vision. The lack of realism is a strength, and it is also a weakness.

THE SEEDS OF THE NEW VISION

Reading the tea leaves of the present, the successor to the sixth stage will be "connectedness." Whether or not that word has any resonance in the future, what it signifies will. Connectedness is an umbrella term for the needs that the sixth stage doesn't directly address or cannot adequately meet. It will mean a different set of values, and a distinct set of goals.

Already, there are hints that the sixth stage is not fulfilling people, at least not in relation to expectations and promises. "A Newer, Lonelier Crowd Emerges in Internet Study." That according to a story in *The New York Times*, which went on to say that the more hours people spend on the Internet, the less they interact with real human beings and the more isolated they feel. These findings are in direct contrast to those who claim that the Internet provides new, vibrant communities for people who need them. But in several major studies, Internet usage is directly correlated to spending less time with family and friends, less time in stores, and less time in social environments.

This perspective about the Internet is only one sliver of a larger set of concerns that rumble through the culture, popping up in an academic study here, an article there, heard in bits and pieces on various self-help infomercials or on morning television shows, and Oprah Winfrey's daily afternoon hour watched by millions. People say they feel adrift, gripped by a pervasive sense that things aren't quite right, an uneasy feeling that for all the material abundance, happiness seems unattainable. Each of these chords has a different tenor. Some point to an unsettling lack of community, a loss of that mythic village. Others mourn the absence of civic spirit, the feeling that we are all in this together. A growing number of critics note the multiple forces in contemporary society that pull people apart and dilute our sense of connection.

Robert Putnam, a Harvard political scientist, has called this phenomenon "bowling alone." He begins with the axiom that the vibrance of the United States stems from what the French writer Alexis de Tocqueville saw as a unique American predilection to form voluntary associations. These associations, ranging from the Masons to the PTA, from the Elks to bowling leagues, created a strong civic society, and hence help explain the success of the United States. Putnam is one of a number of observers who believe that the past thirty years have witnessed a steep decline in "civic engagement," a decline that he feels has troubling consequences. If nothing else, according to Putnam, the tendency of Americans to "bowl alone" in ad hoc groups instead of as part of regular bowling leagues reflects a wider erosion of community. And if nothing else, the rising chorus of writers and academics who assert that there is an endemic loss of connectedness tap into a widespread set of concerns that the bonds that link people to each other are weakening.[2]

These notes of ennui float through the sixth stage, but like arrows against fortress walls, they tend to fall listlessly to the ground without making any discernible dent in the current ethos. That only increases the sense of futility and despair. In addition, as many are quick to point out, there have always been complaints that traditional values are eroding, that communities are collapsing, and that, all in all, society is going to hell in a handbasket. It's sometimes hard to distinguish between a normal, predictable quotient of human dissatisfaction and a deeper manifestation that the way things are simply won't do in the long run.

The types of people who voice discontent further undermine the case. Because those who confess to feeling dislocated tend to be people who aren't doing as well under the regime of the sixth stage, their expressed desire for alternative mores can be dismissed as sour grapes. Meanwhile, those who are profiting, literally and metaphysically, from the New Economy vision vocally celebrate its potential. Until there is a substantial shift in the attitudes of these people, the sixth stage will continue to be formidable. Only when the scales tip and a critical mass of people begin to express discontent and actively seek alternatives can the change from one stage to the next occur.

Still, everywhere there are murmurs. In spite of the market ethos that pervades the culture, average Americans claim, in survey after survey, that they are less interested in material affluence than in family and friendships, that they are less focused on career and work than on living simple, moral lives. They aver that the teachings of the Bible carry far more weight in their lives than the exhortations of the market or the dreams of the Internet. It's hard to know how much these sentiments accurately reflect people's inner lives. Do they say that they value relationships more because they do, or because they think that they should? Do they claim to pay more heed to the Bible because they believe that they ought to, but guiltily know that they don't? Whatever the case, the fact that people express such feelings is indication enough that the sixth stage leaves certain needs unfulfilled.[3]

Psychologists, biologists, and social scientists have begun to recognize what folk wisdom has long known. People thrive on face-to-face contact. Human beings need intimacy for their emotional and physical well-being. That need is almost on a par with physical needs for food, water, and shelter. Studies across race, class, income, and geography, in the United States and throughout the world, demonstrate that social isolation leads to depression, increased health risks, greater risk of early mortality, and general feelings of unhappiness. According to Lisa Berkman of the Harvard School of Public Health, "The extent to which we maintain close personal relationships, and the degree to which we feel a part of our community or have deep abiding social and psychological resources help to determine how protected we are against biological, environmental, or interpersonal assaults."[4]

In his study of happiness in market democracies, Robert Lane of Yale concluded that the more affluence generated by the economy, the less that affluence leads to happiness. According to researchers like Lane, happiness can only be measured subjectively. That is, when people are asked if they're happy, do they say that they are? If they do, then they are. Psychologists recognize that some societies place a greater premium on happiness, and that the United States is on the extreme end of the scale when it comes to the expectation of happiness. You'd expect that from a utopian culture. Americans believe in the possibility of happiness, and they believe that something can be done to maximize it.

But according to surveys, Americans aren't that happy. Given the heady vision that animates the market and the Internet, that's surprising. The explanation, says Lane, is simple. "The reason markets in advanced economies fail to do much to promote, let alone maximize, well-being is that the things that contribute most to well-being, especially companionship and family life, are market externalities. And commodities, it seems, are poor substitutes for friends." Lane establishes that there is an inverse relationship between the amount of disposable income and the level of happiness in a society. Money, it would appear, really doesn't buy happiness. Lane, however, is subtler than that. For poor societies, money does raise contentment, because for the very poor, the things money can buy are necessities that they struggle for daily, such as adequate food, clean water, and shelter. When basic material needs are met, the law of diminishing returns sets in, and more money buys less happiness.[5]

If these arguments are true, then the material orientation of the New Economy can only go so far in extending the sphere of happiness. Many people don't believe that, and they attack the motives of those who do. Lane and Putnam have been characterized as defeatists who see the clouds behind every silver lining. Many market theorists, not to mention Internet visionaries, contest the claim that companionship and family life are market externalities. The very dominance of the Internet, they say, is a testament to the need for more connection, and these visionaries interpret signs of malaise as bumps on the road to a golden age in which the New Economy enriches the body and the soul and links consumers to products and people to one another.

It is too soon to tell just how far the sixth stage will go in the direction that its visionaries predict. Many of the problems may in fact work themselves out. Yet it's difficult to brush away the signs of unease as growing pains. No matter how loud the visionaries trumpet the virtues of the New Economy, many people don't like it, aren't satisfied by it, and are looking for something else.

Take the following examples:

- Americans in the millions responded to a book about community written by a not-very-popular White House resident named Hillary Clinton, who went around the country with the message that "it takes a village to raise a child" and was greeted with standing ovations, even by people who otherwise would not have invited her over for tea.

- Or this. The Disney Corporation announced a plan to build a model community that replicated the 1950s idyll of the American small town. Named "Celebration," the town was built in Orlando, Florida, near Disney World, and had far more applicants than the 2,500 slots available. The subsequent history of Celebration is hardly cause for it, but the pull of that dream remains strong, and for every vacancy, there are dozens of families waiting in line.

- The Oprah Winfrey show, which offers a daily vision of a world governed by emotional honesty and openness, draws millions of viewers and influences millions more. Related messages can be heard on other shows.

- The sales of New Age books, which strike a decidedly antimarket tone, rival the sales of business books. Self-help guides to relationships proliferate, with titles like *Connect: 12 Vital Ties That Open Your Heart, Lengthen Your Life, and Deepen Your Soul*, which promise to help people communicate with one another. These books rarely get reviewed in major newspapers and magazines; they get ridiculed in movies and televisions; and they are usually invisible in Northeast-generated pop culture. But from infomercials to morning television, from bookstores to online discussions groups, they have a huge, hungry audience.

- The sales of Christian-themed books dominate best-seller lists, even though they are read by few of the people who make the culture of the sixth stage. The serial novels of Jan Karon depict the life of a small North Carolina town, uncontaminated by malls, computers, and urban values. In short, she writes about a town that is the antithesis of the sixth stage. Sharing space on the lists, the dark, apocalyptic fantasies of Tim LaHaye describe a near future when the Antichrist returns and a few pure souls struggle to stay alive and true while awaiting the Second Coming.

- There is a spiritual revival occurring in workplaces. Even *Business Week* acknowledges that "neither economic efficiency nor scientific rationalism has diluted the overwhelming force of religious beliefs, rituals and myths." Each year, for example, several hundred Xerox employees, a company at the center of Silicon Valley, participate in a "vision quest." Emulating the Native Americans of the Southwest, they go into the desert for twenty-four hours and try to have a spiritual experience. A poll of managers nationwide finds that they want more meaning in their lives, even at the expense of earning less. Other polls find that when a company respects the spiritual needs of its workers, those workers are more productive. In special seminars, employees are urged to talk about their fears of failure and are taught better ways to communicate with one another. Traditional religions are also thriving in the workplace, and companies have hired full-time chaplains and other assorted clergy.[6]

- In the midst of the New Economy, there has been explosive growth in the nonprofit sector. Nonprofit organizations are the descendants of the voluntary associations of the nineteenth century. During the 1920s, following the spirit of the Progressive era, the federal government created a tax category to promote organizations that operate for religious, charitable, or educational purposes. During the 1990s, as the federal government receded, nonprofits proliferated. There are now more than 1.5 million nonprofits which employ more than 10 percent of the American workforce. Nonprofits are funded by billions of dollars of foundation money, and if not for the success of the New Economy, this money would not have been generated. Some nonprofits are groups like the National Football League and the National Rifle Association, which take advantage of the loose language of legislation to qualify for nonprofit status. Many more, however, are staffed by people who are poorly paid, if paid at all, and dedicated to helping others, improving communities, and caring for the environment.

- There is also the phenomenon of downshifting. Throughout the country, people are dropping out of high-pressure, fast-paced, lucrative jobs because they don't think that their needs are being addressed. Some of these people probably downshifted because they realized that they were never going to be particularly successful; there's nothing more stressful than knowing that you are mediocre at what you're doing. But many others left voluntarily while their careers were still on the upswing. "Downshifting has simplified our lives," says Steven Varelmann of Cincinnati. "We leased our house in the city, sold most of what we owned, and moved to a small house on Lake Waynoka. The goal is to concentrate our energy on what is important in life: being happy, free from extraneous diversions and stress." Some downshifters have formed groups that encourage people to take a step back and reconsider their priorities, and some of these groups overlap with "New Age" movements. "False success," says James Dillehay in *InnerSelf* magazine, "means abandoning what is in your heart for the lure of money and security. When we primarily strive for more and more money and possessions, we will never get enough to satisfy." Dillehay was an affluent vice-president of a chain of stores in the Midwest, yet he left that life to follow the teaching of an itinerant Sufi. Other articles in *InnerSelf* offer personal testimonies of people who "lived for the office" and then quit to focus on matters of the spirit and family.[7]

In some respects, downshifters are updating an old American passion play. The back-to-the-land spirit animated hippies in the 1960s, as it did Henry David Thoreau in the mid-nineteenth century. In the face of industrialization, urbanization, modernization, and computerization, people fear that they are losing touch with the intangibles, such as friends and a connection to the land. They feel squeezed for time, unmoored, and they yearn to reconnect to what they think they have lost.

But the downshifting movement is also a reaction to contemporary materialism. According to Juliet Schor, in the 1990s, nearly 20 percent of all adult Americans "made a voluntary lifestyle change . . . that entailed earning less money." Support groups throughout the country give people the opportunity to share their stories about downshifting and "simple living." In gathering together, people recognize that they are not alone and that others have come to a similar impasse. The Center for a New American Dream, for instance, calls on people to give up financial security in order to gain time and personal freedom. "The good life," begins one of the center's newsletters, "is now defined by many as a life of continuous acquisition. Millions fawn over Bill Gates and Michael Jordan, in part because of what they have accomplished, but perhaps even more because of the greatness of their wealth and status possessions." The center documents the costs of the imperative to become affluent, evident in rising levels of personal bankruptcy and in the despair of people such as teachers and nurses who do vital work but aren't financially compensated. The center also works with the World Wildlife Fund and Worldwatch Institute, as well as other major nonprofit organizations dedicated to various environmental causes.[8]

- Concern about the environment is the flip side of the technological revolution. The old tension between science and nature has reappeared. The more we advance scientifically, it seems to some, the more havoc we wreak on the earth. Between the protests in Seattle, the rise of the Green Party in the United States (marginal, but still millions), the move toward recycling, and the concern over the greenhouse effect and global warming, people have serious doubts about what lies at the end of the market rainbow.

Relative to the larger culture—which pulses with messages of the market, these items don't yet amount to much. Oprah, downshifting, and workplace pastors are isolated phenomena, reflecting dissatisfaction but making only occasional dents in the dominant vision. But the degree to which they are reflected in the culture may not represent the degree to which they mirror people's lives. The dots of discontent may not form a coherent pattern, but in time, as the dominant culture dissipates, they will be connected.

Whether or not you take New Age movements seriously, are a fan of Oprah, a reader of Tim LaHaye, or an ardent downshifter who believes that environmental destruction is imminent, these currents exist, and they are more than marginal and more than representative of a lunatic fringe. They amount to a rejection of the sixth stage, as much a part of the visionary cycle as the Founding Fathers and the Progressive critics. In time, the disparate, and often desperate, criticisms will evolve into a new stage that will supplant the New Economy.

THE SEVENTH STAGE

The New Economy is an economic and technological success. It has achieved much of what its visionaries predicted. In all likelihood, the sixth stage will end not because it will fail to enrich us materially. It will end because of what millions of people believe it does not and cannot offer: spiritual fulfillment, intimate relationships, and community.

In the next stage, these will be the watchwords. The goals will be to increase intimacy; enhance self-awareness; carve out time and space for friendships, family, and community; establish ecological harmony; create demographic balance; and promote greater understanding of the nonmaterial aspects of human existence. The heroes of the seventh stage will be those who devote themselves to these goals. The culture will reward people who come up with innovative ways to improve cities and suburbs, who learn from the mistakes of the twentieth century, and whose primary goal is improving the quality of life, whether or not such improvement yields a profit.

The visionaries of the next era will look to restructure work and rewrite law in order to lessen the tension between career and family. They will probe the boundaries between science and spirituality with the same zeal, and with the same financial support, that theoretical physicists now probe the nature of existence. They will explore the nature of spiritual fulfillment. They will investigate why humans have a chemical need for interpersonal relationships. They will invent new bottles to hold the ancient wine of human needs.

Forecasting the rise of connectedness assumes that the streams of discontent discussed above will eventually converge and form a torrent that will overwhelm the sixth stage. It's impossible to know exactly how long it will be before the New Economy template decays, but strains of dissatisfaction circulate through the same channels that all other information does. The Information Age allows for a faster dissemination of ideas, and it makes it easier to notice patterns. That means that the shift to connectedness could reach critical mass more quickly than at times in the past. Because of the Information Age, the next stage may be closer than it seems.

The utopian vision of connectedness will dream of a society in which people focus on their own emotional growth with the same fervor, sophistication, and intensity that they now focus on enhancing the New Economy. The seventh stage will be animated by the same belief that everything is possible and all is attainable. The emphasis will be on the nonmaterial needs of life, but the visionaries of the seventh stage will contend that connectedness will also answer material needs. They will claim that spiritual fulfillment can create economic prosperity, because (so the reasoning will go) spiritually fulfilled people recognize that each individual prospers most when emotional confusion, fears, and various internal demons are no longer impediments. "Yes, you can have it all" will still be relevant, except that the "all" will refer to the perfect community, one that is the product of each of its members working in conjunction with each other and with regard for the physical environment.

Drawing on traditional religious theology, New Age teachings, psychology, therapeutic techniques, medical research, and communitarian philosophies, the seventh stage will create a new framework for the culture. Instead of the language of the market, the seventh stage will resound with the language of spirituality. Instead of valuing profit and commercial transactions, the seventh stage will stress contentment and relationships. Instead of technology, the seventh stage will be marked by techgnosis, the realm where science blurs and spirituality blooms, and where computers begin to approximate consciousness.[9]

The seventh stage will reward those who manifestly contribute to the creation of connectedness. Teachers who provide insight into the workings of the human psyche will find themselves at the center of the culture instead of at the periphery. Community consultants, who draw on lessons learned from urban planning, sociology, social work, family counseling, psychology, local politics, and churches, will be involved in the architecture and construction of buildings, in hospital management, workplace organization, and Internet businesses. Politicians who craft legislation that helps people devote time and space to focus on the nonmaterial, on family life and personal growth, will have electoral success. And companies that integrate these needs into their business plans will thrive.

Connectedness will be as ambiguous and complicated as the previous stages. Its visionaries will talk as though they have found a new path to the ideal society, but that won't mean that society will approximate utopia. There will be a disconnect between the vision and people's daily experience. The seventh stage will have its winners and losers, just as in the past. If teachers (broadly defined) gain accolades, then entrepreneurs may receive a cold cultural shoulder. Investment bankers may thrive financially but find that their interests are not treasured by the culture at large, nor are their values treated with respect. If the culture lauds people who devote their energy to projects that enhance the quality of life but offer minimal financial rewards, what of those who make different choices or who have other values? Corporate CEOs may continue to innovate and enhance the sphere of the market and the Internet, but their pictures will not grace the covers of national magazines, their stories will not be offered as inspiring primers, and they will not be sought for their counsel and wisdom. If the culture makes icons of people who are adept at bringing people together, then what of the loners or the individualists who thrive alone? Scientists and technologists may invent ever more extraordinary devices and delve more deeply into the physical laws underpinning the universe, but they will labor in the shadows unless they link their work to spirituality and to the mysteries of emotions and relationships which continue to defy the efforts of science and its instruments to quantify them.

In short, connectedness will not be some New Age paradise. It will be a different prism. Those who are in sync with its values will have success and accolades. Those who don't will find the world an uncomfortable place, and they will react against it. If past patterns hold, there will be tension between those who benefit from the vision and those who don't. The utopian promise of connectedness will be no more and no less far-fetched than the previous visions. It will be no more realistic, and it may be as totalitarian, but because a sufficient number of people with a sufficient amount of power and influence will be driven by it, it will cause tectonic cultural changes.

If the vision of connectedness strikes an odd note, that's because at present, its values are out of place. They clash with the New Economy as intensely as Anne Hutchinson clashed with the men of Massachusetts Bay. Religious beliefs, New Age language, the political philosophy of the Green Party, and psychotherapeutic ideas arouse strong reactions because they are at best tangential, and at worst antithetical to the culture of the New Economy. The goal of all the stages may be the same, but the competition between the different approaches is fierce and acrimonious.

Unfortunately, the result is an endless cycle of utopian visions. American culture is dynamic, yes, but it also sets up an ongoing split between those who make the culture and thrive, because they are in harmony with the present stage, and those who either cannot or will not orient their lives behind the reigning paradigm. People who don't accept the current vision suffer from alienation and a dearth of avenues to attain the respect and recognition that they crave.

When they finally triumph, they have a stockpile of accumulated grievances. Having suffered from the scorn of the old regime, they aren't about to cut it much slack. The Progressive reformers were so embattled with the robber barons that they couldn't appreciate the beneficial results of expansion, and the proponents of the New Economy were so aggressively anti-government that they failed to recognize what government had done well. The champions of the seventh stage, having clawed and fought against the New Economy, are likely to be as intolerant of their critics as were the visionaries of the past. They will disdain alternate perspectives, and those who dissent from the mores of connectedness will become bitter and alienated. The cycle will begin again, and the culture will lurch from the seventh stage to the eighth, and so on into the future.

The past isn't binding, but it carries weight. We are mired in this cycle, and there's no reason to believe that we are about to break free of it. There are worse fates. This cycle has brought the United States prosperity and power. But we can do better.

AN ALTERNATIVE

Rather than being stuck in a never-ending pattern, there is another possibility. It's unlikely; it requires a leap of faith even to imagine. In fact, it requires us to envision a world unlike the one we have been living in. In order to believe that the future could be different, we have to believe that an impractical idea could become a lived reality. That is a tall order, but no taller than getting on a rickety ship in the mid-seventeenth century and migrating to New England. In the United States, there is precedent for believing that the unprecedented is possible.

Instead of tilting from stage to stage endlessly, the next stage could be an era when the desire to have it all is tempered by a recognition that no one template is sufficient. It could be a time when we recognize, collectively, that though the dreams have been constant, they remain a will-o'-the-wisp. And not just for the United States. No society has figured out how to satisfy the preponderance of human needs, and no culture has yet discovered a way to provide for the spirit and the body in equal measure. There's an old adage: fool me once, shame on you; fool me twice, shame on me. In some sense, we have fooled ourselves at least six times. At the very least, then, we ought to step back and take stock of what we have been doing.

The missing element is a general recognition of the utopian impulse, how deep and abiding it is, and how both dynamic and unrealistic society tends to be. Each time a new stage arises, the accumulated wisdom of the past is cast aside, and ideas that don't accord with the prevailing vision are given short shrift. That closes off an immense range of options, and forces innovation to occur inside the boundaries of the current stage, whatever it might be. As vibrant as the culture is, it can be self-defeating and unnecessarily rigid.

If we had a better perspective on what drives our culture, we might be able to pursue our goals more effectively. It's true that utopias are utopias because they are never realities. But the impulse to construct social orders that come close to providing for a wide spectrum of needs can only be for the best. We don't need to set the bar lower. We need only to recognize that the same process that has brought us close has also limited how far we can go.

Cleaving to a vision du jour has an undeniable appeal. It creates the illusion that life is fairly simple. It also establishes a hierarchy of goals and values which people can use to orient their lives. Once again, the United States has always been a nation that revolves around an idea. It makes sense, therefore, that historically the dominant ideas have been simple and all-encompassing. Each had to apply to the greatest common denominator. The various visions have been for American society what Christianity was in the Middle Ages: an organizing set of principles that gave meaning to life and channeled people's energies accordingly.

So what is the way forward? For one, we could use a dose of humility to temper the utopianism. Not humility about the goal, but a humbleness about the means. The drive to address the entire spectrum of human needs is essential to our culture, but we could benefit by being less naive about the next thing. As it stands, connectedness will suffer from fatal flaws. The seventh stage may allow for a level of understanding about the psyche, emotions, relationships, and community, but by focusing laser-like on the needs of the spirit, it will probably undervalue material needs. By overemphasizing the non-material, the culture will leave other drives and interests unattended to. And by believing that connectedness will be the path that will finally lead to the longed-for utopia, its visionaries will brook dissent no more willingly than the Puritans tolerated Anne Hutchinson. Faced with such a brittle edifice, people will react against it, and eventually they will overturn it.

That would be a loss. Ceaselessly striving for an idyll, we do not honor what has worked in the past, and our fingers are always ready to pull the trigger on what is working in the present. The moment an idea fails to live up to its greatest potential is the moment it begins to fade. We do not adequately allow for limited success.

So first, we need to understand the cycle. Then, perhaps, it will be clear that no one paradigm can possibly provide for all human interests, wants, and desires. Instead of stages that are dominated by a simple template, we might try, collectively and individually, to construct a culture that combines the past visions, explicitly and deliberately. Instead of cramming everything into one cultural framework, we might become more nuanced and more malleable. Market mores clearly work for business, so discarding them would be foolish. Religious traditions, New Age teachings, and psycho-therapeutic techniques answer nonmaterial needs. The only way to address the entire spectrum is to combine visions, to blend the spiritual yearnings of connectedness with the material mores of the New Economy, to honor the need for unity and the need for individualism, to respect that the dream of a City on a Hill has befuddled human beings forever and that if the path were clear, others would have walked it.

We do ourselves a cultural disservice by not embracing multiple stages simultaneously. No one of them alone will satisfy, and there's no guarantee that several in conjunction will, either. But if you saw someone doing the same thing over and over and still complaining of dissatisfaction, you might suggest that this person reassess and come up with a revised approach. The same can be said for societies.

This alternate vision for the future, of a society that embraces multiple strategies on the path toward a better world, is as utopian as any vision in the past. It imagines us jointly and collectively arriving at an awareness of how we have evolved, of what our goals are, and then making innumerable decisions that transform the culture. It has the conceit of believing that the future is something each of us can influence, and it honors the idea that with each passing generation, it is possible to draw nearer to the dream of a society that values community, treasures family, spurs individuals to know themselves and learn more about the nature of free will, embraces material comforts, celebrates the mysteries of life, deals directly with death and mortality, seeks a balance between the needs of the many and the demands of the few, respects the role of government and the glory of the market, and expands the sphere of human consciousness.

It is profoundly improbable. It envisions a society that learns from its past, takes stock of its present, and takes time to consider its future. It is a dream that rests on an optimistic appraisal of American society. Our divisions are real, the inequities undeniable, and there is still a yawning chasm between the ideal society of universal prosperity and communal harmony, and the world we actually live in. But from the billionaires who tout the New Economy to the critics who excoriate it, we share a yearning for a better world that keeps us together, and whether or not we recognize it, we share a heritage of four centuries of American dreams.

Yes, this alternate vision is improbable, but so were all the other visions, and all the other stages that comprise American culture. The Puritan journey was astonishing; the American Revolution was unlikely; the creation of a union, the expansion of the late nineteenth century, and the New Deal, all unrealistic. The New Economy and the Internet, who could have imagined?

The United States is a country that rises and falls on utopian dreams that are never quite realized. It is a country fueled by goals that it never attains and driven by visionaries who can't accept that they will fall short. The cycle of vision giving way to vision, of stages rising and then being supplanted, has been a source of vitality. One day, perhaps, this cycle will come to an end, and a new one, with a potential we can barely imagine, will be born. One day, we may find that elusive formula that makes us both happy and rich, and we may discover that we knew the answers all along but lacked the means to integrate them. This, too, is a dream—for a better world, an unexplored future, and a new frontier. It may remain a dream, but in a visionary nation, anything is possible.

NOTES

INTRODUCTION

1. Many people have argued about the role of utopia in American society. Recently, Andrew Delbanco wrote about the tendency of Americans to dream of a better world, and how the result is often a certain melancholy. Paul Berman has written about the ebb and flow of the utopian impulse in the '60s generation. Russell Jacoby has argued that contemporary society is marked by the end of the utopian vision, and that the endless trumpeting of the Internet or the New Economy makes marketing sense but isn't really a vision. In his view, the utopian visions of the present are so thin and so derivative of utopian visions of the past that they don't really qualify as utopian visions at all. In a somewhat different vein, Francis Fukuyama has argued that with the end of the Cold War, there are no new visions, simply the triumph of the Western liberal vision. These are only the more recent works of a large corpus. Jacoby is certainly right that the utopian vision is lacking in the work of contemporary writers and intellectuals, and he also notes that politics is no longer a sphere for visionaries. But, as I discuss in later chapters, that is symptomatic of the shift from the government paradigm to the market and the Internet, and not an absolute end of utopianism. See Russell Jacoby, *The End of Utopia: Politics and Culture in an Age of Apathy* (New York: Basic Books, 1999);

Francis Fukuyama, *The End of History and the Last Man* (New York: Avon, 1993); Andrew Delbanco, *The Real American Dream: A Meditation on Hope* (Cambridge: Harvard University Press, 1999); Paul Berman, *A Tale of Two Utopias: The Political Journey of the Generation of 1968* (New York: Norton, 1996).

2.   There is nothing particularly novel about this approach, and many historians and philosophers have tried to describe societies in terms of stages. The nineteenth-century German thinker Georg Friedrich Hegel was a major proponent of a historical "dialectic." He saw historical evolution as a process of a thesis giving way to an antithesis, which in turn eventually gave rise to a synthesis, and he claimed that the present is a result of multiple historical stages. Hegel's intellectual children include sociologists such as Max Weber, who devoted considerable energy to identifying the key forces at work in societies at specific times. And more recently, scholars such as Benedict Anderson have talked about the degree to which all nations are "imagined communities," the product of self-conscious ideas and dreams and not simply organic units that emerge naturally. Michael Lind divided American culture into four revolutions in his book, *The Next American Nation* (New York: The Free Press, 1995). In short, the seven stages that I discuss are particular to this book, but the impulse to characterize society in terms of distinct ideas prevalent at distinct times is not.

Chapter One

1.   According to Samuel Eliot Morison, *The Oxford History of the American People*, Vol. 1 (New York: Oxford University Press, 1972), pp. 80–81.

2.   John Smith, "The Starving Time in Virginia," in Richard Dorson, ed., *America Begins: Early American Writings* (New York: Pantheon, 1950), pp. 138–142; Alden Vaughan, *American Genesis: Captain John Smith and the Founding of Virginia* (Boston: Little Brown, 1975).

3.   This account is drawn from several sources, including Bernard Bailyn et al., *The Great Republic: A History of the American People*, Vol. 1 (Lexington, MA: D. C. Heath, 1992), pp. 44–45;

Clarence Ver Steeg, *The Formative Years: 1607–1763* (New York: Hill & Wang, 1964), pp. 26–27.

4. Accounts of various laws come from Thomas Jefferson Werten-baker, *The Puritan Oligarchy: The Founding of American Civilization* (New York: Grosset & Dunlap, 1947), pp. 172ff. Also, Edmund Morgan, *Visible Saints: The History of a Puritan Idea* (Ithaca: Cornell University Press, 1963).

5. Quoted in Perry Miller, *Errand into the Wilderness* (Cambridge: Harvard University Press, 1984), p. 11.

6. Edward Johnson, *Wonder-Working Providence 1628–1651*, J. F. Jameson, ed., (New York, 1910), pp. 58–85; Increase Mather, "The Mystery of Israel's Salvation (1667)," in Alan Heimart and Andrew Delbanco, eds., *The Puritans in America: A Narrative Anthology* (Cambridge: Harvard University Press, 1985), pp. 237–46; John Winthrop, "A Modell of Christian Charity 1630," in Edwin Gaustad, ed., *A Documentary History of Religion in America to the Civil War* (Grand Rapids, MI: Eerdmans, 1982), pp. 106–107. Also, Philip Gura, *A Glimpse of Sion's Glory* (Middletown, Conn.: Wesleyan University Press, 1984).

7. Winthrop quoted in Ver Steeg, pp. 49–51; Cotton quoted in Sydney Mead, *The Lively Experiment: The Shaping of Christianity in America* (New York: Harper & Row, 1963), p. 13.

8. The text is taken from David Hall, ed., *The Antinomian Controversies 1636–1638: A Documentary History* (Durham, N.C.: Duke University Press, 1990).

9. Quoted in Richard Bushman, *From Puritan to Yankee: Character and the Social Order in Connecticut, 1690–1765* (Cambridge: Harvard University Press, 1967), p. 210.

10. Richard Hofstadter, *America at 1750: A Social Portrait* (New York: Vintage, 1971), pp. 217ff; Sydney Ahlstrom, *A Religious History of the American People* (New Haven: Yale University Press, 1972).

11. "Edwards and the Great Awakening," in Miller, *Errand into the Wilderness*, op. cit., p. 161.

CHAPTER TWO

1. Yehoshua Arieli, *Individualism and Nationalism in American Ideology* (Cambridge: Harvard University Press, 1964), pp. 190ff.

2.   Text of the resolution in Richard Hofstadter, ed., *Great Issues in American History: Volume II: From the Revolution to the Civil War, 1765–1865* (New York: Vintage Books, 1958), p. 8. Also, see Edmund and Helen Morgan, *The Stamp Act Crisis: Prologue to Revolution* (New York: Collier Books, 1962); for Patrick Henry, see Bailyn et al., *The Great Republic*, op. cit., p. 231.

3.   Soame Jenkyns in Hofstadter, *Great Issues in American History*, op. cit., p. 13.

4.   Esmund Wright, *Franklin of Philadelphia* (Cambridge: Harvard University Press, 1986); Paul Johnson, *A History of the American People* (New York: HarperCollins, 1997), pp. 134–137. Also, see Franklin's writings, such as *Idea of the English School* (1751), *The Way to Wealth* (1757), and *Autobiography* (1771).

5.   Gordon Wood, *The Creation of the American Republic, 1776–1787* (New York: Norton, 1969), pp. 114–118.

6.   Merrill Peterson, *Adams and Jefferson: A Revolutionary Dialogue* (New York: Oxford University Press, 1976), p. 5.

7.   David Hackett Fischer, *Paul Revere's Ride* (New York: Oxford University Press, 1994), p. xvii. Also, Hackett Fischer, *Albion's Seed* (New York: Oxford University Press, 1989); Barry Alan Shain, *The Myth of American Individualism: The Protestant Origins of American Political Thought* (Princeton: Princeton University Press, 1994).

8.   The observation was made by the English diplomat Sir Augustus John Foster, quoted in Edmund Morgan, *American Slavery, American Freedom: The Ordeal of Colonial Virginia* (New York: Norton, 1975), p. 380. Also, Winthrop Jordan, *White Over Black: American Attitudes Towards the Negro, 1550–1812* (New York: Norton, 1968).

9.   Quoted in Morison, *Oxford History of the American People*, op. cit., p. 271.

10. The most thorough examination of this ideology is offered in Bernard Bailyn, *The Ideological Origins of the American Revolution* (Cambridge: Harvard University Press, 1967).

11. Jefferson quoted in Peterson, *Adams and Jefferson*, op. cit., p. 7. Also, Noble Cunningham, *In Pursuit of Reason: The Life of Thomas Jefferson* (New York: Ballantine Books, 1987). Patrick Henry quoted in Johnson, *A History of the American People*, op. cit., p. 149.

12. J. Hector St. John de Crevecoeur, *Letters from an American Farmer and Sketches of Eighteenth-Century America* (New York: Penguin, 1981), pp. 90–91.

13. Thomas Paine, *Common Sense*. On Paine, see Eric Foner, *Tom Paine and Revolutionary America* (New York: Oxford University Press, 1976); Pauline Maier, *American Scripture: Making the Declaration of Independence* (New York: Knopf, 1997), pp. 31–35.

14. Maier, *American Scripture*, passim.

15. Kevin Philips, *The Cousins' Wars: Religion, Politics, and the Triumph of Anglo-America* (New York: Basic Books, 1999); Jack Rakove, *Beginning of National Politics: An Interpretive History of the Continental Congress* (Baltimore: Johns Hopkins University Press, 1979); Gordon Wood, *The Radicalism of the American Revolution* (New York: Knopf, 1991).

16. That is the thesis of Wood's *Radicalism of the America Revolution*, op. cit.

17. Richard Beeman et al., eds., *Beyond Confederation: Origins of the Constitution and American National Identity* (Chapel Hill: University of North Carolina Press, 1987). George Washington's letter to John Jay, August 1, 1786, reprinted in Hofstadter, *Great Issues*, op. cit., pp. 82–83.

18. Morison, *Oxford History of the American People*, op. cit., pp. 390ff; David Szatsmary, *Shays' Rebellion: The Making of an Agrarian Insurrection* (Amherst: University of Massachusetts Press, 1980).

Chapter Three

1. Thomas Paine, *Common Sense*, p. 3

2. For a heroic look at Hamilton's life, see Richard Brookhiser, *Alexander Hamilton: American* (New York: The Free Press, 1999).

3. The literature on the Constitution would take a lifetime to wade through. For a sampling, see Leonard Levy, *Original Intent and the Framers' Constitution* (New York: Macmillan, 1988); Jack Greene, *Peripheries and Center: Constitutional Development in the Extended Polities of the British Empire and the United States, 1607–1788* (New York: Norton, 1986); Jack Rakove, *Original Meanings: Politics and Ideas in the Making of the Constitution*

(New York: Knopf, 1996); Charles Beard, *An Economic Interpretation of the Constitution* (New York, 1913).

4. From Debates in the Ratifying Convention in Virginia, June 4 and 5, in Hofstadter, *Great Issues in American History*, op. cit., pp. 116–124. Also, William Wirt Henry, *Patrick Henry: Life, Correspondence, and Speeches* (New York: Charles Scribner's Sons, 1891), pp. 378–85.

5. *The Federalist Papers* (New York: New American Library, 1961). Also, on Madison, see Jack Rakove, *James Madison and the Creation of the American Republic* (Glenview, Illinois: Scott, Foresman, 1990).

6. Quoted in Rakove, *Original Meanings*, op. cit., p. 131.

7. Washington, "Farewell Address," in Hofstadter, *Great Issues*, op. cit., pp. 215–20. Also, J. R. Pole, *The Idea of Union* (Alexandria, VA: Bicentennial Council of the Thirteen Original States Fund, 1977), pp. 9–18; Joseph Charles, *The Origins of the American Party System* (New York: Harper & Row, 1956).

8. Bray Hammond, *Banks and Politics in America* (Princeton: Princeton University Press, 1957), p. 122; Drew McCoy, *The Elusive Republic: Political Economy in Jeffersonian America* (New York: Norton, 1980), pp. 185ff; David Mayer, *The Constitutional Thought of Thomas Jefferson* (Charlottesville: University Press of Virginia, 1994), pp. 200–20.

9. Marshall Smelser, *The Democratic Republic* (New York: Harper & Row, 1968).

10. Merrill Peterson, *The Great Triumvirate* (New York: Oxford University Press, 1987); Robert Remini, *Henry Clay: Statesman for the Union* (New York: Norton, 1991); Irving Bartlett, *Daniel Webster* (New York: Norton, 1978); Robert Remini, *Andrew Jackson and the Course of American Freedom* (New York: Harper & Row, 1981); David Potter, *The Impending Crisis* (New York: Harper Torchbooks, 1976), pp. 5–11; Jean Edward Smith, *John Marshall: Definer of a Nation* (New York: Henry Holt, 1996); George Dangerfield, *The Awakening of American Nationalism, 1815–1828* (New York: Harper Row, 1965).

11. Arthur Schlesinger, *The Age of Jackson* (Boston: Little Brown, 1945); Sean Wilentz, *Chants Democratic: New York City and the Rise of the American Working Class* (New York: Oxford Univer-

sity Press, 1984); Lee Benson, *The Concept of Jacksonian Democracy: New York As a Test Case* (Princeton: Princeton University Press, 1961).

12. Jackson, Proclamation to the People of South Carolina, December 10, 1832, in Hofstadter, *Great Issues*, op. cit., pp. 282–88. Also, William Freehling, *Prelude to Civil War: The Nullification Controversy in South Carolina, 1816–1836* (New York: Harper & Row, 1966).

13. Webster, Speech, in H. S. Commager, *Living Ideas in America* (New York: Harper & Row, 1964), pp. 283–85.

14. Michael Holt, *The Political Crisis of the 1850s* (New York: Norton, 1978); Eric Foner, *Free Soil, Free Labor, Free Men: The Ideology of the Republican Party Before the Civil War* (New York: Oxford University Press, 1970); William Gienapp, *The Origins of the Republican Party, 1852–1856* (New York: Oxford University Press, 1987); Ronald Walters, *The Antislavery Appeal: American Abolitionism After 1830* (Baltimore: Johns Hopkins University Press, 1978).

15. For Lincoln, see Carl Sandburg's multivolume biography, *Abraham Lincoln: The Prairie Years* (New York, Harcourt, Brace, and Company, 1926) and *Abraham Lincoln: The War Years* (New York, 1939); Stephen Oates, *With Malice Toward None: The Life of Abraham Lincoln* (New York: Harper & Row, 1977); David Herbert Donald, *Lincoln* (New York: Simon & Schuster, 1995); Gary Wills, *Lincoln at Gettysburg* (New York: Simon & Schuster, 1996); Priscilla Wald, *Constituting Americans: Cultural Anxiety and Narrative Form* (Durham, N.C.: Duke University Press, 1995) pp. 47–72.

16. Lincoln's Inaugural Address, March 4, 1861, in Hofstadter, *Great Issues*, op. cit, pp. 389–97.

CHAPTER FOUR

1. For the best account of the creation of a transcontinental railroad, see David Bain, *Empire Express* (New York: Viking, 2000); also, Albro Martin, *Railroads Triumphant: The Growth, Rejection and Rebirth of a Vital American Force* (New York: Oxford University Press, 1992).

2. Eric Foner, *Reconstruction: America's Unfinished Revolution* (New York: Harper & Row, 1988); Kenneth Stamp, *The Era of Reconstruction* (New York: Knopf, 1965).

3. Quoted in Albert Weinberg, *Manifest Destiny: A Study of Nationalist Expansion in American History* (Baltimore: Johns Hopkins University Press, 1935), p. 112. Also, see Frederick Merk, *Manifest Destiny and Mission in American History: A Reinterpretation* (New York: Knopf, 1963).

4. Dee Brown, *Bury My Heart at Wounded Knee: An Indian History of the American West* (New York: Simon & Schuster, 1981).

5. Roger Daniels, *Coming to America: A History of Immigration and Ethnicity in American Life* (New York: HarperCollins, 1990), pp. 212ff. Also, statistics in Paul Johnson, *History of the American People*, p. 514.

6. Statistics in Bailyn et al., *The Great Republic*, Vol. 2, op. cit, pp. 80–81.

7. Ron Chernow, *Titan: The Life of John D. Rockefeller* (New York: Random House, 1998); Daniel Yergin, *The Prize: The Epic Quest for Oil, Money, and Power* (New York: Simon & Schuster, 1991).

8. Alan Trachtenberg, *The Incorporation of America: Culture and Society in the Gilded Age* (New York: Hill & Wang, 1982); William Serrin, *Homestead: The Glory and Tragedy of an American Steel Town* (New York: Random House, 1992); Samuel Hays, *The Response to Industrialism: 1885–1914* (Chicago: University of Chicago Press, 1957); sections from Henry George, *Progress and Poverty* (1879) and Henry Demarest Lloyd, *Wealth Against Commonwealth* (1894) found in Richard Hofstadter and Beatrice Hofstadter, *Great Issues in American History, Volume III: from Reconstruction to the Present Day, 1864–1981* (New York: Vintage, 1982).

9. Printed in Richard Heffner, ed., *Documentary History of the United States* (New York: New American Library, 1952), pp. 154–65.

10. Jean Strouse, *Morgan: American Financier* (New York: Random House, 1999).

11. For a contrasting perspective, see Richard Hofstadter, "The Spoilsmen: The Age of Cynicism," in *The American Political Tradition and the Men Who Made It* (New York: Vintage, 1973), pp. 211–39.

12. Quoted in Weinberg, op. cit., p. 241.

13. "The March of the Flag," Speech of September 16, 1898, in Albert Beveridge, *The Meaning of the Times and Other Speeches* (Bobbs-Merrill Company, 1936).

14. Quoted in John Milton Cooper, *The Warrior and the Priest: Woodrow Wilson and Theodore Roosevelt* (Cambridge: Harvard University Press, 1983), p. 38. Also, see George Mowry, *The Era of Theodore Roosevelt and the Birth of Modern America, 1900–1912* (New York: Harper & Row, 1958); H. W. Brands, *TR: The Last Romantic* (New York: Basic Books, 1997); Ernest May, *American Imperialism: A Speculative Essay* (Chicago: Imprint Publications, 1991); Howard Beale, *Theodore Roosevelt and the Rise of America to World Power* (Baltimore: Johns Hopkins University Press, 1956).

15. "Platform of the American Anti-Imperialist League," in Hofstadter, ed. *Great Issues in American History,* Vol. III, pp. 194–96.

16. Richard Hofstadter, *The Age of Reform* (New York: Random House, 1955).

CHAPTER FIVE

1. Martin Van Buren, Message to Congress, September 4, 1837, in Henry Steel Commager, ed., *Living Ideas in America* (New York: Harper & Row, 1964), pp. 323–24.

2. Henry Demarest Lloyd, "Lords of Industry," *North American Review* (June 1884), pp. 550–51; Albert Bushnell Hart, *National Ideal Historically Traced, 1607–1907* (New York: Harper & Row, 1907), pp. 246–52.

3. Roosevelt, Message to Congress, December 3, 1901, in Henry Steele Commager, *Documents of American History* (New York: Appleton, Century, Crofts, 1973), p. 201.

4. Roosevelt's last Annual Message to Congress, December 8, 1908, in William Miller, *Readings in American Values* (Englewood, N.J.: Prentice Hall, 1964), pp. 295–98. Also see William Harbaugh, ed., *The Writings of Theodore Roosevelt* (New York: Bobbs-Merrill Company, 1967).

5. Lewis Gould, *The Progressive Era* (Syracuse: Syracuse University Press, 1973); John Morton Blum, *The Progressive Presidents:*

Roosevelt, Wilson, Roosevelt, Johnson (New York: Norton, 1980); Robert Wiebe, *The Search for Order, 1877–1920* (New York: Hill & Wang, 1967); Arthur Link and Richard McCormick, *Progressivism* (Arlington Heights, Ill.: Harlan Davidson, 1983).

6. Quoted in Cooper, *The Warrior and the Priest,* op. cit., pp. 193–195. Also, August Heckscher, *Woodrow Wilson: A Biography* (New York: Collier Books, 1991); Arthur Link, *Woodrow Wilson: Revolution, War, and Peace* (Arlington Heights, Ill.: Harlan Davidson, 1979).

7. David Kennedy, *Over Here: The First World War and American Society* (New York: Oxford University Press, 1980).

8. Hoover, Speech, October 22, 1928, in Hofstadter, *Great Issues,* op. cit., pp. 330–32; Peter Temin, *Lessons from the Great Depression* (Cambridge: MIT Press, 1989).

9. Frank Freidel, *Roosevelt: A Rendezvous with Destiny* (Boston: Little Brown, 1990); William Leuchtenberg, *The Perils of Prosperity, 1914–1932* (Chicago: University of Chicago Press, 1958).

10. Roosevelt, "Commonwealth Club Speech," September 23, 1932, in Hofstadter, *Great Issues,* op. cit., pp. 335–40.

11. William Leuchtenberg, *Franklin D. Roosevelt and the New Deal, 1932–1940* (New York: Harper & Row, 1963); Anthony Badger, *The New Deal: The Depression Years, 1933–1940* (New York: Hill & Wang, 1989); Ellis Hawley, *The New Deal and the Problem of Monopoly* (Princeton, N.J.: Princeton University Press, 1966).

12. Quotations come from Leuchtenberg, *Franklin Roosevelt,* op. cit., pp. 331–36; David Kennedy, *Freedom from Fear: The American People in War and Depression, 1929–1945* (New York: Oxford University Press, 1999), pp. 280–81 and passim.

13. Alan Brinkley, *The End of Reform: New Deal Liberalism in Recession and War* (New York: Knopf, 1995).

14. James T. Patterson, *Mr. Republican: A Biography of Robert A. Taft* (Boston: Houghton Mifflin, 1972); Gary Wills, *A Necessary Evil: A History of American Distrust of Government* (New York: Simon & Schuster, 1999); Harry Truman's State of the Union Message, January, 1949, in Commager, *Living Ideas in America,* pp. 357–60.

15. Johnson, Speech, May 22, 1964, in Bruce Schulman, *Lyndon B. Johnson and American Liberalism: A Brief Biography with Docu-*

ments (Boston: Bedford Books, 1995), pp. 174–76; Robert Dallek, *Flawed Giant: Lyndon Johnson and His Times, 1961–1973* (New York: Oxford University Press, 1997); Robert Caro, *The Years of Lyndon Johnson: The Path to Power* (New York: Knopf, 1982). Irving Bernstein, *Guns or Butter: The Presidency of Lyndon Johnson* (New York: Oxford University Press, 1996). Also, Richard Goodwin, "The Shape of American Politics," *Commentary* (June 1967).

16. Quoted in Michael Sandel, *Democracy's Discontent: America in Search of a Public Philosophy* (Cambridge: Harvard University Press, 1996), p. 283.

17. Todd Gitlin, *The Sixties: Years of Hope, Days of Rage* (New York: Bantam Books, 1987); Doris Kearns Goodwin, *Lyndon Johnson and the American Dream* (New York: St. Martin's Press, 1976); Godfrey Hodgson, *America in Our Time: From World War II to Nixon, What Happened and Why* (New York: Random House, 1976).

18. Joseph Nye, Philip Zelikow, and David King, *Why Americans Don't Trust Government* (Cambridge: Harvard University Press, 1997); David Frum, *How We Got Here: The '70s* (New York: Basic Books, 2000); Theodore White, *Breach of Faith: The Fall of Richard Nixon* (New York: Dell, 1975).

19. Garry Wills, *A Necessary Evil*, op. cit.

20. William Martin, *With God on Our Side: The Rise of the Religious Right in America* (New York: Broadway Books, 1996), pp. 174–87. Reagan, Remarks, October 28, 1980, in Hofstadter, *Great Issues*, op. cit., pp. 526–30. Also, Lou Cannon, *President Reagan: The Role of a Lifetime* (New York: Public Affairs, 2000); Edmund Morris, *Dutch: A Memoir of Ronald Reagan* (New York: Random House, 1999); Matthew Dallek, *The Right Moment* (New York: Norton, 2000).

21. Haynes Johnson and David Broder, *The System: The American Way of Politics at the Breaking Point* (Boston: Little Brown, 1996); Elizabeth Drew, *On the Edge: The Clinton Presidency* (New York: Simon & Schuster, 1994).

22. Jonathan Rauch, *Government's End: Why Washington Stopped Working* (New York: Public Affairs, 2000); Thomas Geoghegan, *The Secret Lives of Citizens: Pursuing the Promise of American*

Life (New York: Pantheon, 1999); John Judis, *The Paradox of American Democracy* (New York: Pantheon, 2000).

CHAPTER SIX

1. Clinton, State of the Union Address, *The New York Times* (January 28, 2000).

2. M. Corey Goldman, "Brave new economy," CNNfn.com (May 22, 2000).

3. Robert Frank, *Luxury Fever: Why Money Fails to Satisfy in an Age of Excess* (New York: The Free Press, 1999), pp. 34–38; "The Boom," *Business Week* (February 14, 2000); also see statistics compiled by the Center on Budget and Policy Priorities at www.cbpp.org.

4. For statistics, see "The Vanishing Voter," a project of the Joan Shorenstein Center on the Press, Politics, and Public Policy at the Kennedy School of Government, Harvard University, www.vanishingvoter.org.

5. Jeffrey Madrick, *The End of Affluence: The Causes and Consequences of America's Economic Dilemma* (New York: Random House, 1995); Ruy Teixara and Joel Rogers, *The White Working Class and the Future of Government* (New York: Basic Books, 2000); Theda Skocpol, *The Missing Middle: Working Families and the Future of American Social Policy* (New York: Norton, 2000); Barbara Ehrenreich, "Nickel and Dimed," *Harper's Magazine* (January 1999).

6. Edward Chancellor, *Devil Take the Hindmost: A History of Financial Speculation* (New York: Farrar, Straus and Giroux, 1999), pp. 217–25, 345–47; John Kenneth Galbraith, *American Capitalism: The Concept of Countervailing Power* (Boston: Houghton Mifflin, 1952) and *The Affluent Society* (Boston: Houghton Mifflin, 1958); Alfred Chandler, *Scale and Scope: The Dynamics of Industrial Capitalism* (Cambridge: The Belknap Press, 1990).

7. Friedrich Hayek, *The Road to Serfdom* (Chicago: University of Chicago Press, 1994); Henry Hazlitt, *Economics in One Lesson* (New York: Harper, 1946) and *The Failure of the "New Economics"* (Princeton: Van Nostrand, 1959); Milton Friedman, *Capi-*

talism and Freedom (Chicago: University of Chicago Press, 1963).

8. Peter Drucker, *The Age of Discontinuity* (New York: Harper & Row, 1969) and "New Economists: The Cambridge Tendency," *The Economist* (December 24, 1988).

9. Gordon Wood, "Was America Born Capitalist?" *The Wilson Quarterly* (Spring 1999); David Potter, *People of Plenty: Economic Abundance and the American Character* (Chicago: University of Chicago Press, 1957).

10. Taken from a brochure on Electronic Commerce Risk Management. See www.arthurandersen.com.

11. *The New York Times* (April 16, 2000).

12. David Brooks, *Bobos in Paradise: The New Upper Class and How They Got There* (New York: Simon & Schuster, 2000); Daniel Gross, *Bull Run: Wall Street, the Democrats, and the New Politics of Personal Finance* (New York: Public Affairs, 2000).

13. Lendol Calder, *Financing the American Dream: A Cultural History of Consumer Credit* (Princeton, N.J.: Princeton University Press, 1999); Tom Frank, *The Conquest of Cool* (Chicago: University of Chicago Press, 1997).

14. www.winnsborotx.com/116.htm.

15. Robert Samuelson, *The Good Life and Its Discontents: The American Dream in the Age of Entitlement* (New York: Times Books, 1995), pp. 4, 67–69.

16. Benedict Anderson, *Imagined Communities* (London: Verso, 1983).

17. "Bank Reform . . . Finally on the Right Road," *The Economist* (November 1999); Greg McDonald, "Bank Industry Faces Dramatic Changes," *Houston Chronicle* (November 5, 1999); Stephen Labaton, "Congress Passes Wide-Ranging Bill Easing Bank Laws," *The New York Times* (November 5, 1999).

18. For example, David Sanger, "The Personality Cults of Impersonal Economics," *The New York Times* (May 16, 1999). Daniel Gross, in *Bull Run*, shows how "New Democrats" like Rubin came to have a controlling voice in the Clinton administration.

19. Frank Bruni, "The Republicans Debate," *The New York Times* (December 3, 1999); John Flanigan, "Saved by Greenspan's Exuberant Money Policy," *The Los Angeles Times* (January 24, 1999);

"Almighty Alan Greenspan," *The Economist* (January 11, 2000).

20. John Cassidy, "The Fountainhead," *The New Yorker* (April 24/ May 1, 2000); Richard Stevenson, "Inside the Head of the Fed," *The New York Times* (November 15, 1998); David Sicilia and Jeffrey Cruikshank, *The Greenspan Effect: Words That Move the World's Markets* (New York: McGraw-Hill, 2000); Justin Martin, *Greenspan: The Man Behind the Money* (New York: Perseus Books: 2000).

21. See, for example, Michael Wolff, *Burn Rate: How I Survived the Gold Rush Years on the Internet* (New York: Simon & Schuster, 1998), as well as his columns in *New York* magazine. Both he and James Cramer, who helped create TheStreet.com and also writes for *New York* magazine, are part of the journalistic-Wall Street-New Economy nexus. Also, for an academic who shapes this world, see Lester Thurow, *Building Wealth* (New York: HarperCollins, 1999), and Thomas Friedman, *The Lexus and the Olive Tree* (New York: Farrar, Straus & Giroux, 1999).

22. Charles Morris, *Money, Greed, and Risk: Why Financial Crises and Crashes Happen* (New York: Times Books, 1999); John Cassidy, "The Productivity Mirage," *The New Yorker* (November 27, 2000).

23. This debate can be found everywhere. See Robert Schiller, *Irrational Exuberance* (Princeton: Princeton University Press, 2000); Raveendra Batra, *The Crash of the Millennium: Surviving the Coming Inflationary Depression* (New York: Harmony Books, 1999); Donald Cassidy, *When the Dow Breaks* (New York: McGraw-Hill, 1999); "Reactions to Stock Carnage: The Bubble Has Burst," *Salon.com* (April 14, 2000); Thomas Bass, "Black Box," *The New Yorker* (April 26, 1999); Jeff Madrick, "How New Is the New Economy?," *The New York Review of Books* (September 23, 1999); Alan Murray, "The Economy Is New: Human Nature Isn't," *The Wall Street Journal* (July 24, 1999); Chip Bayers, "Think Beyond Commerce," *Wired* (March 2000); James Cramer, "Look Out Below," *New York* magazine. (December 4, 2000); Miguel Helft, "Economic Engine Trouble," *The Industry Standard* (December 4, 2000).

24. Robert Samuelson, "What Greenspan Doesn't Know," *Newsweek* (May 1, 2000).

25. Ramesh Ponnuru, "Taking on the Biggest," *National Review* (June 5, 2000).

26. See www.edisonschools.com for information. Milton Friedman, "Public Schools: Make Them Private," *The Washington Post* (February 19, 1995).

27. Jacques Steinberg and Edward Wyatt, "Boola, Boola," *The New York Times* (February 13, 2000).

28. "Special Report: Market-Driven Higher Education," a conference sponsored by *University Business Magazine* (October 7, 1999); James Traub, "The Campus Is Being Simulated," *The New York Times Magazine* (November 19, 2000).

29. Barry Yeoman, "Steel Town," *Mother Jones* (May/June 2000).

30. "Charting the Pain Behind the Gain," *The Wall Street Journal* (October 1, 1999); Bruce Ackerman and Anne Alstott, *The Stakeholder Society* (New Haven: Yale University Press, 1999); Statistics from the U.S. Census Bureau at www.census.gov.

31. Louis Uchitelle, "The American Middle, Just Getting By," *The New York Times* (August 1, 1999); Arlie Hochschild, *The Time Bind* (New York: Henry Holt, 1997); Robert Frank, *Luxury Fever: Why Money Fails to Satisfy in an Age of Excess* (New York: The Free Press, 1999); Katherine Newman, *Falling from Grace: The Experience of Downward Mobility in the American Middle Class* (New York: The Free Press, 1988); Barbara Ehrenreich, *Fear of Falling: The Inner Life of the Middle Class* (New York: Harper Perennial, 1989); Christopher Lasch, *The Culture of Narcissism: American Life in an Age of Diminishing Expectations* (New York: Norton, 1979).

32. Robert Reich, "The Bankers' Regime," *American Prospect* (November/December 1998).

33. See Thomas Frank, *One Market Under God: Extreme Capitalism, Market Populism, and the End of Economic Democracy* (New York: Doubleday, 2000).

34. Andrew Kohut, "Globalization and the Wage Gap," *The New York Times* (December 3, 1999); David Samuels, "Letter from Eugene: Notes from Underground," *Harper's Magazine* (November 1999); John R. MacArthur, *The Selling of Free Trade: NAFTA, Washington, and the Subversion of American Democracy* (New York: Hill & Wang, 2000).

35. William Finnegan, "After Seattle," *The New Yorker* (April 17, 2000).

Chapter Seven

1. John Hagel and Marc Singer, *New Worth: Shaping Markets When Customers Make the Rules* (Cambridge: Harvard Business School Press, 1999), p. xii.

2. Rick Levine et al., *The Cluetrain Manifesto: The End of Business as Usual* (Cambridge: Perseus Books, 2000); Philip Evans and Thomas Wurster, *Blown to Bits: How the New Economics of Information Transforms Strategy* (Cambridge: Harvard Business School Press, 2000); Jeremy Rifkin, *The Age of Access: The New Culture of Hypercapitalism Where All of Life Is a Paid-for Experience* (New York: Tarcher-Putnam, 2000).

3. Susan Greco, "Get $$$ Now.com," *Inc.* (September 1999); Charles Piller, "The Cutting Edge," *The Los Angeles Times* (January 24, 2000).

4. Quoted in Guy Kawasaki, *Rules for Revolutionaries: The Capitalist Manifesto for Creating and Marketing New Products and Services* (New York: HarperBusiness, 1999).

5. Scott McNealy, "Online Revolution Already Is upon Us," *San Diego Union-Tribune* (January 27, 1999).

6. Paul Andrews, *How the Web Was Won: Microsoft from Windows to the Web* (New York: Broadway Books, 1999), p. 85.

7. Bill Gates, *The Road Ahead* (New York: Viking, 1995); John Wallace and Jim Erickson, *Hard Drive: Bill Gates and the Making of the Microsoft Empire* (New York: HarperBusiness, 1992); Robert Cringely, *Accidental Empires: How the Boys of Silicon Valley Make Their Millions, Battle Foreign Competition, and Still Can't Get a Date* (New York: HarperBusiness, 1996); Gary Rivlin, *The Plot to Get Bill Gates* (New York: Times Books, 1999).

8. Jim Carlton, *Apple: The Inside Story of Intrigue, Egomania, and Business Blunders* (New York: HarperBusiness, 1998); David Kaplan, *The Silicon Boys* (New York: Morrow, 1999).

9. Kara Swisher, *aol.com* (New York: Times Business, 1999); Nicholas Negroponte, *Being Digital* (New York: Knopf, 1995); Michael Lewis, *The New New Thing* (New York: Norton, 1999); Kevin Kelly, *New Rules for the New Economy* (New York: Penguin, 1999); Alan Deutschman, "The Sand Hill Road Gang," *GQ* (June 1999); Michael Wolff, "The E-Decade," *New York*

(December 15, 1999); Michael Dell, *Direct from Dell* (New York: HarperBusiness, 1999); Joshua Quittner, "An Eye on the Future," *Time* (December 27, 1999); Steven Levy, "The New Digital Galaxy," *Newsweek* (May 31, 1999); Adam Sachs, "The e-Billionaire Nobody Knows," *GQ* (May 2000).

10. "Silicon Envy," *The Economist* (February 20, 1999); "Cult of Personality Rules High-Tech PR," *O'Dwyer PR Services Report* (November 1997); Warren Burger, "Hot Spots," *Wired* (February 2000).

11. For instance, see Robert Schiller, *Irrational Exuberance* (Princeton: Princeton University Press, 2000); Scott Kirsner, "Reboot: Charles Schwab & Company," *Wired* (November 1999); Steve Lohr, "Technology Sell-Off May Bring Shakeout of Dot-Com Concerns," *The New York Times* (April 17, 2000); Michael Wolff, "Dot-Com Bomb," *New York* (May 1, 2000).

12. For instance, Jerry Kaplan, *Startup: A Silicon Valley Adventure* (New York: Penguin Books, 1994); Charles Ferguson, *High Stakes, No Prisoners* (New York: Times Business, 1999); Po Bronson, *Nudist on the Late Shift* (New York: Random House, 1999).

13. The quotation comes from Richard Stallman, in Robert Young, *Under the Radar: How Red Hat Changed the Software Business and Took Microsoft by Surprise* (Scottsdale, AZ: The Coriolis Group, 1999), pp. 108–109.

14. Andrew Shapiro, *The Control Revolution* (New York: Public Affairs, 1999); Francis Fukuyama, *The Great Disruption* (New York: The Free Press, 1999).

15. *The Industry Standard* (June 12, 2000).

16. Damien Cave, "Killjoy," *Salon.com* (April 10, 2000).

17. Ricardo Pimentel, "Internet Defies Defining," *The Arizona Republic* (May 16, 2000); Malcolm Gladwell, "Clicks and Mortar," *The New Yorker* (December 6, 1999).

18. Steven Jones, ed., *Virtual Culture: Identity and Communication in Cybersociety* (New York: Sage Publications, 1997); David Porter, ed., *Internet Culture* (New York: Routledge, 1997); Sherry Turkle, *Life on the Screen: Identity in the Age of the Internet* (New York: Simon & Schuster, 1997); Mark Slouka, *War of the Worlds* (New York: Basic Books, 1995); Rob Kitchen, *The*

World in the Wires (New York: John Wiley, 1998); Stacy Horn, *Cyberville: Clocks, Culture, and the Creation of the Online Town* (New York: Warner Books, 1998).

19. Lawrence Lessig, *Code and Other Laws of Cyberspace* (New York: Basic Books, 1999), pp. 62ff.

20. Susan Fisher, "Creating the Online Town," *Upside* (January 2000).

CHAPTER EIGHT

1. Quoted in Dinty Moore, *The Emperor's Virtual Clothes: The Naked Truth About the Internet Culture* (New York: Algonquin Books, 1995), pp. 61–62.

2. Robert Putnam, *Bowling Alone: The Collapse and Revival of American Community* (New York: Simon & Schuster, 2000). Also see Francis Fukuyama, *Trust: The Social Virtues and the Creation of Prosperity* (New York: The Free Press, 1995); Michael Sandel, *Democracy's Discontent: America in Search of a Public Philosophy* (Cambridge: Harvard University Press, 1996); Amitai Etzioni, *The New Golden Rule: Community and Morality in a Democratic Society* (New York: Basic Books, 1996); Richard Sennett, *The Corrosion of Character: The Personal Consequences of Work in the New Capitalism* (New York: Norton, 1999); Robert Wuthnow, *Sharing the Journey: Support Groups and Americans' New Quest for Community* (New York: The Free Press, 1994); Benjamin Barber, *Jihad vs. McWorld: How the Planet Is Both Falling Apart and Coming Together and What This Means for Democracy* (New York: Times Books, 1995).

3. See the special issue of *The New York Times Magazine* (May 7, 2000). Also, Alan Wolfe, *One Nation, After All* (New York: Viking, 1998).

4. Sophia Glezos, "Social Relationships, Connectedness, and Health," a summary of a presentation by Professor Lisa Berkman, May 22, 1997 (National Institutes of Health. www.ol.nih.go/obssr/social.htm.)

5. Robert Lane, *The Loss of Happiness in Market Democracies* (New Haven: Yale University Press, 2000); also, David Myers, *The American Paradox: Spiritual Hunger in an Age of Plenty* (New Haven: Yale University Press, 2000).

6. Michelle Conlin, "The Growing Presence of Spirituality in Corporate America," *BusinessWeek* (November 1, 1999). Also, special issue, "21 Ideas for the 21st Century," *BusinessWeek* (August 23, 1999); Dinesh D'Souza, *The Virtue of Prosperity: Finding Values in an Age of Techo-Affluence* (New York: The Free Press, 2000).

7. www.innerself.com. Steve Varelmann's comments at: members.aol.com/svarelmann/homepage.

8. www.newdream.org. also, Juliet Schor, *The Overspent American: Upscaling, Downshifting, and the New Consumer* (New York: Basic Books, 1998); Frank Levering and Wanda Urbanska, *Simple Living: One Couple's Search for a Better Life* (New York: Penguin, 1992).

9. Erik Davis, *Techgnosis: Myth, Magic, and Mysticism in the Age of Information* (New York: Harmony Books, 1998).

INDEX

Adams, John, 34, 35–36, 39, 40, 45, 53
Adams, Samuel, 35, 38
Amazon.com, 139, 158, 161, 171, 173, 175
America Online (AOL), 173, 175, 185, 187–88
American culture, 8, 9, 14
  changes in, 103, 105–6, 195
  dynamism of, 198, 210–11
  fragmented, 135
  influence of frontier on, 78
  Internet in, 157, 161, 166
  producers of, 132–33, 152
  Progressivism in, 87
  self-determination in, 35
  stage one, 13–30, 69, 178
  stage two, 24, 29, 31–47, 69, 178
  stage three, 48–66, 68, 69, 180
  stage four, 69–83, 181, 182
  stage five, 84–116, 131, 183, 198
  stage six, 119–57, 122, 125–27, 131–42, 151–52, 198–99
  stage six: encompasses previous stages, 177–84
  stage six: erosion of, 196–97
  stage six: future of, 165, 184–89
  stage six: opponents of, 152–57
  stage six: origins of, 128–31
  stage six: rejection of, 207
  stage six: replacement of, 197–200
  stage six: successor to, 200–207
  stage seven, 158–89, 194–97, 207–11, 212–13
  stages of, 5–7, 92–93, 114–15, 116, 177–84, 189, 198, 211–15
  utopian yearning of, 177
  Washington-centric, 99, 109
American identity, 31, 51–52, 57–58, 62, 178
American Revolution, 6, 31, 45, 47, 48, 49, 127, 184, 214
  anarchic quality to, 43
  compared to present, 131
  individualism of, 46
Amish, 22
Andreesen, Marc, 179
Anglicans, 14, 15, 16, 23
Anti-Federalists, 49, 50, 98, 107
Anti-Imperialist League, 81, 83
Antinomianism/Antinomians, 21, 22, 27, 29, 30, 45, 156
Apple (co.), 139, 160, 167, 168, 169, 170–71, 194
Articles of Confederation, 43, 46, 47, 49
Asimov, Isaac, 182
Ask Jeeves, 1–3, 4, 134, 158, 163–64
Augustine of Hippo, Saint, 18

Bank of the United States, 58
Banks/banking, 58, 84, 90, 93, 95, 108, 135–36
Bartiromo, Maria, 139
Bellamy, Edward, 75
Bentsen, Lloyd, 136
Berkman, Lisa, 202

Bessemer, Sir Henry, 74
Beveridge, Albert, 79
Bezos, Jeff, 139, 171
Bill of Rights, 31, 102
Birnbaum, David, 3
Booth, John Wilkes, 65–66
Borah, William, 91
Boston, 16, 23, 30, 32, 35
Bradford, William, 16
Branch Davidians, 115
British Empire, 33, 34, 38, 39
Bryan, William Jennings, 77, 90, 183
Buchanan, James, 62
Buchanan, Pat, 137, 152–53
Buckley, William, 130, 185
Burr, Aaron, 54
Bush, George, 110, 111
Bush, George W., 125
business, 88, 96
    and government, 85, 86, 90, 91, 97
    and Internet, 158–59, 160

Cahill, Tim, 181
Calhoun, John C., 57, 59, 61
Calvert, Cecilius, 21
Calvin, John, 24
capitalism, 76–77, 129, 131, 134, 140
captains of industry, 73, 76, 86
Carnegie, Andrew, 74–76, 77, 81, 82, 85,
    126, 140
Carter, Jimmy, 106, 108
Case, Steve, 173, 187
Cavuto, Neil, 139
"Celebration" (town), 204
Center for a New American Dream, 206–7
Central Intelligence Agency, 98
Chambers, John, 172
Charles I, 16, 20, 33
Chicago, 70, 72, 73
Christian conservatives, 108, 114, 153
cities, 72–73, 82, 93, 182
Citigroup, 136
City of God (Augustine of Hippo), 18
City on a Hill, 9, 22, 27, 69, 79, 116, 123,
    137, 160, 197, 213
    commonwealth of law, 30
    Puritan vision of, 6, 18, 19, 24, 29
    society approximating, 88

Civil Rights Act of 1964, 102
Civil War, 6, 60–66, 67, 68, 70, 91, 180,
    184
Clark, Jim, 139, 172
Clay, Henry, 57, 58, 60, 61, 62, 95
Clayton Antitrust Act, 90
Clinton, Hillary, 203
Clinton, William Jefferson, 6, 111, 112,
    113–15, 122–23, 135, 136–37,
    143–44
Coercive Acts, 38
Cohen, Abby Joseph, 141
Cold War, 98, 130–31, 134, 136, 153, 180,
    194
colleges and universities, 29, 145–48
colonies/colonists, 30, 33–34, 36, 40, 43
    governance of, 41
    tension with England, 35, 38
    rights of, 39
    visions of, 36
Common Sense (Paine), 40–41
Communism, 98, 103, 107, 130–31, 153
community, 3, 7, 106, 198, 200, 203, 208,
    209, 214
    Internet and, 185–89, 200
Compromise of 1850, 61, 62
computer, 3–4, 127, 140, 165, 170, 177,
    198–99
    see also personal computer (PC)
computer industry, 166–71
Confederacy, 64, 65, 66
Congress, 47, 52, 86, 90, 91, 95, 99, 101,
    109, 110, 111, 135, 138
connectedness, 7, 193–215
Constitution, 6, 49–51, 59, 88, 89
    framers of, 46, 48, 156
    interstate commerce clause, 87
    ratification of, 49–50, 51
    and role of government, 86
Constitutional Convention, 46–47, 49
Continental Congress, 38, 43, 44, 45, 46
Coolidge, Calvin, 92
Cotton, John, 23, 24, 25, 26
covenant, 19, 23, 24, 30, 36
covenant of works, 25–26
Cramer, James, 139, 173
Crevecoeur, J. Hector St. John, 40
Cromwell, Oliver, 21

Crucible, The (Miller), 18
cyberspace, 165, 179, 185, 187–88

Davis, Jefferson, 64
Debs, Eugene V., 89
Declaration of Independence, 31, 38,
    41–42, 43, 60–61, 62, 116, 134, 159
Dell, Michael, 173
Dell Computers, 173, 175
democracy, 43, 46, 49, 183
    excesses of, 44, 45, 48
Democratic Party/Democrats, 60, 62, 90,
    115, 183
Department of Defense, 98, 113, 166
Department of Labor, 96
Dewey, George, 80
Dillehay, James, 206
disillusionment, 5, 7, 83
    and change of vision, 21, 198
    in government, 103, 104, 106, 108
    in Puritan vision, 27
    in Revolutionary vision, 45–47
    with sixth stage, 185, 189, 197, 201–2,
        207, 208
Doerr, John, 173
Dominion of New England, 32
Douglas, Stephen, 61, 62, 63
downshifting, 205–6, 207
Drucker, Peter, 130
Dukakis, Michael, 110
Dyson, Esther, 172

economic crises, 44, 82, 87, 93
economic expansion/growth, 69, 73,
    75–77, 79, 81, 85, 93, 124–25, 126,
    174–75, 198
    government and, 104
    New Economy, 140–42
economic policy, 56, 136–37, 155
economy, 70, 84, 92, 97, 105, 142, 189,
    195, 196
    in American culture, 125
    government and, 71, 98, 128–29, 130
Edison Schools, 145
education, 144–48
Edwards, Jonathan, 28–29
Ehrlichman, John, 105
Eisenhower, Dwight, 99

Ellison, Larry, 139, 163, 172, 181
Employment Act of 1946, 98, 99
English Constitution, 40
English law and religion, common legacy
    of, 34, 36, 38
Equal Rights Amendment, 102
European Union, 143, 153, 163
expansion, 67–83, 87, 116, 181, 182, 183,
    197, 211, 214

federal government, 6, 46, 49, 59, 64, 82
    and economy, 71, 79, 128–29
    and education, 145–46
    epitomized by those involved in
        economic issues, 136–39
    powers of, 50, 51, 52, 54, 56, 90–92, 95,
        98
    primacy of, 66
    role of, 77–78, 86–88, 90, 91, 96, 97, 98,
        99, 108, 109, 111, 113, 114, 115–16
Federal Reserve Act of 1913, 90
Federal Reserve Board, 128–29, 136,
    137–38, 152
Federalist letters, 50–51
Federalists, 45–46, 47, 49, 50–51, 54
    clash with Republicans, 53, 54, 55–56
Filo, David, 172, 181
financial system, 76–77, 88, 90, 93
Ford, Gerald, 107
Forster, E. M., 198
Founding Fathers, 6, 35, 42, 88, 135, 143,
    197–98, 207
Franklin, Benjamin, 34–35
free market, 109, 110, 130–31, 135–36,
    138–39, 143
    see also market (the)
free trade, 130, 137, 153–54, 155
freedom, 6, 31, 32, 37, 38, 39, 40, 41, 79
    individual, 29, 56, 69
Frick, Henry Clay, 75, 77
Friedman, Milton, 129, 130, 131, 145,
    185
Friedman, Thomas, 139, 155
frontier, 45, 69, 78

Galbraith, John Kenneth, 128
Galt, Edith Bolling, 91
Garrison, William Lloyd, 60–61

Gates, Bill, 155, 167–68, 169, 171, 179, 181, 206
George, Henry, 75
George III, 30, 33, 38, 39–41
Gerstner, Lou, 139
Gibson, William, 165
Gilbert, Sir Humphrey, 13
Gilded Age, 73, 74, 76, 77, 79, 85, 86, 87, 92, 152, 169
    businesses during, 134
    visionaries, 140
Gilder, George, 172–73
Gingrich, Newt, 107, 112
Gladwell, Malcolm, 184
Glass-Steagall Act, 95, 135–36
globalization, 153, 154, 155, 156
Godkin, E. L., 75
Goldwater, Barry, 107
Gore, Al, 125, 135, 183
Gospel of Wealth, 76, 81, 85, 104, 126, 159, 198
government, 6, 7, 8, 84–116, 152, 211
    activist, 102–3, 111
    age of, 85, 95, 101
    aid, assistance from, 85, 93–94, 99, 103
    apex of, 93–103
    by elite, 49, 53
    fear of, 59, 98
    as instrument to fulfill American dream, 95, 98
    language of, 135–36
    market vision in, 136–39
    opponents of, 104, 106, 108, 109, 110, 112–13
    reaction to, 128–31
    recession of, 92
    rise of, 85, 86–93
    size and scope of, 98, 102, 104, 109–10, 131
    Web and, 183
    see also federal government
government agencies, 91, 95–96, 98
government era/paradigm, 6, 85, 103, 125, 140, 168, 198
    assault on, 108–9
    end of, 104–16, 197
government programs, 102, 105, 106, 112–13, 115

government regulation, 73, 82–83, 85, 86, 87, 90, 102, 104, 115, 168
    economic, 71, 128–29
Grant, Ulysses S., 69
Great Awakening, 27–28, 29, 30, 32, 34, 40
Great Britain, 39, 55
Great Depression, 84–85, 93, 95, 97, 128, 135, 136
Great Migration, 18–19
Great Society, 6, 8, 85, 100–102, 103, 105, 106, 107, 110, 111, 116, 123, 129, 134, 153, 156, 184
"Great Triumvirate, The," 57, 61, 135
Greenspan, Alan, 137–39, 140, 141, 152
Gross, Bill, 181
Gross National Product (GNP), 174
Grove, Andy, 169

Haldeman, H. R., 105
Hamilton, Alexander, 49, 50–51, 53, 54, 56, 64
Harding, Warren, 94
Harlem Renaissance, 93
Hartford Convention, 55–56
Hayek, Friedrich, 129
Hazlitt, Henry, 129
Hearst, William Randolph, 80
Heinlein, Robert, 193
Henry, Patrick, 33, 38, 39, 45–46, 50
Hewlett-Packard (HP), 167
Homestead, 74, 75, 77, 78
Hoover, Herbert, 92, 93, 94, 96
Howells, William Dean, 75
Huntington, Samuel, 51
Hutchinson, Anne, 22, 24–27, 28, 156, 185, 210, 213
Hutchinson, Thomas, 24, 25

imperialism, 69, 78–79, 81
incarceration, 149–50
independence, 34, 36, 37, 38–39, 40, 41–42, 143
individualism, 6, 31–47, 48, 49, 79, 93, 99, 115–16, 143, 185, 213
    government and, 104
    in popular culture, 56
    of Puritans, 20

rhetoric of, 96
of sixth stage, 178–82
in West, 58
Industry Standard, The, 161, 175, 181
inequities, 66, 75, 126, 137, 196, 214
information, 127, 135, 184, 199
  in education, 147–48
  Internet and, 158–59, 161–62
  in market ideal, 123
  Perfect, 1–2, 4, 134
Information Age, 147, 158, 183, 189, 195,
  208
Information Revolution, 123
International Monetary Fund, 152, 154
Internet, 1, 3, 4, 5, 7, 122, 125, 126, 133,
  134, 141, 151, 156, 157, 158–89, 195,
  197, 214
  access to, 166
  and community, 185–89, 198
  and connectedness, 200
  in future, 184, 185
  and government, 183
  and happiness, 202–3
  in higher education, 146
  individualism of, 179
  religion on, 178
  speculation about implications of,
    163–65
  vision of, 124
  Wild West analogy, 181
Internet companies, 165, 171, 175
Iran-Contra, 110

Jackson, Andrew, 56, 57–58, 59
Jacksonian era, 52, 57–58, 64
Jamestown, Virginia, 14–15
Jay, John, 45, 50–51, 53
Jazz Age, 93, 96
Jefferson, Thomas, 24, 34, 39, 47, 53, 64,
  68, 95, 99, 140
  and Constitution, 50
  and Declaration of Independence, 42
  owned slaves, 37, 169
  president, 53–55
Jobs, Steve, 139, 167, 169–71, 182, 194
Johnson, Andrew, 69, 114
Johnson, Lyndon, 100–101, 104, 105, 107,
  116

Joy, Bill, 182
Jungle, The (Sinclair), 83

Kelly, Kevin, 172
Kennedy, John F., 99–100, 101, 140
Keynes, John Maynard, 128, 129
Keynesian economics, 128–29
Kissinger, Henry, 136, 137
Krugman, Paul, 130

LaHaye, Timothy, 108, 204, 207
Lamont, Thomas, 136
Lane, Robert, 202, 203
Laud, William, 16, 18, 24
law (the)/laws, 30, 41, 42, 91, 95, 96, 102
League of Nations, 91–92
Lee, Robert E., 66
Lewis, Michael, 172
liberty, 6, 24, 29, 31, 32, 37, 41, 48, 79, 85,
  131
  conceptions of, 38–39
  in Declaration of Independence, 42
  government threat to, 104, 115
  language of, 69
  society oriented around, 36
Liddy, G. Gordon, 105
Lincoln, Abraham, 62–66, 68, 91, 180
Lloyd, Henry Demarest, 75, 85
Lodge, Henry Cabot, 91
Louisiana Purchase, 55

McCain, John, 138
McKinley, William, 78, 80, 86
McNealy, Scott, 139, 163, 168, 181
Madison, James, 37, 45, 50–51, 53, 55
Manchester School, 128
Manifest Destiny, 60, 69, 78
market (the), 7, 116, 128, 179–80, 197
  and happiness, 202–3
  information and, 159, 160
  Internet and, 165
  as utopian paradigm, 128–31
market ideal, 122–31, 140, 201–2
  individualism in, 178
market vision, 115, 119–57, 213
  reach of, 142–50
  Reagan bridge to, 109
  those left out of, 150–57

Marshall, John, 58
Marshner, Connie, 108
Mason, George, 50
Massachusetts Bay colony, 16, 18, 20, 22,
    23, 24, 30, 69, 114, 123, 156, 210
  church membership in, 25
  as noble experiment, 18
media, 140, 154–55
Mellon, Andrew, 136
Mexico, 60, 70, 137
Microsoft, 158, 167, 168–69, 172, 175, 179
Milken, Michael, 176
Millennial Church of Believers, 22
Miller, Arthur, 18
Money magazine, 160
More, Sir Thomas, 13
Morgan, J. P., 76, 77, 81, 87, 140
Morris, Gouverneur, 45

Nader, Ralph, 153, 156
Napoleonic Wars, 55
Nasdaq, 124, 125, 132, 141
Nasser, Jacques, 139
Native Americans, 14, 23, 27, 57, 67, 71,
    72, 80, 81
needs, material/non-material, 4, 142–43,
    197
needs satisfaction
  in New Economy, 197–200, 207–8
  in seventh stage, 208–9, 212–13
Negroponte, Nicholas, 172
New Age, 7, 204, 206, 209, 210, 213
New Deal, 6, 93–98, 99, 100, 101, 103,
    104, 106, 107, 111, 116, 127, 128,
    129, 156, 214
  repeal of laws of, 135–36
New Democrat, 111
New Economy, 2–3, 4, 5, 6, 7, 115,
    122–24, 126–27, 131, 132–33, 137,
    138, 146, 173, 201, 211, 213, 214
  community in, 186–89
  creators of technology of, 165–77
  creed of, 134
  debate about, 141–42
  differing views of, 180–83, 188–89
  dissatisfaction with, 156, 208
  fading, 184, 185
  and free trade, 153

future of, 195–97
  and government, 183
  high-tech companies driving, 174,
    175
  as idea/as reality, 155
  individualism in, 178–79
  inequalities in, 137
  information in, 147–48
  Internet in, 158, 160, 164–65
  replacement of, 197–200
  rhetoric of, 152
  seventh stage supplanting, 207–11
  stock market in, 176
  those left out, 133, 151–52, 155, 195
  values clash, 210
New England, 6, 20, 29, 30
  and Federalists, 53, 55, 56
  religion in, 27–30
  settlers, 14–16, 18–20
New Freedom, 90
New World, 13–14, 16, 21
New York (city), 70, 73, 77
Nixon, Richard, 104, 105, 107, 137
nonprofit sector, 205
North (the), 60, 73
  and Civil War, 60–61, 65, 66
  and slavery, 63, 70
North, Oliver, 110
North American Free Trade Agreement
    (NAFTA), 153, 154, 155
Nullification Crisis, 59

Oklahoma City bombing, 115
Omidyar, Pierre, 171
Oracle (co.), 139, 168, 171, 172
Orwell, George, 193–94
O'Sullivan, John, 70
Otis, James, 33

Paine, Thomas, 38, 39–41, 48–49, 99, 140
Panic of 1837, 84
paradigm(s), 22, 36–37, 79, 213
  collapse of, 197
  government, 85, 113, 125
  market, 124–25, 126, 128–31, 148, 152,
    156
  new 39, 48
paradigm shifts, 5, 21, 27–28, 82, 185, 195

Parliament, 30, 32, 33, 35, 38
Paterson, William, 45
Peace Corps, 99–100, 103, 125
Penn, William, 21
Pennsylvania, 21, 22, 30, 44, 71, 73
Perkins, Francis, 96
Perot, Ross, 131, 137, 152
personal computer (PC), 166–68, 170,
    171, 173, 194
Philadelphia, 21, 34, 46, 49, 51, 73
Philippines, 80, 81, 82, 83
Pilgrims, 14, 16, 22
Plymouth colony, 16, 22
Polese, Kim, 140
popular culture, 1, 56, 58, 108, 166
poverty, 75, 85, 101, 106, 126, 150–51,
    195
prisons, privatizing, 149–50
Progessive Era, 149, 205
Progressive Party, 88–89, 92
Progressives, 82–83, 84, 88–90, 97, 104,
    116, 131, 135, 156, 184
    moral purity of, 182
    reformers, 94, 98, 103, 211
Progressivism, 87–88, 94, 134, 152
Pujo, Arsene, 87
Pulitzer, Joseph, 80
Puritans, 8, 14, 32, 34, 88, 90, 114, 126,
    127, 135, 182, 184, 197, 214
    disputes among, 20
    emphasis on work and rectitude, 35
    freedom in, 37, 39
    vision of, 6, 16–30, 21, 30, 36, 63, 93
Putnam, Robert, 201, 203

Quakers, 14, 21, 23, 28, 35

railroads, 67–68, 71
Rand, Ayn, 138–39
Reagan, Ronald, 6, 92, 102, 107–10, 111,
    112, 131, 137, 169
Reaganism, 130, 151
Reaganomics, 110
recessions, 55, 84, 92
Reconstruction, 68, 72
Reform Party, 137
regulatory state, 102, 104, 105, 116
Reich, Robert, 152

religion, 8, 13–30, 39, 85, 114–16, 127,
    213
    in American identity, 178
    in Franklin, 35
    government and, 104
    in market vision, 148–49
    in popular culture, 56
    in Progressivism, 88, 90
    in seventh stage, 209
    in workplace, 205
Religious Right, 108, 114, 115
Republic, 39, 43, 53
    utopian vision of, 54, 55
Republican Party, 60, 61–62, 63, 64,
    68–69, 80, 180
    and government, 106
    and New Economy, 130
    new wave of, 107
Republican Revolution, 112–13
Republicanism, 36, 45, 47, 48, 53–54
Republicans, 52, 54, 56, 91, 92, 93, 94, 99,
    104, 115
    and Civil War, 66
    clash with Federalists, 53, 55–56
    and New Deal, 97
    and role of government, 98, 112–13
Revere, Paul, 31, 37
Revolutionary Era, 63, 99, 115, 140
Revolutionary vision, 32–45
Rhode Island, 20, 23–24, 25, 27
rights, 31, 32, 36, 37, 39, 41, 42, 43, 48, 102
Road Ahead, The (Gates), 169
robber barons, 73, 75, 77, 81, 82, 85, 92,
    104, 135, 169, 181, 211
    critique of, 182
Rockefeller, John D., 73–74, 77, 81, 83, 140
Roosevelt, Franklin Delano, 94–95,
    96–97, 98, 105, 116, 140
Roosevelt, Theodore, 73, 79–81, 82, 83,
    94, 103, 116
    and rise of government, 86–88, 89, 90
Rubin, Robert, 136–37, 139

Sachs, Jeffrey, 130
Salem, Enrique, 33
Samuelson, Robert, 134, 141
Schiller, Robert, 141
Schor, Juliet, 206

Schumpeter, Josef, 129
Schwab, Charles, 76
Seattle, Washington, 153–55, 156, 157, 207
Second Continental Congress, 41–42
Second Great Awakening, 56
Securities and Exchange Commission, 95–96
Seven Years War, 32
Seward, William, 62
Shakers, 22
Shays, Daniel, 46–47
Sherman Antitrust Act, 82
Shriver, Sargent, 101, 140
Silicon Alley, 147, 174
Silicon Valley, 1, 6, 147, 155, 167, 169, 172, 173–74, 187
Sinclair, Upton, 83
slavery, 37, 39, 49, 54, 57, 58, 60, 70, 97
   abolition of, 68, 71
   and Civil War, 60–61, 62–64, 65, 66
   Lincoln and, 63
   states' rights and, 59
Smith, Adam, 128
Smith, John, 14–15
Social Security, 113, 143
Social Security Act of 1935, 96
Socialist party, 89, 92
society
   alternate visions of, 104
   government and, 105–6, 110, 114
   idyllic, 88
Sons of Liberty, 33, 35, 37
South (the), 56, 60, 64, 68, 180
   and Civil War, 60, 65, 66
   economic expansion, 73, 77
   slavery, 61, 63, 70
   states' rights, 50
South Carolina, 59, 64
Soviet Union, 98, 107, 110, 130, 153
spirituality, 28, 156, 178, 204–5, 208, 209, 210, 213
Stamp Act Congress, 33
Stamp Act of 1765, 32–33, 35, 36, 38
Standard Oil Company, 73–74
Stanford, Leland, 68
state constitutions, 41, 43
state governments, 44–45, 46, 109
states' rights, 50, 54, 57, 58–60, 66

Steffens, Lincoln, 182–83
stock market, 3–4, 92, 122, 125, 126, 132, 135–36, 143, 176, 177, 189
   in New Economy, 141
   possible collapse of, 195–96
   risk in, 124
   and the Web, 4, 174–76
stock market crash, 93, 110
Stoddard, Solomon, 28
Summers, Lawrence, 130, 141
Sun Microsystems, 139, 167, 168, 171, 173
Supreme Court, 52, 58, 83, 97

Taft, Howard, 88, 89
Taft, Robert, 98–99, 104
Tarbell, Ida, 83
Taxation, 32–33, 43, 46, 59
technologies, new, 131, 134, 140, 159, 179–80, 182, 185, 194
technology, and productivity, 177
Tennant, Gilbert, 28–29
Tennessee Valley Authority, 96
Territorial expansion, 70–72, 78–79, 81
Texas, 60, 70
Thoreau, Henry David, 206
Thurow, Lester, 139
Tillam, Thomas, 18–19
Tocqueville, Alexis de, 201
Torvalds, Linus, 179
Truman, Harry, 98
Turner, Frederick Jackson, 78
Twain, Mark, 75

union, 6, 44, 45, 69, 97, 198, 214
   Civil War and triumph of, 60–66
   debates regarding, 53–60
   of people or of states, 49–50
   struggles over, 180–81
   vision fades and is replaced, 68–73
   vision for, 48–52
United Nations, 91
United States, 43, 47, 54, 56, 214–15
   expansion, 69, 70
   idea of, 212
   reality of, 42
   religious society, 30
   shared vision in, 134–35
   visionary nation, 4–5

U.S. Army, 71, 80, 83
unity, 48–66, 68, 84, 116, 213
    in New Economy, 180
utopia(s), 5, 9, 13, 18
    connectedness, 209, 210
    in economic expansion, 75
    Internet and, 157
    and reality, 197
Utopia (More), 13
utopian dynamism, endless cycle of, 184,
    207, 211, 213, 214
utopian impulse, 5, 8, 22, 212
utopianism, 1, 116, 169
    humility tempering, 212–13
    Internet, 160–63
    intolerance in, 22
    market, 128–31
    in New Economy, 126–27, 183–84
    religious, 27–28
    technological, 162
utopian vision(s), 6, 126, 200, 214
    of connectedness, 208–10
    in Constitution, 51
    endless cycle of, 4, 210–11
    fall short, 156
    market, 155
    New Economy as, 142
    of republic, 55

values, 64, 201, 212
    of community, 186
    in connectedness, 200, 210
    market, 122, 126, 128, 133, 134, 144
    in New Deal, 96–97
    New Economy, 126–27
Van Buren, Martin, 84, 85, 92, 93
Vietnam War, 103, 104, 105
Virginia, 15, 17, 30, 32, 33, 34, 39, 44, 65
virtual communities, 184–89, 198
vision(s), 30, 155
    alienation from, 211
    alternative, 211–15
    combining, 213–15
    contested, 156
    cycle of, 5–7, 8–9, 49
    disconnect between reality and, 209–10
    disenchantment with, 68
    in Internet, 160, 161, 162–63

    for new nation, 48–52
    Puritan, 16–30, 36, 63, 93
    seeds of new, 200–207
    shared, in U.S., 134–35
    of sixth stage, 184–89
    unrealizable, 185
    winners/losers, 66
    see also Utopian vision
visionaries, 4–5, 7, 8, 214
    creating technology of New Economy,
        165–77
    Gilded Age, 140
    government, 106
    Lincoln as, 64
    New Economy, 139–40, 185, 188, 189,
        197, 198, 203, 207
    Revolutionary Era, 140
    vision articulated by, 135
    of stage four, 69, 73–83
    of stage five, 116
    of stage six, 139–40, 185
    of stage seven, 208, 209–10, 213
Voting Rights Act of 1965, 102

Wall Street, 93, 108, 132, 137, 139, 140,
    151, 187
    high-tech companies, 174
    loss of influence, 176
War Hawks, 55
War of 1812, 55, 57
War of 1898, 80
War on Poverty, 101
Washington, D.C., 99, 101, 109, 110, 115
Washington, George, 37, 45, 46, 47, 49,
    50, 52, 53
Watergate scandal, 104–5
"Wealth" (Carnegie), 74–75
Web (the), 3–4, 135, 164, 165–66, 169,
    170, 171, 180, 194
    access to, 163
    and community, 198–99
    expansion of, 197
    in future, 184, 185
    and government, 183
    individualism of, 179
    mysticism of, 178
    stock market and, 4, 174–76
Web makers, 165–77

Webster, Daniel, 57, 63
Webster, Noah, 58
Welch, Jack, 139
welfare programs/state, 101, 104, 108, 113
Wells, H. G., 193
West (the), 58, 60, 61, 81, 83, 181
    settlement of, 70, 71–72
Whigs, 52, 60
White House, 54, 92, 99, 109, 140
White House Conference on the Family,
    108
Whitefield, George, 28, 29
Williams, Roger, 22–24, 28
Willow Creek Community Church,
    148–49, 178
Wilson, Thomas Woodrow, 88, 89–92, 94,
    95, 116, 129

Winning of the West, The (Roosevelt), 80
Winthrop, John, 16–17, 18, 19, 20, 22, 23,
    24–25, 26, 27, 29
World Trade Organization (WTO), 152,
    153–55
World War I, 72, 90–91
World War II, 98
Wozniak, Steve, 170
Wrubel, Robert, 1–2, 3, 4, 7, 163

Xerox, 167, 204–5

Yahoo!, 158, 172, 175, 178
Yang, Jeff, 172, 181
"you can have it all" mentality, 4, 134,
    143, 209
Young, James, 119–22, 127, 150